AJ51B

A

Voyage

to California,

the Sandwich Islands, &

Around the World

in the Years

1826–1829

A Voyage to California, the Sandwich Islands, & Around the World in the Years 1826–1829

by
Auguste Duhaut-Cilly

Translated and edited by
August Frugé and Neal Harlow

UNIVERSITY OF CALIFORNIA PRESS
BERKELEY LOS ANGELES LONDON

University of California Press
Berkeley and Los Angeles, California

University of California Press, Ltd.
London, England

First University of California Press printing 1999

Library of Congress Cataloging-in-Publication Data

Duhaut-Cilly, Auguste Bernard, 1790–1849.
    [Voyage autour du monde, principalement à la Cali-
fornie et aux îles Sandwich, pendant les années 1826,
1827, 1828, et 1829. English]
    A voyage to California, the Sandwich Islands, and
around the world in the years 1826–1829 / Auguste
Duhaut-Cilly ; translated and edited by August Frugé
and Neal Harlow.
        p.   cm.
    Originally published: San Francisco : The Book
Club of California, 1997.
    Includes bibliographical references and index.
    ISBN 0-520-21752-7 (cloth : alk. paper)
    1. Duhaut-Cilly, Auguste Bernard, 1790–1849—
Journeys.   2. Voyages around the world.
3. California—Description and travel.   4. Hawaii—
Description and travel.   5. Héros (ship)
I. Frugé, August, 1909–   .   II. Harlow, Neal,
1908–   .   III. Title.
G440.D85D85   1999
910.4'5—dc21   98-36122
                                              CIP

Printed in the United States of America
9 8 7 6 5 4 3 2 1

The paper used in this publication is both acid-free
and totally chlorine-free (TCF). It meets the minimum
requirements of American Standard for Information
Sciences—Permanence of Paper for Printed Library
Materials, ANSI Z39.48-1984.

TABLE OF CONTENTS

LIST OF ILLUSTRATIONS

8. [*Page 120*] The game of takersia or takersié as played by the Mojave Indians. From Baldwin Möllhausen, *Diary of a Journey from the Mississippi to the Coasts of the Pacific*, London, 1858.

9. [*Page 183*] Aleutian sea otter canoe, or baidarka, and hunters. From Charles M. Scammon, *The Marine Mammals of the Northwestern Coast of North America*, New York, 1874.

10. [*Page 188*]. View of the Russian establishment at Bodega (Ross) on the coast of New Albion in 1828. Lithograph from sketch by Auguste Duhaut-Cilly. A view of Fort Ross rather than Bodega.

11. [*Page 203*] View of the harbor and valley of Honolulu on the Island of Oahu. Lithograph of sketch by Auguste Duhaut-Cilly.

EDITORS' INTRODUCTION

I. THIS BOOK AND SOME OTHERS

THIS BOOK HAS BEEN KNOWN but not known—known about, that is, but seldom looked at because its true quality has been hidden from readers of English. The original itself is probably the richest and most vivid eyewitness account ever written about early California. Bancroft wrote that the author's "opportunities for observation were more extensive than those of any foreign visitor who had preceded him." What Bancroft did not make clear, having seen only an Italian translation, is that the author was a talented writer and artist.

The original volumes are quite scarce, while the only English version, published serially in 1929, is incomplete and rendered difficult to read by an honest but unfortunate attempt to follow the French syntax in a literal way. The meaning behind the words is obscured, the literary style muffled, and a fine personal narrative, complete with several heroes and a villain, is effectively lost. Our task, then, is to restore life to an excellent book.

Master of a trading ship, the *Héros,* Auguste Duhaut-Cilly, or du Haut-Cilly, whom the Californians called Don Augusto because they could not pronounce his name, spent nearly two years, 1827 and 1828, on the coast of California, seeing it from one end to the other before proceeding to the Sandwich Islands, China, and home around the world. His long account, mostly written on board ship, was published in two volumes in 1834–35. The author was also an artist by avocation and put into the book four lithographs of his own sketches. These, strangely enough, are known to us mostly from copies made by an Italian engraver in 1841.

As an observer, this captain had many advantages. A foreigner who could see with the perspective of an outsider, he was also a coreligionist, friendly to the Franciscan padres and trusted by them. As he himself wrote (Chapter 9): "They were happy to deal with a captain of their own faith. Never would they have discussed these matters with an American or an Englishman."

A veteran of the Napoleonic wars at sea, Duhaut-Cilly was an educated man with literary tastes who could read and converse in at least three languages, Spanish and English as well as French. And his badly chosen trading stock, which he had expected to sell in three or four months, forced him to spend a much longer time visiting all the California ports and pueblos, most of the missions more than once, and even the Russian establishment at Bodega and Ross. Thus his trading misfortune is our good fortune in this fine book.

Duhaut-Cilly saw the California missions at almost the last time they could be seen at the height of their development and before the disaster of secularization. At San Gabriel in June 1828 he attended the reading by Dominican and Franciscan friars of the decree expelling Spaniards from the two Californias. To the *comisario prefecto* of the missions, Vicente de Sarría, he offered passage to Manila (declined) and he was also a near-witness of the escape of Padre Ripoll and Padre Altimira from Santa Barbara. A few years later, in 1832, the great missionary Antonio Peyrí left San Luis Rey, which he had built into perhaps the most successful mission of all. Duhaut-Cilly's account of his visit there in the summer of 1827 may be the fullest and most charming description ever written of a mission in its glory days.

The villain of the story was the supercargo, a man called Monsieur R____ by his captain. Jean-Baptiste Rives had spent some years in the Sandwich Islands and had come to London with King Liholiho, who died there of the measles. In Paris Rives negotiated with some merchants to send a trading ship, the *Héros,* to California and the Islands. At the same time, and unknown to the captain and his principals, Rives promoted the dispatch of a competing ship, the *Comète,* which sailed a few months later. This little tale of two ships—they met in Monterey—is a story within the story.

Almost nothing has been known about the captain/author/artist. By good fortune we have obtained from his descendants in France, and from several obscure periodical sources, some pertinent information about the man and his family, about his experiences in war and in peace. The family has also allowed us to reproduce the captain's portrait, made by a celebrated painter of the time, who also portrayed Franz Liszt and Victor Hugo.

THERE WERE OTHER EARLY and talented visitors, including three great explorers, La Pérouse in 1786, Vancouver in 1792–94, and Frederick William Beechey, whose visit was almost contemporary with that of Duhaut-Cilly. All three left valuable accounts: La Pérouse was the first foreign visitor; Vancouver, like Duhaut-Cilly after him, made the land journey to Santa Clara; Beechey, a fine observer, seems to have gone there by boat. But none of the three saw California south of Monterey and so all had only limited opportunities to observe. Other early visitors, such as Langsdorff (1806), Kotzebue (1816), and Roquefeuil (1817), the latter a friend of Duhaut-Cilly, saw only San Francisco or Monterey.

Richard Henry Dana's *Two Years before the Mast* is surely the finest literary production by an early visitor, a classic of American letters. Dana spent more than a year on the coast but as an ordinary seaman did not have a captain's freedom to move about, never getting to Santa Clara, San Luis Rey, San Gabriel, or to the pueblos of Los Angeles and San Jose. And he arrived in 1835, when the missions were no longer what they once had been.

The book most nearly comparable to the present one is *Life in California* by Alfred Robinson, who arrived as a very young man in 1829 and stayed long enough to convert to Catholicism and marry a daughter of the de la Guerra family of Santa Barbara in a ceremony witnessed by Dana. The first part of Robinson's book, published in 1846, describes his visits to the ports of California and his horseback travels to the missions between San Francisco and San Diego. As a personal narrative account it has many parallels with that of Duhaut-Cilly although shorter and with less detail. And of course there is a striking difference in attitude and sensibility between the young Yankee trader and the veteran French sea captain. The latter part of Robinson's book sets forth the political events of the 1830s and early 1840s, something not given by Duhaut-Cilly, who left California several months before Robinson arrived.

Other American accounts, such as *Seventy-Five Years in California* by William Heath Davis, are concerned mostly with the later years after secularization of the missions. And Davis was a sort of insider, who could not see with the fresh eyes of a Yankee or a Frenchman; from him we do not learn what the country and the people looked like.

Abel du Petit-Thouars stopped at Monterey in 1837 and wrote usefully about recent California history, with pertinent documents, but had little opportunity to observe the country and its people. Another Frenchman, Eugène Duflot de Mofras, made an official tour in 1841 and published a lengthy description of California and Oregon. Translated by Marguerite Eyer Wilbur as *Travels on the Pacific Coast* and handsomely printed by the Fine Arts Press, Santa Ana, in 1937, this account is much better known than that of Duhaut-Cilly, but Duflot de Mofras was a latecomer, and much of his account is rather factual in the manner of a report. It is not clear how much he saw for himself and how much he took from others.[1] As narrative it is dull stuff compared to the vivid and personal account of Duhaut-Cilly.

OUR CAPTAIN'S SHIP, THE *Héros,* sailed from Le Hâvre on 10 April 1826, and proceeded to Rio de Janeiro and around the Horn to Valparaíso. After several stops along the Peruvian coast she reached San José del Cabo in Baja California in the latter part of the year and San Francisco in early 1827. Most of that year was spent on the California coast, after which came a backward journey to Peru to dispose of the

---

1. Duflot de Mofras calls the church at San Luis Rey "the most beautiful, the most symmetrical" mission in California, and he prints a handsome engraving with two equal towers, one of which never existed.

tallow taken in trade and then several more months in California. The Sandwich Islands were reached in September 1828 and Canton in late December, after which the *Héros* sailed around the Cape of Good Hope and arrived home on 19 July 1829.

Duhaut-Cilly possessed a literary flair; his long account of the voyage, including more than 500 octavo pages on the Californias and the Sandwich Islands, is a clearly written first-person narrative, but it is written in neither English nor Spanish, the two common languages of California history. The only English version, that of Charles Franklin Carter in the *California Historical Society Quarterly* in 1929, omits the Baja California and Hawaiian chapters. It is accurate enough word for word, but its attempt at literalness fails to bring out the special quality of the Frenchman's writing, its vivid immediacy. Carter also omitted the fine description of Canton, where the *Héros* stopped on the way home to sell furs and sandalwood. And the reader is given little help with unfamiliar matters.[2]

Two partial accounts of the voyage were published before the captain's full account. Edmond Le Netrel, lieutenant (second mate) on board the *Héros,* turned his journal over to the editors of the *Nouvelles annales des voyages,* Paris, who in 1830 published parts of it. This account is brief, rather thin, and adds only a few things to the longer book, but Le Netrel is more forthcoming than his captain about their trading difficulties, although he does not mention Jean Rives, who carried off and lost a part of the cargo. And the lieutenant tells us that in Honolulu the captain reluctantly allowed the crew to entertain Hawaiian women on board provided that the day's work had been finished first and that the visiting ladies not proceed past the main mast.[3]

The naturalist and physician on board the *Héros,* Paul-Emile Botta, wrote three short sets of "Observations": on the inhabitants of California, on the inhabitants of the Sandwich Islands, and divers obser-

2. The Hawaiian portion of the book, in a version by Alfons L. Korn, appeared in the *Hawaiian Journal of History* 17 (1983):1–39. We did not come upon this until we had completed our own version. The two are quite different stylistically and in editorial treatment.

3. Le Netrel's account, in an English version by Blanche Collet Wagner, was published in Glen Dawson's *Early California Travels Series* in 1951.

vations made at sea. These also were published in *Nouvelles annales des voyages* in 1831. Put into Italian, they later appeared in the Italian version of Duhaut-Cilly's book, translated by Botta's father, Carlo Botta, a well-known historian and poet.

The elder Botta had emigrated to Rouen in Normandy where the son studied medicine under Gustave Flaubert's father; in later years the younger Botta had a long career as archaeologist and French consul in the Near East, became a friend of Benjamin Disraeli and of Layard, the excavator of Nineveh, and met Flaubert himself when the great writer made his tour of the "orient" in 1850. Young Botta also picked up, perhaps in Canton, the habit of opium smoking.[4]

II. TWO VOYAGES AND A TRAITOR

IN HIS INTRODUCTION Captain Duhaut-Cilly tells the genesis of the trading voyage and names its sponsors in Le Hâvre and Paris. The initial impetus came from Rives, who had acted as a sort of secretary to King Liholiho of the Sandwich Islands and had accompanied him on his ill-fated visit to London. It is worthy of note that Duhaut-Cilly never names this man but refers to him throughout the book as Monsieur R____. This supercargo was, in the eyes of his captain, the villain from whose treachery and misrepresentations flowed the chief troubles of the voyage. Among the captain's several comments on Monsieur R____ is the following, made in Santa Barbara (Chapter 10): "his teeth blackened by an excessive use of tobacco, and his monkey head surmounting a meager body of four feet eight. . . ." The reader may compare this description to the unfriendly pen portrait made by Jacques Arago a few years earlier.[5]

---

4. An English version of Botta's California observations appeared in the *Early California Travels Series* in 1952. A translation of the Hawaiian observations, together with an attractive account of Botta's later life, may be found in Edgar C. Knowlton, Jr., "Paul-Emile Botta, Visitor to Hawaii in 1828," in *Hawaiian Journal of History* 18 (1984):13–38.

5. Jacques Etienne Arago accompanied Louis de Freycinet on a scientific voyage around the world in the *Uranie* in 1817–1821, visiting the Sandwich Islands in 1819. He left a narrative account, as did Freycinet himself and Madame Freycinet. It has been said, but we cannot verify, that Arago disliked Rives, in part because Rives would not leave the room when Arago wished to be alone with the attractive wife of the Hawaiian prime minister.

Rives claimed to own land in the Islands and to speak for the Hawaiian rulers in granting special trading privileges to the nation or company of his choice. A privately funded trading voyage was organized. Although doubts about Rives' veracity arose before the ship set out, the backers determined to go ahead with the venture in the hope that it would open a new field for French commerce, not only in the Islands but also in California and on the Northwest Coast of America. It was then that Duhaut-Cilly was asked to command the ship with Rives as supercargo.

That the trading cargo was badly chosen may have been the fault of Rives, who did not know California, or it may have resulted simply from the inexperience of the French. The captain does not speak of this directly, but the reader may deduce the difficulty from the slowness of sales to individuals and the small results of dealing with the missions. In contrast, Alfred Robinson writes of eager purchasers and appears to have done excellent business with the padres. The experienced Yankee firm of Bryant, Sturgis must have known what to offer.

Le Netrel, who describes the cargo as ill-chosen, writes of poor morale among the crew as the months stretched into nearly two years and as it became necessary to turn back as far as Peru to sell the tallow taken in trade. These products must not have been salable in France as they were in Boston. Spirits rose, he says, when at last they turned toward the Sandwich Islands, China, and home.

Although we are never told the financial results of the voyage, it seems clear that it could not have been a success in spite of the captain's heroic efforts to recoup for his owners. Not only did he sail back to Lima, as also to Mazatlán, but he called on the missions one more time, visited the Russians at Ross, and then embarked a deckload of horses and resold them at a profit in Honolulu. There he took on a load of sandalwood for China, and in Canton loaded miscellaneous goods for France.

Before turning back to Peru, the captain chartered the brig *Waverly* and instructed his supercargo to take a part of the remaining goods to the Columbia River and Sitka. But instead of sailing north, Rives went south, where the merchandise seems to have been impounded by the Mexicans. Rives, who now knew that he was *persona non grata* in

1. Jean-Baptiste Rives. Pen portrait by Jacques Arago. 1819.

the Islands, took off into Mexico, where he died of cholera a few years later. The government of that country eventually paid an indemnity to the heirs of Rives, who had not owned the merchandise.

This little disaster was not his responsibility, Duhaut-Cilly tells us, but we cannot help wondering why he left Rives in charge instead of placing a trusted crew member over him. But the crew numbered only thirty-two, and it may be that he could not spare an officer.

Rives is mentioned in a number of contemporary accounts and in modern studies, but there is no full and balanced study of his strange career. As noted above, in Paris he promoted two private expeditions to the Pacific, that of the *Héros* and, unbeknownst to its captain and principals, a second venture organized by a government official, Catineau-Laroche. Several months after the *Héros* had departed Le Hâvre, another ship, the *Comète,* sailed from Bordeaux for the Sandwich Islands, carrying a risk cargo of trade goods and also a small agricultural colony headed by the official's young nephew, Philippe-Auguste de Morineau, who planned to work the lands supposedly owned by Rives and to make use of his influence.

The *Comète* also carried three Catholic missionaries known as the Picpus Fathers and three lay brothers. Duhaut-Cilly tells us that he had previously declined the request of the government to transport them on the *Héros,* knowing that they would be vehemently opposed by the American Protestant missionaries, who already had a foothold in the Islands and had gained influence with the Island chiefs. This opposition, combined with the fact that Rives was now being blamed for the death of Liholiho in London, meant that the Frenchmen of the *Comète* were not welcome in Honolulu. They seem to have gotten ashore by a ruse and might have been put back on the ship had not her captain departed quickly with his trade goods still on board.

The French missionaries were still there, keeping a low profile, when Duhaut-Cilly arrived in September 1828. He compared them favorably to their American rivals and had hopes for their success, but in 1831 they were expelled and sent to California. A second group was also sent away, and Catholic priests were not allowed in the Islands until 1839 when Captain Laplace in the frigate *Artémise* trained his guns on Honolulu, demanded freedom of entry for French priests and merchants, and carried off a guarantee of $20,000.

When the *Héros* sailed into Monterey Bay for the second time in August of 1827, there they found the *Comète,* come to California after its hasty flight from Honolulu. It was then that Duhaut-Cilly learned about "this strange expedition," as he called it. Had it been a success, he says, it would have utterly ruined the business of his own voyage. Through the duplicity of Rives and the government official, the outfitters of the *Comète* had known all about his plans and had taken advantage of the knowledge. He now felt constrained to forbid any business dealings between Rives and Captain Plassiard of the *Comète.* And he adds, with no little satisfaction, that the captain was in difficulty, not knowing what to do with his cargo. Later, in Valparaíso, the *Comète* was sold as unseaworthy.

III. THE CAPTAIN

AUGUSTE BERNARD DUHAUT-CILLY was born in Saint-Malo on the coast of Brittany in March 1790, a few months after the beginning of the great French Revolution. His father belonged to the noble family of Bernard du Haut-Cilly of Saint-Brieuc and Saint-Malo, while his mother bore the resplendent name of Marie-Anne Bossinot de la Belle Issue. She also bore eleven children, one every two years beginning in 1784. Two of the boys, Auguste and Malo, two years older, became notable sea captains.

At some time the old patronymic of Bernard (as shown in the coat of arms) seems to have been deemphasized and the noble particle incorporated into the rest of the name, which thus became Duhaut-Cilly. We may speculate that the change may have been made in the post-revolutionary years when, for a time at least, some families did not stress their noble origins. But fashions and particles revert, and the descendants of the family, now living in several parts of France, call themselves du Haut-Cilly. Both before and after our captain's time, the family produced many persons notable in commerce, war, and government.

In February 1807, at the age of not quite seventeen, Auguste Duhaut-Cilly, as he later called himself, embarked as a volunteer on the ship *Revenant,* newly fitted out and commanded by the celebrated corsair Robert Surcouf, another Breton from Saint-Malo. It was a

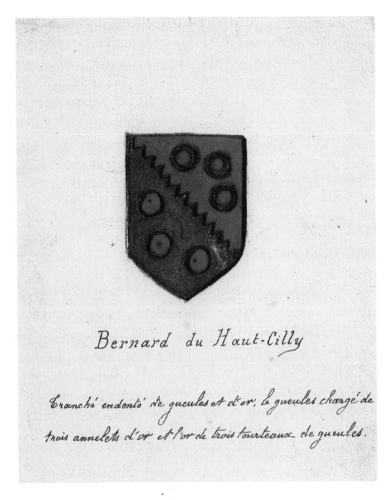

Bernard du Haut-Cilly

Tranché endenté de gueules et d'or, le gueules chargé de trois annelets d'or et l'or de trois tourteaux de gueules.

2. Coat of arms of Bernard du Haut-Cilly.

time when the outgunned French navy, assisted by privateers, was doing its best to harass the superior British sea forces and to capture British merchantmen, including ships of the East India Company in the Indian Ocean. As a young man in his teens Auguste took part in a number of sea battles, some successful, some not, in the waters around Mauritius and Réunion, then called Ile de France and Ile Bourbon. In 1813 he was aboard the frigate *Aréthuse* when it bested a number of British ships off the coast of West Africa. For his part in this action he was later made a knight of the Legion of Honor.

When peace came in 1814 he elected, unlike brother Malo, to leave the navy and transfer to the merchant marine, sailing out of Le Hâvre in Normandy. Then in his twenties and early thirties, he commanded a number of ships on voyages to the West Indies, to South America, and to the Indian Ocean. By 1826, when he was made master of the *Héros,* he was a seasoned navigator, bearing the title of *capitaine au long-cours,* as shown on the title page of his book. Both ends of the journey around the world were familiar waters; only the central part, from Peru to California and China, was new to him.

Duhaut-Cilly was sufficiently familiar with Cape Horn to set down at some length his reasoned opinion that passage of the Horn from east to west was less difficult in winter than in summer. And he was justifiably proud that he accomplished a voyage of more than three years without losing a man, returning with a ship as bright and clean as when he departed. Indeed, his book may be looked on, in part, as an *apologia* for his conduct of the voyage. Against this interpretation, it must be noted that the book shows clear signs of having been written during the voyage, a fact that helps to account for its vividness and sense of actuality.

Some biographical accounts tell us that the captain's health suffered so much from the long voyage that he found it necessary to retire from the sea. But there are no details, and he tells us only that he sustained a broken collarbone when his horse fell with him in San Diego. His book is full of opinions and reactions so that we may form a good idea of the man's attitudes and character, but he is notably reticent about the facts of his personal life. His last twenty years were spent as a private citizen in Saint-Servan, next door to Saint-Malo, where he served for several years as mayor of the town. There he died of cholera in 1849. One of his sons died at nearly the same time.

Auguste Duhaut-Cilly was married to Elise (or Elizabeth) Bourdas, and they had six children, none of whom seems to have left direct descendants. But some of his brothers and sisters procreated well enough to keep the family going. We learn, but only in a couple of footnotes and almost accidentally, that the captain's young brother-in-law, Albert Bourdas, was with him on the ship, and there is a hint at the end of Chapter 7 that his wife may also have been on board.

Duhaut-Cilly was a loyal Frenchman who fought for the Empire against the British, but he was no imperialist or admirer of the military life, which he calls confining to the human spirit. His political convictions are complex and not easily stated. As shown in many passages, he was sympathetic to peoples who sought political freedom but was not sure what that freedom should be. And he had few illusions about the violent after-events of successful insurrection. "Those like us," he wrote (Chapter 11), "who were born in the midst of revolution, only we know how difficult it is to construct dams strong enough to hold back such torrents." He had harsh words for the "ugly designs" of the Mexican patriots. "It was not difficult to see that, in expelling the rich Spaniards from Mexico or in cutting off their heads, the real purpose was to get hold of their fortunes." This son of the Revolution goes on to make a rather good anti-revolutionary statement. If there is contradiction in his attitudes, it is the ambiguity of a thoughtful man, who believed in freedom but did not blind himself to its excesses. "This patriot" and "this republican," he wrote of certain Mexican officials in California, and the meaning is clearly sarcastic.

There are other complexities, perhaps even contradictions. The practical sea captain, whose nautical success must have derived from strict discipline, could not escape the intellectual currents of his romantic age. His description of a Baja California rancho in Chapter 5 might have come right out of Jean-Jacques Rousseau, with its praise of the simple life away from the corruptions of civilization. And his sympathy for the noble savage, and for some not so noble, seems to reflect a reading of his Breton neighbor and friend, René de Chateaubriand. But what could be more modern than his remark that Captain Cook visited but did not discover the Sandwich Islands? He blames the whalers and other foreigners for provoking the savagery of the Northwest Coast Indians. Everywhere he shows sympathy for the native races whether he admires them (the Hawaiians) or thinks them degraded (the Indians of California).

Duhaut-Cilly, like La Pérouse before him, calls the Indians slaves of the missions, using the word rather loosely, and wishes success to those who try to run away. Two condemned Indians, whom he had agreed to transport south, are allowed freedom on board the *Héros* ("There is no slavery in France") and of course they escape. Another Indian, Valerio, by the evidence a criminal type, is portrayed as a freedom fighter.

But if the Indians were slaves, what were the padres? Duhaut-Cilly has only admiration for the latter as men, as Christians, and as caretakers, especially for the good administrators such as Peyrí and Ripoll. If there is contradiction here, it may have been in the situation itself rather than in one man's thinking. Those of us who are free of contradictory attitudes may criticize.

This educated sea captain was an excellent observer. What he saw with his own eyes, and that was much, is described in clear and believable fashion. The reader may trust what he says, we think, as long as the information is firsthand. Only when he relates stories told by others do we need to read with a skeptical eye. His account of the Indian Valerio, hearsay gained at third hand through his young brother-in-law, is scarcely believable. And in Chapter 14 his report of a reprisal expedition against the Indians is surely wrong in several respects. Captain Beechey, who was in California at the time and saw the returned captives in San Jose, has a more reliable account.

Sometimes credulous of stories that provoke his sympathies for the downtrodden, Duhaut-Cilly could be skeptical enough of other matters. In San Diego he is merely amused by the old story, perhaps new at that time, of the rattlesnake, the roadrunner, and the cactus corral. In Chapter 16 it is not clear how much faith he puts in an Indian's story about the use of rattlesnake venom to poison arrows and the testing of its effectiveness on old women of the tribe. Did he know that his leg was being pulled?

The account of the Sandwich Islands is lively and opinionated. The Hawaiian natives, except perhaps for the overfed chiefs, get high marks for appearance and intelligence. Whether one accepts the characterization of the American Protestant missionaries, written from a Catholic point of view, may depend on one's own prejudices. The indictment is not easy to pass off. Much of this seems to have come from Richard Charlton, the British consul, with whom Duhaut-Cilly made at least two excursions and whom he admired and trusted. Here and elsewhere this one-time Napoleonic sea fighter writes of his old enemies with both praise and censure in what appears to be a fair and balanced way.

That Duhaut-Cilly saw people and places with an observant eye may derive in part from his avocation as an artist. Four of his sketches are reproduced in the original book: depictions of Monterey, San Luis Rey, Honolulu, and Bodega (Ross). About the latter we have the captain's own testimony (Chapter 18): "Arising early the next day I positioned myself on a hillside to the east and sketched the citadel, as shown in the plate that accompanies this volume." In an earlier chapter he writes of sketching, not for the first time, the peak of Tenerife, but this is not reproduced in the book. How many other drawings were made, we cannot know; if they were preserved, they may have perished when the family home was destroyed in World War II.

Nor can we know, alas, just what Duhaut-Cilly's original drawings looked like; the versions we see have been changed, little or much, by the lithographer.[6] But all are charming, and we may assume that they are accurate in the same way that his firsthand verbal descriptions are honest and clear. He was an amateur but talented artist in both word and picture. In the sketch of San Luis Rey the men on horseback are perhaps the artist's, or the lithographer's, decoration, but the church looks right although not quite what we see today. And the Indian huts are probably accurate in design if not in precise location. The citadel at Ross must have been pretty much as our captain saw it on that early morning in 1828.

No one has given us a better idea of what California looked like 170 years ago.

A. F.

6. The same four sketches may be found in the Italian translation of 1841 but they are not identical, being the work of another engraver.

VOYAGE

AUTOUR DU MONDE,

PRINCIPALEMENT

A la Californie et aux Iles Sandwich,

PENDANT LES ANNÉES 1826, 1827, 1828, ET 1829;

PAR A. DUHAUT-CILLY,

CAPITAINE AU LONG-COURS, CHEVALIER DE LA LÉGION
D'HONNEUR, MEMBRE DE L'ACADÉMIE D'INDUSTRIE
MANUFACTURIÈRE, AGRICOLE ET COMMERCIALE
DE PARIS.

Illi robur et æs triplex

. . . .

Horace

TOME PREMIER.

PARIS,

Chez ARTHUS BERTRAND, LIBRAIRE, rue Hautefeuille, 23;

Saint-Servan,

Chez D. LEMARCHAND, LIBRAIRE.

1834.

3. Title page of the original edition.

EDITORIAL NOTE

CAPTAIN DUHAUT-CILLY's *Voyage autour du monde, principalement à la Californie et aux Iles Sandwich* . . . was published with the dual imprint of Paris and Saint-Servan in 1834–35, five and six years after his return from the Pacific. There were two volumes and a total of more than 850 small octavo pages. The first four chapters take the ship from Le Hâvre to Baja California. These we have combined into one chapter, with the inclusive number of 1–4, omitting passages of no present interest. The visit to the two Californias is described in more than fourteen chapters, all included here, and that to the Sandwich Islands in a long chapter and a half, numbers 19 and 20. Our chapter 21–23 contains the more relevant parts of three original chapters on the voyage across the Pacific to China and around the Cape of Good Hope to the home port.

The original chapter numbers are retained—at the cost of some awkward inclusive numbering—in order that scholars interested in details of spelling or in the French words may more easily find their way.

Our editorial intention has been to include everything that relates to the Californias and Hawaii, and also the passages that reveal the quality of this particular voyage around the world. The translation is intended to be accurate to the meaning of the original text, sentence by sentence, but does not follow it word for word nor does it reproduce the French syntax. Anything else would betray the author. His original is vivid and direct, sometimes poetic (as in the evening approach to Waialua in Chapter 20), and deserves to appear in English as it once did in French, as a compelling personal narrative. The writing, however, has one fault; it is sometimes redundant, using ten words where seven would suffice. We have eliminated most of the redundancies and tried to put the sense of this true adventure narrative into clear and direct English. Nothing has been added and no meanings intentionally changed; the only omissions, except where noted, are several tabulations of compass bearings from mooring spots.

Somewhere in his book the captain apologizes for his "infernal" nautical language. A number of descriptions, he says, will be of no interest to most readers but will be appreciated by the navigators who may follow him. Not all of these passages have been retained here, but it is they that, in this age of careening technology, are the most difficult to put into another language. Even though he lived in the age of sail, the Italian translator of one hundred fifty years ago complained of this problem. We do the same, and acknowledge that we have often been rescued by William Falconer and William Burney, whose *New Universal Dictionary of the Marine* (London, 1815) is a true treasury of nautical terms and practices as they were known to sailors of Napoleon's time.

Notes signaled by asterisks are those of Captain Duhaut-Cilly. Numbered notes are by the editors. The majority of these were written by Neal Harlow, a smaller number by August Frugé. The translation and introduction were prepared by Frugé with emendations by Harlow. From the beginning this has been a joint enterprise, conceived and carried out together.

The spelling of personal and place names has been silently corrected whenever feasible; a few spellings of unusual interest are mentioned in the notes. As authority for the names of California friars we have used Maynard Geiger's *Franciscan Missionaries in Hispanic California* (1969). Hawaiian names are spelled as in Ralph S. Kuykendall's *The Hawaiian Kingdom* (1938, 1980). Accents are not used on names generally spelled without them, such as San Jose (Alta California) and Santa Barbara. Words printed in parentheses are translated or copied from the original; a few words and several summaries in square brackets have been interpolated by the editors. The chapter titles are ours; the chapter summaries of the original have been dropped.

Work on this edition was first begun more than ten years ago; it was put aside in favor of other tasks and was then resumed in 1994. The original text was translated completely. When we chose later to emphasize California and Hawaiian history rather than the voyage as a voyage, the decisions on what to retain were made from the English version.

❂ ❂ ❂

Many generous people have helped in the preparation of this book. Doyce B. Nunis, Jr., read the manuscript as it was produced and gave us the benefit of his great wit and erudition. Nora Harlow and Pat Morris read the manuscript and made many helpful suggestions; Nora also read proof and compiled the index. Gary Kurutz and Harlan Kessel of the Book Club of California helped in more ways than can be cited here. Various parts of the manuscript were read critically by Susan Frugé, Mabel Jackson, Verle Ludwig, and James A. Sandos. All saved us from errors of one kind or another. The errors that remain are ours.

Anne Kraatz of Paris introduced us to the du Haut-Cilly family (so spelled today) there and also searched a number of archives, helping us to learn more about our captain-author than was previously known in this part of the world.

M. and Mme. Alain du Haut-Cilly of Paris allowed us to reproduce the portrait of their ancestor as well as the family coat of arms. A most useful manuscript genealogy was copied for us by Mme. Christiane Tourres, née du Haut-Cilly. Dr. Douglas Pepin of Woodland, California, permitted us to reproduce the four lithographs in his copy of the original book.

We have profited greatly by the help of several libraries: the Bancroft Library in Berkeley, whose late director James D. Hart provided the French and Italian texts; the Huntington Library of San Marino, which provided a number of nineteenth-century French periodicals; and the San Bernardino County Library, where Richard Erickson obtained by inter-library loan many books and articles that we could not otherwise have consulted. Robert Ryal Miller of Berkeley did some useful research for us in the Bancroft Library. Ms. Danielle Le Marc-Combe, bibliothécaire of the Service Historique de la Marine in Brest, provided a short manuscript biography of Captain Duhaut-Cilly. M. Ph. Mangon of Saint-Malo and Mr. and Mrs. B. P. Reardon of Lion-sur-Mer did some searching for us. Among others who helped are Richard Dillon, Paul Kahn, Art Kidwell, Albert Muto, Norman Neuerburg, and Robert Y. Zachary. We are deeply grateful to all.

A

Voyage

to California,

the Sandwich Islands, &

Around the World

in the Years

1826–1829

4. Captain Duhaut-Cilly.

My goal in writing about this voyage is neither to display a brilliance of style nor to impress the reader with profound observations. My sole ambition is to be useful to those who will follow me to the distant shores whose description is the principal purpose of this account. If my colleagues can employ it as a source of information and find in it what they need, then I will have all the reward I desire for my pains.

○　○　○

In 1824 the king of the Sandwich Islands, Liholiho, impelled by curiosity and perhaps also by some thought of gain, journeyed to England on board a whaling vessel that had stopped in at one of his islands.[1] He was accompanied by his wife, his ministers, Kalanimoku and Boki, and by a Frenchman named R____, who served him as

1. The English ship *L'Aigle*. The king's name is spelled Rio-Rio by Duhaut-Cilly. Here, as in later chapters and whenever possible, we spell Hawaiian names as given in R. S. Kuykendall's *The Hawaiian Kingdom,* vol. 1, Honolulu, 1980.

interpreter and secretary.[2] In London the king became an object of curiosity and ridicule. The great entertained him for their own amusement and showed him off like a rare animal; journalists took advantage of his presence to fill their papers with witty and comical stories; capitalists, banking on his ignorance, devised schemes that never came to fruition; and the government generously paid his expenses, hoping to profit thereby and obtain from him special advantages for English commerce, which might anticipate fine profits from the fertility of the Sandwich Islands. But before negotiations could begin, Liholiho and his wife both came down with the smallpox and died.[3]

The king's retinue, along with his embalmed body and that of the queen, were sent back to the Sandwich Islands on board the frigate H.M.S. *Blonde,* and a consul was accredited with the title of consul general to all the Islands of the Pacific Ocean. Mr. R____ stayed behind in London and sought to gain personal profit from his position, spreading the report that King Liholiho, before dying, had conferred on him the power to contract in his name or in that of his successor an exclusive commercial treaty with any government or any company that might wish to undertake the venture. Although the moment could not have been more favorable, since many enterprises of the kind were being set up in London at this time, and some of them on more absurd claims than this one, his intrigues came to naught.

Thwarted in his hopes he came to Paris, where his family lived, and there began once more to talk of the authority granted him and of the splendid profits that might be had from an expedition to the Sandwich Islands, California, and the Northwest Coast of America. A shipper who had no credit or business standing was the first to take up the project but had to turn to others for the necessary funds, and these others did not wish his name associated with their more respectable names; displeased at this, he was pushed aside and played no further part in the enterprise.

2. Jean-Baptiste Rives, who is discussed below and in the editors' introduction. For reasons that the reader may ponder, Duhaut-Cilly continues to refer to him only by the initial of his surname.

3. Kuykendall and other authorities say that the disease was the measles.

The expedition that I am about to describe was undertaken by the Messrs. Javal, bankers, and Martin Laffitte of Le Hâvre, and by Jacques Laffitte,* whose concern for the general good, rather than the wish to increase his own great fortune, moved him to provide capital in the hope of opening a new branch of trade and a new outlet for French commerce.

An agreement in which Mr. R____ granted, in the name of the government of the Sandwich Islands, great privileges to the interested parties, was signed in Paris at the end of 1825. He promised, among other things, profits of several times the investment in exported merchandise; the right to exploit large tracts of land that he claimed to own in these islands; a monopoly in sandalwood, which is the principal source of wealth there; and many other dazzling things. Without lending entire faith to such glittering prospects, these gentlemen thought they could discern the possibility of establishing with this archipelago relations that might become of considerable importance to our commerce as a whole. But scarcely had they begun to get the project under way when a fuller knowledge of Mr. R____'s character led them to fear they might have too lightly put trust in a man whose words betokened more clearly every day a lack of prudence and a want of capacity that proved all too true thereafter.

Nevertheless, not wishing to repudiate a contract, the leaders of the enterprise proceeded with the plans but decided to take away from Mr. R____ the entire management of the operation; and it was then that they proposed to me that I take charge of it and also be in command of the ship that they would provide. Flattered by this mark of confidence and being naturally inclined toward adventurous undertakings, I closed my eyes to the problems that such a long absence might cause me and without further hesitation made a firm commitment. My instructions gave me authority to act for all the interested parties; I was to require that Mr. R____ fulfill punctually all provisions of the contract; I was to keep an eye on whatever he did; in other words, he would be responsible to me in all matters, I having the right, if need be, to withdraw all authority from him.

* The same who, later, became minister of state.

I repaired to Bordeaux where I purchased a fine ship of 370 tons, named her the *Héros,* and brought her to Le Hâvre to complete the fitting out and to load the cargo. The minister of marine, who had appeared to take some interest in the expedition, promised to provide me with suitable instruments in order that we might contribute something to the knowledge of navigation, but it was in vain that I sought the fulfillment of this promise, and I departed without obtaining anything more than a special passport and a set of marine charts that I gave back on my return. Honored by such an important task, I was still ready to perform it with what skill I had and with enthusiasm, but without these instruments I was limited to nautical observations and to a description of the places that I visited. I should not fail to mention, however, the courtesy of the government in waiving half the import duty on natural products of China that the *Héros* would bring back.

Chapters 1—4

AROUND THE HORN TO THE CALIFORNIAS[1]

April—October 1826

ON THE MORNING OF 10 APRIL 1826 we made ready to sail. The morning was delightful, the risen sun more radiant than usual. The wind, coming at first from the east, shifted suddenly to the west, blowing moderately and bringing not a single cloud. We had made ready to receive on board Mr. Martin Laffitte[2] with his family and friends, and had prepared a luncheon for them. Among the guests was the illustrious Talma, who had gladly accepted the invitation to a meal on the water. The elegant lines of the ship, its full complement of guns, and especially our destination—these surely brought a curious crowd to the dock; but the presence on board of the first tragedian of Europe was the principal reason, I think, for such a great gathering, made up in part of his admirers, still filled with enthusiasm from the evening before, when he had played with such great talent the splendid role of Sulla in the tragedy of that name. The eyes of the viewers,

1. This chapter condenses the first four chapters of the original book. Longer omissions are signaled by asterisks between paragraphs, shorter ones by three dots.

2. A merchant in Le Hâvre and, as noted in the author's introduction, one of the backers of the expedition.

then, seemed more intent on picking him out from among the crowd on the deck than they were in observing the handling of the ship.[3]

During the meal we made several tacks in the roadstead, allowing the ladies to enjoy a splendid view of the harbor of Le Hâvre. A score of fine vessels, departing at the same time as we for divers destinations, were crossing each other in all directions, tacking now this way, now that way, some appearing to follow each other in battle formation, others challenging upwind and causing one to fear a disastrous collision. But the lighter and weaker had at last to give way to the stronger, and the ships swept by each other swiftly, yards passing closely. After allowing our friends to enjoy the spectacle for a time, we hove to near the jetty, and our guests disembarked for the return to land. When the boat carrying Mr. Laffitte and his family was clear of the ship, we saluted them with a salvo of seven guns, not just as a courtesy but also as an expression of gratitude for the good wishes presented to us for a happy voyage. This signal of farewell resounded all the more loudly in our hearts because it was high time to crowd on sail and put out to sea.

In the afternoon the wind freshened, and we experienced the satisfaction of leaving all the other ships behind, even though some of them enjoyed in Le Hâvre the reputation of being fast sailers.

❂   ❂   ❂

On the morning of the 25th I caused the entire crew to gather on the quarter-deck for assignment of battle stations. I had it in mind to reassure the men against a rather strange rumor that was circulating among them before our departure from Le Hâvre. An apprentice whom I had dismissed, doubtless wishing to take revenge on me, was spreading word that I had piratical undertakings in mind. Absurd as the story was, the wives of several of my seamen put sufficient faith in it that they advised their husbands not to make the voyage. In a port where I was so well known, I had no fear that this kind of allegation might be given any credence; but at sea, where the authority of the captain draws its greatest strength from the respect and regard that he inspires, it would be dangerous to allow the smallest suspicion of his

---

3. The great actor was then near the end of his career, dying later that year.

integrity to arise. I therefore seized the opportunity to make myself clear on this subject.

After causing the men to blush at their own credulity, I told them that I had taken arms on board the *Héros* only for our legitimate defense; I pointed out that we might experience the need later on to impress the fierce natives of the Northwest Coast of America or to repel the attacks of Chinese sampans or Malayan proas, and I concluded by authorizing them to turn against me if I should ever make any kind of attack on anyone. But, I added, if our guns are not to be useless arms, we must begin by learning to handle them, and to accomplish that we are now going to undertake some training exercises and will repeat these from time to time. Each then took the station assigned to him, and all conducted themselves with spirit; I saw that for the most part they were no strangers to artillery maneuvers, which several of them had learned on board our warships.

As the vessel was armed with twelve carronades with fixed breaching, eighteen men sufficed to man them, leaving me a dozen for maneuvering and for musket-fire. With men of good will, then, I could withstand all the pirates that we might encounter in certain quarters.[4]

That same day we made our course to pass by the island of Palma. After supper we set up an excellent hurdy-gurdy on the bridge and allowed the crew to dance on the quarter-deck; we also gave each man a glass of punch as encouragement to the exercise, which entertains the men and is at the same time good for their health.

The sailors are madly fond of this diversion. Hardly has permission been accorded when a quadrille is formed near the capstan: the oldest and best seamen choose for dancing partners the youngest and least experienced—that is the custom—and the latter at once strive to take on a feminine aspect, donning long white chemises, fastened around the waist with girdles improvised from rope-yarn; and then we see them take little mincing steps, bending their necks and doing their best to put on coquettish airs. Those, however, who must stand the

---

4. The carronade was a short, large-bore naval gun, named for Carron, the place in Scotland where it was first made. Falconer's *New Universal Dictionary of the Marine* (1815) says that "when within the reach of their point blank, those of a large bore do wonderful execution." The 8.05-inch bore used a ball weighing 68 pounds.

midnight watch prefer the sweetness of sleep to the delights of the ball; they maintain no illusion about the true sex of the bare brawny feet that are pounding over their heads like the paving-rammer whose name* the dancers have adopted. As the deck shakes and resounds above their hammocks, they swear in no very Christian way at those grotesque lovers of Terpsichore. But their vexed tempers and their oaths—mingled with the continual creaking of the ship, produced by every rolling movement, no matter how slight—had no effect on those nymphs perfumed with tar, who persevered with their pleasures. One might say that their willing imagination has transported them to some shady village: To them the caulked planking of the deck becomes a verdant lawn; the light wind in the rigging is an evening zephyr rustling the leaves of the plane trees; and the sound of the sea, which opens before the ship and covers its flanks with something like a girdle of snow, falls on their ears as pleasantly as the babbling of a brook in their home valley.

❀ ❀ ❀

On the evening of 10 May, having been given permission, the crew prepared to celebrate on the morrow that ridiculous ceremony, the baptism of the line. A postillion, mounted on a horse with the head of a fish, came to me and delivered a well-turned letter to which I replied in a manner proper to the circumstances. I will not try to describe the thousand lunacies that a sailor's fertile imagination suggests to him on such occasions; others have attempted without success to determine a convincing origin for this modern bacchanal. I will say only that on the day following delivery of the message, the burlesque God of the Line, with his retinue, advanced toward the stern, where he set himself up as master; and while his assistants initiated into the equinoctial mysteries all those whom he designated, a sailor dressed as Neptune or as some other god of the sea took over the functions of pilot. He acted very nervous about the course that the ship was following, consulted quite often the map, the compass, the sounding line, and, standing close to the helmsman, ordered the most absurd ma-

---

* A demoiselle [damsel] is an instrument made of wood and iron used to drive in paving stones.

neuvers, which the latter had to obey at once. All went off with decency and gaiety, which is rare enough on these occasions when—as when wearing a mask—one thinks he has the right to say and do extravagant things that are not always to the liking of those whose good sense holds them back from taking active part in the orgy.

From the equator to Rio de Janeiro there happened nothing of importance. During this passage of about six hundred leagues, which we made in thirteen days, we enjoyed a constant and favorable wind from the east-southeast; the 20th was especially remarkable for the purity of the sky. The few clouds that appeared, like light balls of cotton, served only to make the horizon stand out distinctly; in its entire circumference it was delineated with an extraordinary sharpness that one sees only rarely between the tropics, where the atmosphere is most often charged with vapor.

❀   ❀   ❀

Opposite Rio de Janeiro is the little city of Praia Grande, where many wealthy men of the capital own pleasant villas. On holiday and Sunday eves they cross the harbor in covered boats and there spend days of leisure with family and friends. Between Santa Cruz and Praia Grande, on a steep hill separated from the mainland by a narrow isthmus, is the convent and church of Boa Viagem. The Portuguese sailors have great faith in the prayers that they say here, while bringing offerings to place at the feet of the Mother of God in this chapel, whose location is so appropriate to their pious pilgrimage. . . .

On an excursion that I made with Dr. Botta* and Mr. R____ we disembarked on this side of the convent of Boa Viagem and, after crossing a kind of isthmus, took our way toward the small bay of Saco Caraï. Our purpose was to collect the beautiful butterflies of the country and to shoot birds and preserve their plumage; we could not have chosen a better place for the endeavor and easily procured a large enough number of both. But all the while we sought what we were

---

* Son of Carlo Botta, whose books have been translated into all languages and are highly esteemed everywhere. This estimable young man, passionately fond of voyages, came on this one as medical officer of the *Héros*. It is to him that I owe the rare good fortune of losing not a man during a journey of three and a half years in every kind of climate and with a crew of thirty-two.

after, we were admiring the astonishing beauty of the place where chance had brought us. We walked for a time between two hedges of dwarf acacias mingled with Bengal roses and serving to enclose large plantations of coffee trees; the red berries made a pleasing contrast with the somber green of the leaves. Soon the path disappeared and we found ourselves in a grove of orange trees, whose branches bent low with the weight of the fruit.

We wondered who owned all these riches and, like the Roman senator whose story is told by Ariosto, we dared not touch what seemed offered to us. But we were not in a fantasy palace of crystal and porphyry; nor was the proprietor a loathsome dwarf with strange and capricious passions. For, turning a clump of trees we saw coming toward us a woman of a certain age accompanied by five handsome young ladies whom she introduced as her daughters, and she invited us in a most gracious manner to come into a charming house, which we had not perceived among the orange, lemon, and banana trees that surrounded it.

In this peaceful retreat, two leagues from the capital city, this amiable family appeared to pass their days with little knowledge of the world, for they asked us news of Rio de Janeiro in the way they might have asked news of Paris. I explained who we were and introduced my companions. At once Dr. Botta was consulted about the health of several people of the house. They said they were ill, it seemed to me, for the pleasure of learning about French medicine; the advice, which I interpreted as best I could, was welcomed in a way that should have pleased the faculty of Paris.

✺　✺　✺

Since entering the region of variable winds the ship has been continually surrounded by an immense number of birds. Among them we observed all the species of petrels, from the very smallest to the giant petrel, called by the Spaniards the *quebranta-huesos* [bone-breaker]. The most interesting of this numerous family is the *damier* [chessboard], so named on account of the singular marking of its plumage, a pattern of black and white squares on its back. In calm weather when the ship is making little headway hundreds of these handsome petrels ride in the wake, right up to the poop, where they resemble a flock of pigeons, being of about the same size and shape. They throw themselves greedily on the pieces of meat and tallow that we throw out, and it is easy to take them on the hook. . . .

All these inhabitants of sky and ocean criss-cross each other in the air, mingle together, separate, and come together again. When a piece of food lands on the water they all rush after it. And then suddenly arrives the despot of this region. The albatross, with his great wings, is the Satan of Milton, looming like a colossus amidst the crowd of rebel angels. These then flee, appetite paralyzed by fear, no longer concerned to dispute the plunder. And the tyrant, when he has devoured it, pauses a few minutes contemplating his strength; then his wings, so carefully folded in three parts, are extended, his feet beat the water, and he runs along the surface for a considerable distance before taking flight.

On occasion we could perceive from a distance something that looked like a large rock; coming nearer we recognized the stripped carcass of a whale, covered with sea birds of all kinds, unknowingly acting as sails and masting for the cadaver while eating it, sailing it far from the place where a whaling ship had abandoned it after taking first profit from its substance. Here again the albatross had the place of honor. . . . And the multitude, the plebe, as a Spaniard would say, do not come back to feed until the master has finished his repast and spread his long wings, like the balancing pole of a tight-rope dancer.

No cries arise from all these birds but when some quarrel erupts among them; except for this they add no sound in calm weather to that produced by the topsails flapping against the mast. But at night a small whistling sound, like a lament, tells us that a halcyon is flying around the ship; the sailors, who know nothing of its sad story, take this as an evil omen and call the bird Devil or Stinky.[5]

❂   ❂   ❂

[The captain enlightens his readers with a long disquisition on the problems of rounding Cape Horn, making a considered case for win-

5. Some say that Alcyone, daughter of Aeolus, and her husband, Ceyx, son of the morning star, were so happy that jealous gods transformed them into birds, she into a kingfisher (halcyon). But Ovid says that Ceyx was drowned at sea and his body found by Alcyone. In her grief she was turned into a bird with a mournful song.

ter as a less difficult time than summer for the passage from east to west with modern—that is early nineteenth-century—equipment. The *Héros* made its way around against contrary winds and current, and in early August reached Valparaíso, where she rode out a storm that destroyed an American ship and killed most of the crew.]

Reaching Chile at the beginning of August we were pleased to think we need not fear those squalls from the open sea that make the harbor of Valparaíso so dangerous in wintertime; but on the 7th the wind shifted to the north, bringing dark and rainy weather. The wind was moderate until the 13th, when it began to blow much harder, breaking all communication between ships and shore. All the signs told us that we were about to experience a great storm and in a situation where quality of ship and skill of officers would be of little advantage. We took all the necessary precautions: sent down the topgallant masts, housed the topmasts, struck the lower yards, so that only the body of the ship and the lower masts were exposed to the wind. But of all our defenses the most reassuring was the large anchor, with its chain of seventeen lines in diameter, which was kept ready to be dropped at the first word.[6]

Every ship in the harbor took the same precautions; all those fine masts that reached for the sky a few days before now looked like old pine trees broken by the tempest and shattered by thunderbolts. The wind continued to rise, and the sea formed great troughs into which ships plunged to their bowsprits and then rose again like rearing horses, showing the red copper of their keels, as brilliant and polished as if they had just come from the shipwright.

At noon on the 14th a violent squall struck the bay, and many cables could not hold; one of ours broke, although quite new, but we dropped our large anchor at that moment and were delighted to observe that neither the wind's force nor the incredible heaving of the sea could strain that splendid long chain, which held the ship as easily as a good line holds a kite in the air. In the security thus allowed us our attention was fixed on what was going on around us. From minute to minute the storm seemed to redouble its strength, and the harbor of Valparaíso was a sinister sight. Mountainous waves broke with a

6. The line or *ligne,* a French measure, equals 2.26 mm or between 1/11 and 1/12 of an inch.

frightful roar on rocks and sand, throwing up into the wind great masses of spray that fell on the roofs of the town. Several ships were already in an alarming state. Some had slipped or broken their cables, collided, and threatened to drag each other onto the shore; masts and yards gave way with a frightful cracking. We saw the bowsprit of one ship plunge down so deep that the weight of the water kept it from rising again; it broke off next to the stem. So a swordfish, they say, in order to save its life, may abandon its sword in the body of the whale it has pierced.

The beach was lined with spectators, most of whom no doubt deplored the cruel fate that seemed to await us, but many were already thinking of the pillage they could make of the unfortunate ships that might be thrown onto the shore. Their wait was not long in vain; a splendid American ship, moored a short distance behind us, broke its three cables at the same time, and two minutes later it struck the shore in the most dangerous spot.

Never was a more dreadful spectacle presented to our eyes; as soon as her hull came against some rocks about fifty paces from the road that ran along the edge of the sea, the waves swept furiously over the body of the ship, each wave going completely over it. By fatal misfortune, the ship was inclined toward the sea, heightening the danger to the unfortunate crew. We saw them trying to climb into the masts, and several succeeded; but this refuge did not long resist the redoubled attack of the waves; the masts fell, engulfing the unfortunate men in the wreckage of masts, sails, and rigging. Men on shore made vain efforts at rescue; those who tried to take out ropes when the waves retreated were bowled over when they returned; several almost became victims of their compassion. In the end, of sixteen men on the *Arethusa* (the name of the ship), there were saved only four, and one of these died of his injuries. From the time when the vessel struck to the time when there was nothing left of her there passed only forty minutes. Soon the beach, from the point of the wreck to the end of the Almendral,[7] a distance of half a league, was covered with the debris of the ship and her rich cargo, which the unrestrained populace

7. The Almendral (almond grove) was a large suburb stretching along the inner shore of the bay.

shamelessly appropriated. But however distasteful we find this sort of rapacity, we should remember that even in France the barbaric practice of plundering wrecks has long been regarded as a right by the people of the coasts of Lower Brittany and Gascony.

❂   ❂   ❂

[Leaving Valparaíso in August 1826, the ship sailed north along the coasts of Chile and Peru, making short stays at Paita, Santa Helena, and the bay of Salango, where they stopped for water and firewood. Before that there was an unpleasant incident involving Mr. R_____.]

A few days later, on the 29th, we were making our way rapidly to the northwest, with a strong wind from the south and a big sea. The *Louise,* a ship from Bordeaux, which had left Valparaíso with us, was about a mile ahead, when cries were heard on deck and word went around that no one could find a young man, servant of Mr. R_____. He had not been seen for an hour, and although every corner of the ship had been searched and he had been called in a loud voice, there was no trace of him. As soon as this dire news reached me, I reduced sail and redoubled the search, but with no success. It was generally agreed that he had left while the crew was eating and had gone alone to the foredeck, where everything led us to believe he had fallen into the sea; the noise of the ship and the sound of the waves had made it impossible to hear his cries even if the ship, in passing over him, had left him able to cry even once. The young man did not know how to swim, and since the ship had gone on at more than nine knots an hour, he must by then have been more than three leagues behind us, and it would have taken us at least six hours to regain the spot; thus any attempt to return would have been quite pointless, and it remained only to mourn his loss. To render him a last respect, I had one cannon fired and put the flag at half-mast. The *Louise,* not knowing the reason for this signal, reduced sail at once and approached us; I informed her captain of the sad event. He confirmed that it would be completely useless to retrace our steps, and we each went our way.

All was silent on board; a feeling of something like terror seemed to have paralyzed our tongues. The foresail had been taken in, and the officer of the watch, as if afraid to interrupt our somber reflection, and himself prey to dolorous thoughts, dared not raise his voice to loosen the brails that held it. Half an hour went by in this sort of trance; I was in my cabin. The tragic death kept appearing in my imagination as a bad omen for the rest of the voyage, when there were heard new cries of a different tone, and I learned that the little unfortunate had just been found in an obscure spot between decks, where he had tried to strangle himself with his necktie. When he was himself again I questioned him about the cause of his despair, and he declared that fear of being maltreated for quite a small misdeed had impelled him to destroy himself. I was not a little surprised to learn that a person who ate at my table, doubtless not expecting that the little rogue would go so far, had been pleased to frighten him with the consequences of his offense and induced him to hide himself. So this individual had coolly watched our alarms, had let me fire the funeral cannon and inform the *Louise* of a misfortune that he knew to be quite false. This callous act, not unrelated to diabolical pleasures, caused general indignation among officers and crew, and I did not hold myself back from showing him my own feelings in public and in a most humiliating way.[8]

❂　❂　❂

On 24 September we unloaded the water casks, filled them with excellent water, and stowed them back on board. We managed the work quickly and easily, with the longboat anchored six cables from shore. Since the sea was not rough, we could have with some effort done the embarking at high tide, but we found it more convenient to leave the boat anchored. The empty casks were rolled along the beach to the running stream, filled, and rolled back to the water's edge; from there the men from the boat parbuckled them on board. . . .

One could not ask a better watering-spot than Salango, and at the same place one can obtain firewood and wood for construction. We cut a few pieces of the latter, including a fine anchor stock, but hav-

---

8. The servant is never mentioned again. We may presume that he went with Rives when the latter deserted the expedition.

ing no other immediate need, I did not wish to be wasteful, and also advised the men not to cut more firewood than needed and to take only mature trees. The supply was so great that it would have been vandalism to cut the young ones that are the future of the forest when without difficulty we could let the ax fall on those that had attained full growth or had already been felled by old age and storms. It is the duty of a captain to explain to his crew that it is barbarous to destroy, without necessity, the gifts of nature. Sailors and—I am ashamed to say this but must speak fairly—experienced mariners also are all too much inclined to ravage the land needlessly when no obstacle stands in the way. I have seen crews set fire lightheartedly to whole forests where they have come to obtain a precious supply of wood. Let Wellington burn sixty towns in a country that he came to protect and defend; let Rostopochin reduce to ashes the noble capital of Muscovy![9] One can conceive that in a ruthless war such cruelties may in some way be necessary; one may even lay them, as at Moscow, to a fierce spirit of patriotism. But to burn forests simply because there is no one there to oppose it, that is worse than vandalism; it is to scorn divine Providence.

✪   ✪   ✪

It took us thirty-two days to go from Salango to the southernmost point of California—that is, to sail a route of about seven hundred fifty leagues. . . . During that time we never had six continuous hours of good weather. The rain fell in torrents, sometimes for twenty-four hours without ceasing . . .

On 8 October especially, a storm came down on us with the greatest fury. We had had little wind during the afternoon, but unsettled weather in all directions and a continuous rain were bad omens for the night that was to follow. Gannets, gulls, and halcyons flew all around the ship, and we captured by hand a small land bird that had strayed

---

9. Wellington's Spanish campaign took place in 1809–12. Count Rostopochin, military governor of Moscow, was accused of instigating the great fire of 1812 as a means of driving out Napoleon.

to sea. In the sea, as in the air, numerous creatures followed the ship or crossed its path. We captured a turtle, a silver-fish, some bonitos and trigger-fish, and a rather large shark, on which the seamen exercised their usual rage. A flat fish, similar to a ray but much larger, swam for a long time in the ship's wake; we wished to harpoon it, but from prudence or instinct it kept itself at a safe distance.

Nightfall brought an end to this recreation and forced us to put aside lines, gigs, and harpoons and prepare ourselves for the bad weather that appeared to be coming. There were several squalls, one after the other, and then about four in the morning we were assaulted by the main storm, which for several hours had held itself stationary in the north. The enormous cloud that had been hiding the tempest came down upon us and enveloped us in such darkness that we ran into each other and could not see sails or masts. The rain fell in sheets, the sound of the deluge mingling with the whistling of the wind, and great claps of thunder climaxed the wild disorder. Under reduced sail, as circumstances required, we pursued our way, with no other concern than that caused by the lightning, which pierced the charged atmosphere and sometimes seemed to go right through the masts.

On this occasion we observed that strange meteoric phenomenon known as St. Elmo's Fire: three little balls of soft fire appeared on the trucks of our masts and for an hour made them look like three torches. These flames, without doubt electrical, appeared more or less bright from moment to moment, and seemed, as far as we could tell through the rain, to leap about the tops of the masts, to move away a few feet, then to return and shine with greater brilliance.

❂   ❂   ❂

At dawn on 27 October we had our first view of the land of California between Point Pulmo and Cape Porfia at 23° 10′ north latitude.[10] The land was high, dominated by tall mountains rising one behind the other, and the wind was contrary to our course for the port

10. They were approaching the east coast of Baja California between La Paz and Cabo San Lucas.

of San Lucas, said by Mr. R____ to be an important place and now lying about ten leagues away to the west-southwest. Consequently, we were forced to tack about, with a good wind from the south-southwest.

The appearance of the coast, as we approached it, seemed quite pleasant—a high and wide plain, wooded but not very green.* Since we were coming to a little known land and one quite new to us, we sought eagerly to make out details; each of us swung his telescope from point to point, seizing avidly on anything that might help his imagination. We made special efforts to recognize signs of habitation; one of us thought he perceived a group of humble cabins; another was certain, he said, that he could see a fine country house, with its flat roof showing above a clump of trees; and a third went even further, describing an elegant bridge suspended over a deep ravine. We much resembled Don Quijote, whose fertile imagination enumerated for his squire the armies of Pentapolín and Alifanfarón.[11] I don't know how far we would have carried this aberration of the senses if a bright ray of light had not suddenly fallen on the coast we were approaching, illuminating it and allowing us to see matters for what they were. A little disconcerted now, we looked at each other, realizing that we had let ourselves be victims of an illusion, and that there were no more vestiges of human habitation on this plain than there were meadows at Paita.[12]

We continued to tack about until the afternoon of the next day, when, raising Cape Porfia to the north 5° west and Cabo San Lucas to the west, we found ourselves toward evening in front of a bay toward which we tacked and where we discerned two ships at anchor. This time it was not an illusion; we could also see several houses near the shore. Not having full confidence in the manuscript maps obtained in Paita, which placed the port of San Lucas quite close to the cape of

* As I learned later, we were looking not at trees but at giant cacti, mixed in with bushes and vines.

11. In chapter 18 of part one of Cervantes' book. The armies were, of course, two bands of sheep.

12. A town in Peru, where they had stopped on the way north.

that name, and since Mr. R____ himself could offer no information on the matter, I had to assume that the maps had misled me as to the position of the port and that we must have reached it sooner than expected.

So I waited for clarification. At sunset several small boats from the ships in the bay came alongside, and I found out that the two ships, one English and one American and both whalers, were anchored not in the port of San Lucas but in the bay of San José del Cabo. It was not without surprise that I learned, quite contrary to my information from Mr. R____, that the port of San Lucas, far from being frequented, was inhabited by only one family, and there had never been more. This discovery dealt a blow to my confidence in this man's knowledge of local conditions; and the doubts that I now conceived about his veracity were only too well verified by what followed.

The officers of the whalers also told me that San José del Cabo was the most considerable town in the environs and the one with the greatest resources for trade, and so I decided to land there. Calm weather came with the evening; our boats and those of the whalers quickly towed us to the mooring place, where we cast anchor at eight o'clock in twelve fathoms of water.

Chapter 5

―――――――― ∘ ――――――――

IN AND AROUND SAN JOSÉ DEL CABO[1]

October—November 1826

THE DAY AFTER OUR ARRIVAL, a Sunday, I embarked in the gig with Mr. R____ and in a quarter of an hour we had reached the eastern shore of the bay, which appeared to be the most convenient spot for a landing; elsewhere the sea was too heavy for our boats to approach without danger.

Putting foot on shore we found ourselves surrounded by about thirty men on horseback; to us, quite unused to their clothes and manners, they had quite the look of a troop of bandits. All were armed with great knives, and several had sabers hanging from their saddles. Most wore only the garb of poverty; the more stylish costume of some was no less singular—short breeches without buttons, open at the knee and terminating in two long, narrow points. The embossed buckskin wrapped around their legs instead of high boots was something new to us.[2] From their mounts, decked out in leather, to themselves covered from head to foot with broad pieces of the same mate-

―――――――――――――――――――――――――

1. The first six paragraphs of this chapter, ruminations on the nature of man and the motives of explorers, have been omitted. Two paragraphs about the exile Pedrin have been fitted in slightly later than their place in the original.

2. Perhaps a kind of chaps or *chaparajos*.

rial, so that one could hardly see their feet, everything about these men lent them a wild and savage aspect.

In spite of this inauspicious exterior, they greeted us politely and talked to us in Spanish. After we had informed them who we were and what had brought us to California, they told us that our ship was the first of our nation to come to this harbor but that they recognized the French as friends, children of the same church; we were welcome and should make ourselves at home. This alliance was ratified by the reciprocal offer of cigars, and while the *mechero* [tinder box] went around for lighting up, they presented us with horses and invited us to accompany them to the mission—that is, to the village of San José.

We mounted and took our way together along a narrow and sandy path, bordered on both sides by several kinds of bushes and by giant cacti. After about a thousand yards we came to a little river of clear water; its two small and shallow streams occupied only a portion of its bed, leaving the greater part dry. The path, several hundred feet farther along, led us to another stream bed quite as dry as the first, and it was from there that the mission of San José del Cabo came into view, a short distance away and consisting of a mean church with no bell tower and about thirty small houses with thatched roofs. The house of the superior appeared larger than the others and was constructed of brick.

It was during this excursion that we met Pedrin, one of the first acquaintances I made in California. He had almost forgotten the French language; it was only after several days of practice that he could once more speak it fluently. He took us to his house, where we stayed for some time and where his wife, proud and happy to entertain countrymen of her husband, greeted us with a fervor that showed a wish to please both her husband and his guests. She was no longer young, but there still existed a tender affection between her and Pedrin, who has found happiness with her and among the numerous children she has given him.

When Pedrin went to sea, it was a time of triumph and glory; children were born, it seemed, only to die on the battlefield. Many parents sought any means they could find to save their sons from this annual harvest but often did so only to see them run dangers of another sort. The breach of the Peace of Amiens[3] found Pedrin in Rio de Janeiro. Stranded when his ship was sold, he was by good fortune signed on as a seaman by an American captain, but a new misfortune awaited. On its way to the Northwest Coast, this ship was wrecked in the environs of Cabo San Lucas, and Pedrin was the only man saved from the catastrophe. He found hospitality among the good people of San José, where gratitude and love caused him to remain. There his good character and prudent conduct gained general approval, and his intelligence procured the comfort in which he lives today.[4]

Our new friend took us to visit the mission superior, Fray Tomás Ahumada of the Dominican order, who received us most graciously and led us to a large room, whose simplicity came close to poverty. A pleasant coolness, maintained by the use of two opposing doors, north and south, was the only luxury we could notice. Much of the room was taken up by a huge table, around which we sat on crudely fashioned benches. Because I was seated opposite the missionary, I was able to contemplate at leisure the beauty and serenity of his venerable features.

Fray Tomás was a man of sixty-five. So perfectly did his peaceful soul harmonize with the freshness of his color and the features of his fine face, so naturally did the exterior fit the moral qualities, that one could never have said whether the character was formed to match the physiognomy or whether the physiognomy was a portrait of the character. When you talked with him, it seemed that he instilled in your heart a measure of the peace in his own. His smile had nothing of gaiety about it but was an outward sign of great spiritual joy; in a word, Fray Tomás was a prototype of the true Christian. After devoting eighteen years to the founding of missions and to advancing the limits of

3. The Treaty of Amiens between England and France was made in 1802 and broken in 1803.

4. In his separate account of the voyage Edmond Le Netrel calls this man Jean Perdrine and says that he had lived in California for six years, hardly long enough to forget his native language or to fit the circumstances of his arrival. Pablo L. Martinez, in *Guía Familiar de Baja California, 1700–1900* (Mexico, 1965), 37, says that Juan Pedro Pedrin, a Frenchman, and his wife, Loreto Ceseña, had many descendants.

civilization in the northern part of Baja California, he was given for his retirement the poor parish of San José, where for four years he has exercised, in one way or another, both spiritual and temporal authority. The only civil magistrate, the *alcalde,* has seen fit to make no decisions without consulting him.[5]

On the advice of Fray Tomás I wrote to Don José María Padrés, commandant of Baja California at the city of Real San Antonio, to inform him of our arrival and to ask authorization to do business with the inhabitants.[6] I wrote also to Don Antonio Navarro, the provincial director of customs and finance, and, having learned that a Frenchman named Bello, a merchant, resided in the same city, I informed him too of our arrival at San José, asking his good offices if needed and putting myself at his service.[7] While awaiting answers to these letters, we occupied ourselves in putting the rigging in order and in painting the exterior of the ship.

During my second interview with Fray Tomás, this good man reminded me that All Saints Day would be celebrated on the morrow, and so on 1 November I went ashore with the officers and part of the crew of the *Héros.* The missionary was awaiting us, and when we arrived the church bells, hanging outside the building, rang to announce the beginning of the service.

The church, both inside and outside, suited the poverty of the mission; it was a kind of storehouse, roofed partly with tile and partly

5. The mission at San José del Cabo was founded by the Jesuits in 1730 and later became a *visita* of Santiago. When the Jesuits were expelled from Mexico in 1778 their missions were turned over first to the Franciscans and, when the latter moved north, to the Dominicans. According to the *Diccionario Porrúa . . . de México,* 5th ed., 1987, Fray Tomás Ahumada spent 27 years in the Baja California missions and returned to Mexico in 1831, where he died in 1842. His mummy is preserved in the monastery of Santo Domingo.

6. Padrés was born in Puebla, took part in the war of independence, and became an ardent republican. An advocate of secularizing the missions, he went to Alta California in 1830 and again in 1834 with the Híjar-Padrés colony. In 1835 he was sent back to Mexico by Governor Figueroa. In Chapter 7, after transporting Padrés to Mazatlán, Duhaut-Cilly gives a brief account of the latter's early life. Real San Antonio is by a modern map about seventy-five miles north of and inland from San José del Cabo.

7. Cayetano Bello, who married Rosario Pedrin, daughter of Juan Pedrin. (Martinez, op. cit., 287.)

with thatch. The only visible ornamentation consisted of some crude paintings done locally, a silver cross, and two lanterns of the same metal. The priest wore his best vestments, made of white satin and surprisingly bright. Mass was conducted by young Indians dressed in red cassocks and white surplices. All the services of the church have fallen to them; the principal citizens consider themselves above this lower class, although born of Indian mothers and Spanish fathers and thus half descended from it. In this they are merely expressing their aversion to servitude, since the two groups are equally attached to their religion. At that time their greatest concern was that the revolution in Mexico should stand against repression of the missionaries and that heresy should not be brought to California. An old woman one day harangued me in similar vein, but from the words she used I gathered that the object of her fears had assumed a completely animal form. Undoubtedly she had taken literally some hyperbole or other figure of speech used by the good missionaries. I assured her that no monster was about to appear and explained to her great pleasure that the new government had declared that the Catholic religion would be maintained forever as the basis of the state constitution.

Some women sang in nasal tones the responses and other parts of the mass. Although there was mingled with the well-known airs a quite original element from their own musical idiom, it was possible to imagine that one was hearing the voices of peasant women in our own country churches. To sustain the illusion one had only to close one's eyes and not notice that they were singing parts and quite in unison, which does not happen with us.

After several days I received an extremely polite response from Don José María Padrés. He granted with pleasure, he said, the permission that I had asked and went on to say that the arrival on this coast of a vessel belonging to such an enlightened (*illustrada*) nation was all the more pleasing to him in that it followed other events looked on by him and his fellow citizens as a happy prelude to recognition of Mexican independence.

The right to do business at San José, granted by the military commandant, was plain and simple, but the director of customs, replying to my letter, imposed an import duty of 25 per cent and a 3½ per cent departure tax. This duty was all the more onerous since they intended to figure it not on my invoice value but on the amount of the sale.

The letter from our compatriot Bello informed me that he had in the port of La Paz a small schooner which he would be sailing to the coast of Mexico, and he proposed that I go there also with the *Héros,* promising that we would do excellent business in the port of Mazatlán.

Our business in the harbor of San José was not large, although we sold at a good price. We were subjected to detailed inspection and barely took in one hundred or one hundred fifty piasters[8] a day. Because this trade was so small, we formed the idea of calling on the merchants of Real San Antonio. Mr. R____ undertook the trip, intending to ask a reduction of the custom charge and hoping also to open a way to more important business. There had come to us a few days before an agent of the customs director, charged with collecting duties on the prescribed basis, but when I told him that I wished to protest the amount, he decided to return, and we agreed that Mr. R____ together with Mr. Le Netrel, second mate on the ship, would go with him. On the day after this was decided I, along with some others from on board, conducted our travelers as far as the village of Santa Rosa, two leagues from San José, where we took leave of each other.

Several days later, needing wood for some large blocks or pulleys, I made an excursion with Pedrin to the farm of his father-in-law, about four leagues to the northwest of the mission. With us went the ship's carpenter and a seaman to help him cut the needed wood. Although we lost our way for a time, attempting a short cut by a path overgrown with grass, we were so well mounted that we arrived in less than two hours.

The road was good until half a league from the *rancho* (farm).* The way was narrow and tortuous, almost everywhere shaded by low trees.

---

8. The Spanish dollar or peso or piece of eight, common currency in a number of countries. It was divided into eight *reales* or bits.

* In California the word *rancho* does not mean precisely a farm but is used to designate a living place in the countryside. One can also say *hacienda, granja,* or *heredad.*

Later it followed the twists and turns of a rock-filled stream, running between great boulders that made the passage dangerous to horse and rider. The rancho occupies the bottom of a valley between two well-wooded mountains that are at least twelve hundred feet high. The name of La Ballena (The Whale), which they call this place, comes from a singular block of granite that lies in the bed of the torrent and has some resemblance, as much in size as in form, to the great cetacean to which the inhabitants compare it. In a country less a stranger to the arts an antiquary might be tempted to look on it as a fine ruin or an unfinished monument, but in California the first thought in the mind of anyone who cares for the grandiose is to make it into an obelisk two hundred feet high.

Toward the upper end of the valley is a level stretch of ground where are built the cabins of the *rancheros* (farmers), several families of them that promise to become more numerous with every passing day. The young rancheros and their wives show no signs of sterility; indeed, proofs of the opposite, both in accomplished deed and in obvious expectations, may be observed on every side. Each family has its own separate cabin, with that of old Carrillo, venerable patriarch of the village, situated at the center. Children, grandchildren, great-grand-children—the respected and respectable old man governs all this posterity with as much kindness as dignity. When I expressed wonder that he could manage to raise and support such a large family, he took my arm with one hand, leaning on it while giving the other hand to the child of his most cherished granddaughter, Doña Estefanita, and conducted me in silence to the highest part of the esplanade, where he had me sit next to him on a large block of stone. Little Pablo picked flowers and threw them at an iguana, which seemed less frightened than amused by this game.

"Take a look, Don Augusto,"* said the old man, "at this fine land. Can there be any place richer and more handsome? If your eyes are better than mine, they should be able to see the whole of an immense

* For a Californian my family name is quite difficult to pronounce; they have always called me by my Christian name.

area. The valley is boxed in here between these two hills, but it then spreads out into a wide plain, covered with shrubs and grass, and stretches to a chain of blue mountains, fifteen or twenty leagues away, which are the interior extension of Cape Porfia. I now can see only through a kind of mist, but I so admired the scene when I was younger that I can describe it from memory. If you will turn your gaze to what is nearer, below us and just over the roof of my dear Estefanita (the child turned his head from the lizard and smiled at the name of his mother), you will see a great park, empty at this moment but soon to be filled with the finest herd in all this province. They have wandered into the nearby woods to escape the heat. Can you hear how they fill the air with their bellowing? The men on horseback who are bringing in the cows—the steers and bulls do not return to the park—they are my sons and grandsons. All join together to take care of the family herd; here only the cabins are private to each household. And among the young men, notice the one whose white drawers extend a hand-breadth below his blue breeches and show so clearly against the black flank of his horse. That is my favorite, my dear Santiago, the best rider (*el mejor ginete*) in the country. Not long ago he went to visit his uncle Ramón Carrillo at the Rancho de Santa Anita, and because he met there a young cousin, rich with fourteen years and two beautiful eyes, we have to build him a house. There you see the cut timber and the adobes (bricks) laid out in the sun; you will know why. And well, Don Augusto, I cannot say that this land is mine, because everything belongs to the government or the mission, but I have the use of it, and my descendants will enjoy it after me. As long as there are Carrillos in Baja California, I do not fear that any other herd will come to graze these pastures.[9] As the family grows the herd will get larger and will suffice for all our needs. It is true that we know how to limit these needs; I allow my children no luxuries; we exchange our tallow, our hides, and our soap only for what will clothe us properly. So be surprised no more at our comfort and take a lesson in happiness."

9. The Carrillos were one of the early families of Baja California. Juan Carrillo, born about 1690, enlisted in the presidio of Loreto by 1715 and subsequently served at other missions.

"Alas!" I replied, "I well appreciate that happiness, but if you knew our Europe, you would soon see that such a sweet life is not for its children."

I enjoyed enormously the conversation of the venerable Californian, but the day was advancing, and we returned to his house. There we found the young ranch women setting a clean table with all the good things of the farm—cheeses, both soft and hard; creams and various milk products; watermelons, with fringes of jet-black seeds showing against the rose-white fruit. The young *rancheras* were also busy cooking the flat cakes of corn and wheat that are called *tortillas;* one of them was mixing the flour into a batter while another rounded some of it into a ball and then flattened it by patting it between her pretty hands; a third spread it on an iron stove where it soon swelled and turned golden; she then served it to us with a covering of cheese and fresh butter. Nearly all these young girls are pretty; a charming gaiety animated their features, showing the openness of their souls and the inner contentment of innocence.[10]

We then took ourselves a few hundred feet away from the rancho to examine the trees that might be suitable for our use. Our choice fell on a fine oak with small and lanceolated leaves and elongated brown acorns; the wood was redder and more finely grained than that of our oaks; these differences may derive more from the climate than from the species.

I had formed the idea of going in the ship's boat to examine the port of Cabo San Lucas; it had been described as quite good and I wished to see for myself whether that was true. I had asked Pedrin to accompany me and had fixed the date of 10 November for the excursion. He arrived on the evening of the 9th to sleep on board, but during the night a bad storm threatened in the east, and I deemed it not prudent to attempt a trip of seven leagues in a small boat or even to keep the

10. In this romantic and Rousseauistic passage we see the belief of the age in the goodness of the simple life next to nature and away from corrupt civilization. Although a sensible and practical man, Duhaut-Cilly was intellectually subject to the illusions of his own time, as we are subject to those of our time.

ship in an unprotected harbor. Calling off the plans, I had Pedrin put on shore at the break of day, and we got up sail and left the bay.

The two foreign whalers made no move to ensure their safety; doubtless they failed to understand the danger that menaced them, a matter on which I will give convincing proof. This sinister-looking storm, however, did not develop and little by little was dissipated. About ten in the morning, lying to about three leagues at sea to observe the weather, we perceived through the telescope a signal atop the house of Fray Tomás. Since the sky was clearing and the storm clouds moving away from us, we headed back to the bay to regain our place there and to learn what the signal meant. We were soon enlightened; before reaching the anchorage we met Pedrin coming to meet us in one of the whaling boats and bringing me letters from Mr. R____ and from Commandant Padrés.

Writing with great politeness, the latter made known to me the great embarrassment in which he found himself. Because he had no ship to carry him to the Mexican port nearest the capital, he found himself liable to miss the opening of the congress-general, to which he had just been elected a deputy. He might dispose of a Mexican schooner now in the port of La Paz, but for two reasons he hesitated to embark in it: he was in very bad health and would suffer from the discomforts of a small ship; and furthermore, this schooner was transporting seven criminals whom he himself had caused to be arrested and who, because of his diligence, would probably be condemned to death. And so he beseeched me to take him to Mazatlán in the *Héros,* promising me the gratitude of his government and leading me to believe that the trip would have a happy effect on my trading business.

Although my owners had not expected me to touch on the west coast of Mexico, I had carte blanche in regard to unexpected matters and saw nothing about this short voyage that might compromise my duties. But before replying in the affirmative, I consulted the letters from Mr. R____ and Mr. Bello, both of whom seemed to expect that I would go to that port. Only one consideration, to my mind, weighed against the advantages of the excursion: the unhealthy state of the coast of Mexico. However, I was assured by everyone that the bad season was past, and I knew that there existed within reach of Mazatlán a well-aired anchorage from where my crew could avoid any but the most essential communication with the shore. With these assurances I could see only advantage in the short voyage.

I therefore replied to Commandant Padrés that, wishing to demonstrate my good will to him and wishing especially to show the new republic the good intentions of the French, I would seize the occasion to serve him, adding that this step, consistent with the recommendations of the minister of the French navy, would please my government, which was always disposed to favor nations that were hospitable to its subjects.

During our stay at San José I was able to spend my time as I wished. The inconsiderable business that we did required my presence only at the beginning. Selling only at retail and at set prices, I could leave to my officers the work of delivering and receiving. On most mornings we sent a boat to shore, which returned with a dozen men who came to spend fifteen or twenty piasters each. I would then go ashore with Dr. Botta, and with our guns we would go hunting in the country roundabout. If some important matter arose on board, I was not far distant; they would run up a signal on the mainmast and I would return at once to the water's edge just as a boat arrived to fetch me. In the afternoon I would take myself to the mission and devote the rest of the day to talk with Fray Tomás, whose conversation was as pleasant as it was interesting.

Chapter 6

SAN JOSÉ AND REAL SAN ANTONIO[1]

November 1826

THE POPULATION OF THIS part of Baja California up to the parallel of Real San Antonio, comprising an area of at least four hundred square leagues, amounts to about five thousand souls and is composed of three classes. The first includes only men, a small number of foreigners and some Mexicans, who conduct commercial business or the affairs of government. This is the smallest group.

The second class makes up four-fifths of the population and bears the name of *gente de razón* (rational people). These are the descendants of Indian women and of the Spaniards who first landed and established themselves in the country. They have fine features, but their slightly dark color, persisting after several generations, betrays their maternal origin.

And last, there is the race of native Indians who have not yet suffered an admixture. In that part of the country I describe and throughout the peninsula, I believe, there are no longer any free Indians; they are all in the service of the missions or of private individuals. In spite of the changes brought about in Mexico by the revolution and the es-

---

1. We have omitted the first part of Duhaut-Cilly's Chapter 6, a few paragraphs on truth and fiction in travel writing and several pages on the birds and animals of the Cape region.

tablishment of independence, they are still looked upon and treated as slaves, called neophytes by the missionaries and domestics by the others. When the missionaries first set up a new establishment, they brought into the mission all the Indians they could collect, taught them, baptized them, and employed them in the construction of buildings and in the cultivation of the land. By an accord with the king of Spain these neophytes were to remain in the service of the missionaries for ten years, working without pay, the missionaries being required only to provide food and clothing. After this trial period they were to be considered civilized, and the mission lands they had cleared were to be distributed among them and they abandoned to their freedom. But at the end of the ten years no move was made to free them, and thus there has been perpetuated for more than a century this kind of servitude.

This policy of the missionaries has caused these unhappy people to lose all the advantages of civilization. Having no personal interest in their labor, they became lazy. And since good behavior did not result in noticeable well-being, they gave themselves over to all those vices that brought on the maladies that in turn destroyed the greater part of the population; the number of births, reduced by servitude, was far from compensating for the number of deaths. So this class comprises today only a sixth of the inhabitants in the part of the country of which I speak.

It is moreover quite certain that the Indian mortality is not caused by the climate but rather by misery and intemperance, for there is perhaps no country on the globe where people generally live as long as do the old people of Baja California. Few of them die before eighty years of age, and many live beyond one hundred; nearly all of them live to see the fourth generation.

The women have strong constitutions (I speak of the gente de razón) and seem to be made for having many children; thus one sees numerous families with fifteen to eighteen children, all by the same mother. Their clothing consists of skirts, or rather petticoats called *naguas,* fastened around the hips, and white shirts with a high neckline, stockings, and shoes. When they go out they add to this simple costume a shawl called a *rebozo,* which covers the head. These shawls of a rather coarse cloth are nearly all made in Mexico. The women have beautiful hair, which they wear long, letting it fall over their shoulders in two large braids.

The men usually go in shirts and full white pantaloons fringed often at the bottom, but when they spruce up or ride horseback they put on a short vest of blue cloth, edged and lined in red, and the short breeches already mentioned, with white drawers extending several inches below them. At these times they also wear around their legs those pieces of tooled leather that they call *botas* or *gamuzas*.

On the 14th Mr. R____ and Mr. Le Netrel returned from San Antonio with Commandant Padrés. They were accompanied by several people who wished to make purchases on board, among them the curé of San Antonio, named Roque.[2] Our trading success was small. To do business we would have had to sell in exchange for leather hides to be delivered in six months, but since we did not yet know how much time we would spend in California, we could not deal under these conditions. We had to limit ourselves to the small amount of silver money and bar silver available to the buyers. Some of them offered pearls, tortoise shell, as well as some gold dust of superior quality, which in this country goes by the name of placer gold.

When I sent Mr. Le Netrel, second mate on the *Héros,* with Mr. R____ my purpose was to obtain all possible information about the country. I requested him to examine carefully all things that appeared to him worthy of attention and to give me a faithful account of them. The brief time he spent on the trip made it impossible to go into much detail, but he accomplished his mission with zeal and intelligence. It is in justice to him that I here include his report, just as he gave it to me on his return.

REPORT OF MR. LE NETREL, SECOND MATE OF
THE *HÉROS,* ON HIS TRIP TO REAL SAN ANTONIO[3]

On the afternoon of Sunday, 5 November, having gone ashore with the captain, who had given me orders to accompany Mr. R____

2. Padre Roque Varela was at Mission San Antonio from 1812 to 1820 and from 1824 to 1827.

3. The report as included here is similar to but not the same as the version given in Le Netrel's own account, published four years earlier.

to San Antonio, I prepared myself for the trip, and at five o'clock in the evening we set out. Besides our guide, José Arcé, deputy to the commissioner of customs, we were conducted as far as the small village of Santa Rosa by a numerous cavalcade: half the crew of the *Héros* and of two whaling ships in the roadstead, they having asked permission of Mr. Duhaut-Cilly to accompany him to the place where we had agreed to separate. Having stopped there a few minutes while the captain gave refreshments to his escort, we got back in the saddle, some returning to the port and others taking the road to the interior.

The way was pleasant and smooth as far as the village of Santa Anita; we rode for about a league alongside the bed of a river that is quite wide but where no water runs except in the rainy season. I saw only one hut, built on a little rise to the left of the road, but it was night, and from the large number of farm animals that we kept encountering, I judged that there must be other dwellings nearby.

At eight o'clock in the evening we arrived at Santa Anita, where we dismounted at the house of a pleasant old man, Ramón Carrillo, who had dined with us at the missionary's house in San José.[4] His house, like those in Santa Rosa, was constructed of wood and earth and covered over with reeds. On the interior wall was painted a large white cross. We were well received and, after refreshing ourselves, continued on our way.

We now climbed a hill with a rather steep grade and then came out on the splendid plain of La Mesa (the table), which is said to be twenty leagues in circumference. At eleven in the evening we arrived at a small settlement of three houses, where Mr. R___ and I lay down on a bed with a leather hide as mattress. Here we slept well until five in the morning, a profound sleep resulting, no doubt, more from the fatigue of the road than from the softness of the bed.

On the 6th we continued to cross the plain of La Mesa on a road that was still quite good but less smooth. In this magnificent terrain we saw here and there a number of houses but no cultivated fields, and we soon came to a ridge called Cuesta Blanca (white ridge) be-

---

4. Probably the uncle mentioned during the visit to the rancho of La Ballena in the previous chapter.

cause it is composed of a whitish soil. Near the top and quite close to us a handsome stag stood still for a few moments and then darted into the woods with the light grace of its kind. On a plain at the foot of this hill I remarked a tree much like our European oak; to judge by the varied forms of the limbs, it could be used for naval construction.

The first village encountered was that of Santiago, which is divided into two parts, one about a thousand yards from the other and each situated on a small rise. The fine river of the same name runs at some distance to the right of the road. In this village there are perhaps twelve or fifteen houses. The surrounding fields are not cultivated, but the people raise cattle and make a large quantity of cheese. Leather is tanned and worked with considerable taste. I saw a cloak of deerskin that was splendidly adorned with a scalloped hem and the other parts decorated in a varied pattern, and was able to buy it for twenty-five piasters.

About two miles beyond Santiago we came to the house of a worthy man who had visited us on board the *Héros*, and here we rested for several hours. Near the dwelling is an enclosure for two hundred bullocks and cows and a little farther on a well-tended field of sugar cane. He makes cheese and *tasajo*.* I judged that we were then about twenty leagues from San José.

While we were at this man's house, two people coming from San Antonio apprised us that Commandant Padrés intended to leave there at seven in the morning. As our group could not arrive until that evening, R____ decided to send a courier to inform him that we were on the way.

At three in the afternoon we remounted our horses and set out. Several times we had to cross the Santiago River, the road cutting across the bends of the stream. We then climbed a very long wooded slope, and the plain that opened up thereafter was much more forested than those we had traversed before. A prodigious number of hares and foxes ran quite close to our horses. At six in the evening we came to a small place called Los Martiros (the martyrs), five leagues from Santiago; here we passed the night in the

---

* Meat that is salted and dried in the sun.

same manner as before. This settlement is composed of three huts built on a small piece of high, sandy ground, a league and a half from the shore of the sea.

On the 7th at two o'clock in the morning we were en route once more under a fine bright moon, and after traveling five miles found ourselves on the shore of the Gulf of California or Vermilion Sea, facing a small bay called Ensenada de Palma (Bay of Palms). We then followed the shore, crossing several rivers of which the largest was called Rio de Tres Colores (River of Three Colors). Once more the road turned inland with another river on our right. This part of the country is neither cultivated nor inhabited.

We climbed a steep hill by a very rough road; descending the other side we came to the river of Los Toros (the bulls), a stream of excellent water running fast and full. Its banks are obstructed by enormous blocks of granite. Here they obtain a large quantity of gold dust, found mixed with the sand of the river bed. We went up still another ridge, where the soil, up to now sandy, became red and hard, pitted with holes and cracks on both sides of the road.

Having made twelve leagues from Los Martiros, we reached at eleven o'clock in the morning a rancho named Agua Caliente (hot water) on account of a spring of thermal water that flows from under a rock twenty-five feet from the house. The heat of the water is about equal to that of bath water.

We were now only two leagues from San Antonio, and there we arrived at six in the evening after crossing a fine plain and surmounting a hill from where we could discern the Vermilion Sea from a distance of about six leagues. We had a letter of introduction from Fray Tomás to Padre Roque, curé of San Antonio, at whose house we stayed. Almost at once we went to pay our respects to Commandant Padrés, who received us with great courtesy.

November 8 was devoted to business, and on the 9th I viewed the so-called city; this I found to consist of about sixty houses, all constructed in the same manner as those we had seen up to now, with thatched roofs and with no furniture except beds of leather, crudely made tables and benches, and chairs of cane covered with leather.

The export trade of Real San Antonio consists of ox hides, tasajo, cheese, maize, and a small amount of cotton. These products are taken to the closest port, that of La Paz, from where they are shipped to Mazatlán and to the ports of Sonora, directly across the Vermilion Sea. There are also operating silver mines in this territory, from which they obtain very fine *pina.**

The people are hospitable and honest, but they also appear to be quite lazy; every time I entered one of their houses I found them either lying down or idle. A great number of children swarm around the houses. These children are precocious smokers; one of them left its mother's breast to take a cigar from me and began to smoke it.

After five days in San Antonio we departed in company with Commandant Padrés, who had obtained passage to Mazatlán from the captain. We spent the night on a plain six leagues from the town; there the men killed a cow to make provisions for the trip, and on the 14th we arrived in San José.

[end of Le Netrel's report]

After the return of our travelers we remained several days in the roadstead of San José in order to serve the people who had come with them and wished to make purchases. I then settled my accounts with the commissioner of customs, the settlement being quite satisfactory. Commandant Padrés had asked me to escort to Mazatlán the schooner that carried the criminals mentioned above, and when I had consented to do so he ordered this small ship to come from La Paz.**

On the evening of the 17th we got under way in company with this schooner and set out to the east-northeast with a fine breeze from the north-northwest. Although Commandant Padrés had assured us that the schooner was a fast sailer, we soon perceived that she could not keep up with us and so we attached a tow-rope to her. With the wind slackening off we did not sight the Mexican coast until the morning of the 19th. The officer commanding the schooner then came aboard

---

* This is the virgin silver after being purged by fire of the mercury with which it was mixed. The more rigorously the evaporation of the quicksilver is managed, the purer the metal. But later I saw proof that the operation is done but imperfectly at San Antonio.

** These men were the crew of a small Mexican schooner and were accused of assassinating the captain and the supercargo.

and, after a short discussion with Commandant Padrés, it was agreed that he would leave our company and make his own way to San Blas. So we cast off the tow-rope and separated.

At daybreak on the 20th we were still about eight leagues from land. There are three principal islands that should have served to identify the harbor of Mazatlán, but at this distance the many hills of the coast looked like an entire group of islands. At noon we had come a little closer and, by observing the latitude, we were able to distinguish true islands from apparent ones. We now had in front of us a three-masted ship heading in the same direction; being closer in than we, she could be at anchor before nightfall. For us this was impossible, and it was not until the next morning that we were able to cast anchor under the island of Venado (deer island) and close to the ship that we had seen on the evening before. She was Genoese and had come from China under command of Captain Thérèse.[5]

5. In Chapter 11, on his second trip to Mazatlán, Duhaut-Cilly identifies this ship as the *Rose* (*Rosa?*). The captain's name may have been Teresa.

Chapter 7

MAZATLÁN AND CABO SAN LUCAS [1]

November—December 1826

ON THE MORNING AFTER OUR arrival, at sunrise, we saluted the Republic of Mexico with thirteen cannon shots, which had to be done slowly with a single poorly mounted gun on that side of the ship. I then went ashore with Mr. R____ and our passenger in order to pay our respects to the authorities of the country, that is, to a lieutenant-colonel who commanded the military forces and to a *capitán del resguardo* (head of the custom guards). The latter told me that the laws of Mexico require a foreign captain to deposit his manifest within forty-eight hours of arrival. If he should disembark even one item, then the entire cargo, down to the last case, must be unloaded and a duty of 46% paid on it whether it be sold or reembarked. I replied that since I had come to Mazatlán only in order to transport a member of the congress, I thought I was entitled to special treatment, and that for this reason I had anchored in the outer harbor. And also that I was determined to remain there until we had cleared this point with the

---

1. From this chapter we have omitted several passages about the Mexican war of independence, about the anchorage in Mazatlán, and about charting the bay of San Lucas.

comisaría general, located in the city of Rosario. Consequently, in order to gain time and to see what we could do about this interruption, it was agreed that Mr. R___ would leave the next day for Rosario, traveling with Commandant Padrés, who was going in that direction.

❍   ❍   ❍

I have already said much about Padrés, but some biographical details learned in Mazatlán induce me to inform the reader. Born in the city of Los Angeles,[2] he was destined to enter the bar and pursued his studies with that in mind until the revolution broke out in Mexico and he had to change his plans. His father, a former magistrate, impelled by the patriotism then felt in the hearts of all Mexicans, asked him to leave his books and take up arms. When Padrés hesitated, his father ordered him to go to the defense of his country. If at first Padrés experienced some irresolution, this was because it cost him much to abandon a course that he had chosen by inclination; but as soon as his destiny was decided he erased from his heart all other ideas but that of serving his country well.

He began as sub-lieutenant in a company of artillery and by dint of study soon made himself capable of performing the new duties entrusted to him. It often happened, said his biographer, that he would study during the night, without anyone being aware, the things that he would have to do in the morning, so that he soon astonished his soldiers and fellow officers, surprised to see that he knew more than they about things of which they thought him ignorant; but he took great care not to reveal the secret of his success. By this means he maintained his self-esteem, gained their regard, and made himself useful to his unit. Thus he soon made the rank of captain, and when the state was no longer in danger he was sent to take command in Baja California with the rank of lieutenant-colonel. There he occupied himself in a close inspection of that whole province and in gathering material for a work he proposed to publish on the geography and to-

2. Puebla de Los Angeles, between Vera Cruz and Mexico City, which came to be known simply as Puebla.

pography and on the commercial and agricultural resources of the peninsula. . . .

In discussing these matters with him I thought I saw an opportunity to present to the Mexican government a project for an agricultural and commercial establishment at Cabo San Lucas; and as he demonstrated a strong interest, I drew up a petition together with a kind of agreement by which he pledged to solicit from the congress the concessions, privileges, and immunities set forth in this document. I even furnished him funds to cover the cost of copying, registration, translation, and the like. I agreed also to prepare a chart of the harbor of San Lucas and to send this to him in Mexico.*

Mr. R____ spent a week on his journey to Rosario, and we were at first quite satisfied with the sales he made there. For my part I put this time to good use and had reason to be pleased that I had come to Mazatlán. At this point, however, there arrived from San Blas a new commandant of the resguardo before whom everyone appeared to tremble. His rigidity and incorruptibility were deemed to be insensible to any consideration. You are lost, people told me; you should not have remained here so long, and the best thing you can do now is to set sail without having any discussion with him. But that is not my way and moreover I had some distrust of this reputation of severity thrown out in advance like the black liquid that a cuttlefish squirts around itself in order to hide from a menacing enemy. So I went to see him at once before anyone could have time to forewarn him, and here I must share a confidence with the reader: from the very first encounter we were in agreement, understanding each other as if our interests were entirely the same.

In spite of this understanding he had to avoid compromising himself, and as I had not yet handed in my manifest and had stayed far beyond the limits of the law, he advised me, in order to gain time, to ask official permission to remain another several days to take on water,

* I kept to the agreement and cannot explain his silence on the results of his overtures. His government may have feared that the project concealed some trap such as plans for the invasion of Baja California.

wood, and provisions. Meanwhile, to avoid all suspicion, he urged me to come to anchor in Mazatlán itself.

[The ship was then moved to an anchorage in the inner harbor, near Creston Island.]

✿ ✿ ✿

We had sold quite a large lot of goods to Don Ignacio Fletes, a merchant at the presidio of Mazatlán, and in order to make delivery to him I had deposited a manifest with the customs; but since this listed a number of prohibited articles our hope of gaining special permission to make delivery was dashed. On the contrary, an order to set sail immediately came to us from the presidio.

Not yet willing to admit defeat, I myself set off on the road to the presidio, nine or ten leagues distant from the port. Although persuaded that this step would be useless, I was delighted to find one more way to put off our departure; it would not be time wasted for our business.

I set out mounted on a good mule and accompanied by a guide. In a direct line it is scarcely six leagues from the port to the presidio of Mazatlán, but one must go around several arms of the sea that penetrate the land, and this adds a good four leagues to the distance. We traveled quite a good road through a forest of bushes, many of which bore beautiful flowers. At the halfway point is a rancho called El Castillo (the castle) and here we stopped for several minutes to refresh ourselves and then took to the road again. As we approached the presidio the trees, until then small, dry, and spindly, became larger and greener. The path ran under an arbor of enormous sandbox trees, on which were frolicking handsome macaws, parakeets, and a kind of brown and green pheasant whose cries were less pleasant to the ear than its plumage was to the eye.

The soil in this region appeared so fertile that I groaned in spite of myself to see it abandoned to the wild growth of nature. No sooner had we left this enchanted grove than we found ourselves all at once on the banks of the Mazatlán River. We crossed on horseback, and to avoid wetting our feet we took them from the stirrups and stretched our legs over the saddle-bows. I could see that this river, now only forty meters wide, becomes a raging torrent during the rainy season. A large part of its wide and deep bed was now dry, but the crumbling banks and the bushes alongside them, smashed down and covered with debris of grass and branches, made clear that there had recently been a great flood. Now the water flowed clear and the taste was excellent.

A few minutes later we reached the town, where we stayed with Don Ignacio Fletes in a handsome house newly built. It is a large square building with no other opening to the outside but a tall porte-cochere under which one passes to enter the courtyard. There is only the ground floor, but the rooms are large, with high ceilings, and very clean. Constructed of adobes, cubes of earth baked in the sun, it is rather crudely made but is covered with plaster and thatched. On the four sides of the interior court a line of columns painted pink supports a set of galleries and lends an air of opulence to the inner dwelling. The outside has the aspect of a prison, or looks rather like those oriental houses that are equally stingy with openings to the outside.

At the presidio of Mazatlán there are several other quite decent houses, but the rest of the town is no more than a collection of huts. The population may amount to as many as 2500 souls. The well-constructed church faces a large square plaza, bordered on three sides by the best houses of the town.[3]

The people of Mazatlán appear sad and miserable. In my opinion the chronic state of illness that affects nearly all of them, together with their indolence, does much to lend them this unhappy look. In few households, I was told, are there fewer than two people with the fever without counting the convalescents, whose aspect is not much more lively. This fever that infects them throughout most of the year is not altogether dangerous, but since they have no medicines and know nothing at all about the simplest remedies or about diet or temperance, it takes root among them, and even when it goes away leaves them weak, morose, and old before their time.

3. The Mazatlán presidio and its adjoining town lay some twenty-five miles westerly of the port on the road to Tepic and San Blas. Much of it was in ruins, but a detachment of soldiers and some administrative officers were still stationed there.

After having spent three days making overtures whose uselessness I anticipated in advance, I made ready to return to the ship. I took the occasion of my sojourn at the Mazatlán presidio to send a letter to France by way of Mexico and Vera Cruz and then returned to the port by the same road I had followed in coming and accompanied by my faithful guide. On the day before my departure for the presidio, I received an official letter (*de oficio*) from the commandant of the port, who informed me that the next day was the festival of Nuestra Señora de Guadalupe and on the same day that of Guadalupe Victoria, president of the republic; and since the Mexicans have a special veneration for this Virgin and also profess a limitless gratitude for the services of this general, he suggested that I might wish to contribute to the splendor of the festival by replying to the salutes that would be fired from the fort. I had consequently left orders aboard ship to fire thirteen guns in the morning and the same number in the evening. The order was executed punctually.[4]

❂   ❂   ❂

On 15 December, having finished all our business, we weighed anchor to return to California. My intention was to go as soon as possible to San Francisco, the most northern presidio of those settlements. But before that I had need to visit the port of Cabo San Lucas and, as I have said, to forward a proposal to Commandant Padrés in order that he might present to his government exact information about the site that I was requesting for a French settlement.

On the 17th we anchored in the roadstead of San José to fulfill the promise I had made to Pedrin and Fray Tomás to take them with me to San Lucas. We passed the night at anchor in the bay and left again on the 18th with these two excellent friends on board.

It is only six leagues from San José to San Lucas. First one goes southwest a quarter south and then southwest a quarter west by the compass. We had light contrary breezes and then calm weather, caus-

---

4. Guadalupe Victoria, whose original name was Manuel Félix Fernández, was the first president of the Mexican republic (1824–1829) after the overthrow of the dictator Iturbide.

ing the passage to be longer than expected, and we were unable to cast anchor until four in the evening. Approaching the anchorage, we spied a brig which announced its colors with a cannon shot. At once we hoisted our own in the same way. It was a ship belonging to the king of the Sandwich Islands, which we knew to be in these waters hunting fur seals. The commander, Captain Samna [Sumner], came on board while we still had sail up, and he immediately recognized Mr. R____.[5]

The news that he gave us from the Sandwich Islands was not reassuring for the rest of our affairs. They knew about our expedition. Mr. R____, far from being awaited as a friend, stood on the contrary accused, if not of having contributed to the death of King Liholiho in England, at least of having watched over his stay there with insufficient care.[6] I even heard Captain Samna say to him in English that if he cared for his head he should abandon all thought of going to the Sandwich Islands. I had moreover a conversation with the officers of the brig, who confirmed the report of their captain, and this caused me not only to doubt the current reputation of Mr. R____ in the Islands but also that which he claimed to enjoy before going with the king to England. He tried vainly to persuade me that Samna, no friend of his, was circulating rumors only to discourage him and to turn him away from going to the Hawaiian archipelago, where the captain feared his influence. My faith in his words had already received more than one blow; this last revelation shook it to the foundations. From this time on I resolved within my own mind to profit from every chance to sell the cargo while awaiting further instructions.

We cast anchor in the bay in ten fathoms of water and within hailing distance of the land. I went ashore at once to reconnoiter and to see whether I could procure firewood and water, necessities that the sailor must seek out before anything else. There were no running streams, but near the beach and behind the small sand dunes that

5. The *Kamahalolani*, Captain William Sumner, was at Cabo San Lucas at that time on the way back to Honolulu with a cargo of 3,160 seal skins.
6. Liholiho's journey to London is described in the author's introduction.

form it we found water at ground level. To obtain an abundant supply it sufficed to sink into the sandy soil a cask that was stove in at both ends; it filled immediately with water of excellent quality. It appeared that throughout the plain that extends to the northwest one can find water a few feet underground.

❂   ❂   ❂

From the statements of Mr. R____ I had fancied that the port of Cabo San Lucas would be much more enclosed than it actually is. It is formed by a pointed cape made up of high rocks; the most notable of these is in the shape of a pyramid. This cape, jutting out some twelve hundred meters to the east, would offer fine shelter from the winds of the south and even from those of the southeast if one could gain this protection by anchoring close in. Unfortunately, it slopes off too abruptly; at a half cable from the rocks at its foot I could not find bottom with a line of seventy-five fathoms.

From the cape to a low black point that I called Padrés on my chart there stretches a long sandy beach that runs first to the north and then curves gradually until it runs in an easterly direction, parallel to the cape. Inside this area there is good anchorage at seven or eight fathoms and within two hundred meters of the land. This bay is much preferable to that of San José but, being open from the southeast to the east, cannot be truly safe except during the season of northerly winds.

The vegetation of the plain of San Lucas is nearly the same as that of San José. That is to say, it is composed of bushes, many of them spiny, and of several kinds of cactus. On one of these we found fruits of a fine red color with an infinity of small seeds held together by a pulp like that of the strawberry, and it has a similar taste.[7]

In this peaceful retreat there was living in patriarchal fashion an uncle of Pedrin surrounded by a numerous family. These sole inhabitants of San Lucas, separated from the town of San José by a chain of arid mountains and by difficult roads, had only rare communication with their neighbors. On festival days parties of young people from

---

7. The *pitahaya agria*.

the ranch, going in turn, mounted their best horses and journeyed to the mission to hear mass and listen to the sermon of Fray Tomás. That was almost the limit of their commerce with the rest of humanity. Were they the less happy for this? I do not think so. In the air around them one sensed the peace of the soul, the absence of present cares, and confidence in the future. But sometimes when they had collected a certain number of ox and cow hides or had made several quintals of cheese, they loaded these products on mules and took them to San José, from where they returned with a supply of those things needed for daily life. For this commercial operation they often chose a time when some ship was in the roadstead at San José; they had once come when we were there. Our arrival in their own port now must have saved them a journey; in return for some oxen we sold them enough provisions to last for a long time.

Besides the fine herds of the rancho, which graze in the woods roundabout, one encounters on this plain a considerable number of wild cattle. Sometimes the bulls come to drink at the water holes and to seek consorts. We saw several of these formidable animals; on seeing men, and especially strangers, they pounded the ground with their hooves, fixed ferocious looks on us while shaking their heads and threatening us with their horns. At such times we found it wise to retreat to the ship or within the ranch buildings. But soon the young *rancheros* descend on them with no other arms than their ropes, their skill, and the quickness of their horses. No sooner has the bull perceived them than, forgetting his thirst and abandoning his loves, he flees bellowing into the brush; and there for a long time one can follow the line of his course by the shaking of the bushes that he surges over like a torrent. Californians on horseback have no fear of attacking these animals; it would be otherwise were they surprised on foot for they would then have no defense against the fury of the beast. Often these bulls lead cows away from the rancho. The young men would destroy all those that appear if they did not have to pay the government—to whom they are deemed to belong—a duty of three piasters for each bull killed. For this reason they content themselves with frightening them off and driving them back into the woods.

On 25 December, having completed our business, we took on board eight cows to provide for our table; they cost us six piasters each. Before leaving, I directed a copy of my map of San Lucas to Fray Tomás, who had returned to San José on the day before, and another to be sent on by him to Don José María Padrés in Mexico. Forthwith we weighed anchor in a light breeze from the southwest. When the good people saw that the *Héros* was setting sail they all ran to the shore and made a thousand signs of friendship, firing off their muskets in farewell. Responding to these signs of interest, I fired off one of our cannon while letting the sails go slack, and we then saw them throwing their hats in the air as a final expression of their good wishes.

On the 29th, the wind having freshened from the southeast, a heavy rain began to fall. We were making good way with the wind behind us when suddenly it veered to the northwest, blowing now from the direction in which we were headed. Catching all the sails, it forced the ship backward. In this position the poop was perpendicular to the waves and the water rushed in three times through the four windows of my cabin, breaking the panes and flooding us before our maneuvers could make the ship fall off and get wind in the sails. Such accidents can happen often enough with young officers who do not appreciate the consequences; but an alert and experienced sailor will avoid them because he will always see some indication of a change in the wind, especially during the day. The event, however, had no grievous consequences; the water ran quickly out through the scuppers placed for this purpose on both sides of the cabin deck. Several wet books, some pieces of furniture damaged, and ten minutes of ill humor on the part of someone I know who was concerned about these minor losses; after that, forgive and forget, and a paternal admonition to the negligent officer of the watch.[8]

8. From this passage we may speculate that the captain's wife may have been on the voyage. In two later footnotes he mentions the presence of his young brother-in-law, Albert Bourdas.

Chapter 8

January–February 1827

THE YEAR 1827 BEGAN UNDER happy auspices; the weather was splendid, and we scudded along toward San Francisco before a favorable
wind. I had no difficulty in trusting the sincerity of the good wishes
expressed to me on the morning of the 1st of January, for it is truly on
board ship that all are united by a common concern, at least in relation to the dangers or successes of the voyage. Each feels that his lot is
linked to that of his fellows, that he shares the same chances, runs the
same risks; but while wishing good fortune to the others, each is
moved less perhaps by philanthropic feelings than by personal con-
siderations. He seeks to read his own fate in the fate of the others, who
reflect it back to him as would the surface of a lake, now smoothed by
the calm of hope but more often agitated by sudden storms of unease
and fear.

On the 2nd of January we passed within sight of Guadalupe Island,
situated in 29° north latitude and eighty leagues from the coast of

---

1. A passage of several pages on the perils of navigating in the fog has been dropped from
this chapter, as shown by the asterisks. Replete with the details of tacking, sounding, and
compass bearings, it was written by the author for navigators who might follow him and will
be, he says, of little interest to other readers.

California. It is five leagues long from south-southwest to north-northeast and about two leagues wide. The island is quite high, particularly to the north where we remarked some large trees. It is uninhabited, but the Russians and the Americans often encamp there to hunt fur seals. The Sandwich Island brig that we encountered at Cabo San Lucas had spent several months there and had collected three thousand sealskins.* [2]

On the afternoon of the 15th the sky was covered with thick clouds and the sea was running high. The weather was almost calm; everything proclaimed a change of wind, and indeed it soon veered from north-northeast to southeast, and as we were then on the parallel of San Francisco we steered directly for that port.

❂ ❂ ❂

[Wishing to follow the lead of Vancouver and Roquefeuil and approach San Francisco from the north, Duhaut-Cilly doubled the Farallons on the west, then sailed toward the coast between these islands and Point Reyes.[3] All went well until the afternoon of the 18th, when a dense fog settled in and hid everything from sight for eight days and nights. Several times, as they tacked cautiously about, officers and crew believed they heard and saw waves breaking over dangerous reefs. Eventually they retraced their course, approached the harbor from the south, and waited, along with the Russian brig *Baikal,* Captain Kirill T. Khlebnikov, for the fog to lift. The reefs later proved not to exist, and Duhaut-Cilly decided that he had been victimized by a mirage.]

On the morning of 26 January we had fair weather at last, and as soon as it was light we made out the entrance to San Francisco Bay, distant about three leagues. The view agreed perfectly with Vancou-

* A fur sealskin of good quality usually brings two piasters in Canton.

2. Guadalupe Island, a Mexican possession off the Baja California coast, was a base for fur seal and sea otter hunting as late as 1844. In this passage the author uses, apparently without change of meaning, the terms *loup marin,* from the Spanish *lobo marino,* sea lion or seal (literally sea wolf), and *phoque,* the ordinary word for seal.

3. The Farallons, three small islands or groups of "sea rocks," are some twenty-five miles west of the Golden Gate and south of the prominent headland of Point Reyes.

ver's description. On the north were steep cliffs of a purplish color; the southern shore, less elevated, was composed of sand dunes mixed with huge scattered rocks, some of which extended several hundred meters into the water at the entrance to the channel.

There was a good breeze, and we lost no time in entering the channel that leads to the great harbor of San Francisco. After passing the first point, where the rocks I have mentioned are found, we reached another and higher point where stands an old Spanish fort,[4] and almost at once found ourselves opposite a cluster of houses that we all took to be a farm. But on examining them more closely and on consulting the accounts of the navigators I have cited, Vancouver and Roquefeuil, I recognized the presidio.[5] As all was in readiness for anchoring, we had only to change course and steer the ship toward the gentle curve made by the southern shore just beyond the fort. A few minutes later, the lead showing seventeen fathoms and a mud bottom, we let go the anchor two hundred fathoms from the beach.

Some men on horseback hastened at once to the shore. I landed with Mr. R____ and there met several soldiers, who offered us horses and invited us to go to the presidio. We set out then, making a long detour to avoid some marshes we had not noticed from the ship, and after a quarter of an hour we arrived at the house of the commandant, Don Ignacio Martínez, lieutenant of infantry, who welcomed us most courteously, congratulated us on our safe arrival, and placed himself and all he possessed at our service—a Spanish expression quite without meaning.[6]

4. The Castillo de San Joaquín at Fort Point, a horseshoe-shaped fortification first completed in 1794, was rebuilt in 1816 and was said in 1820 to mount twenty guns, though none, according to Kotzebue in 1824, were in condition to fire a shot.

5. The presidio, a fortified quadrangle dedicated in 1776, being of highly perishable material and in an exposed place, was extensively rebuilt in 1815 and in 1821. Housing the garrison and their families, it was said by Vancouver in 1792 to resemble a "pound for cattle," and Beechey described it, three months before Duhaut-Cilly's arrival, as being in a dilapidated condition and of the "humblest style."

6. Martínez, *comandante* at San Francisco from 1822, was 57 years old at the time and was to retire in 1831. Though hospitable, he was unpopular as an officer and was several times reproved by his superiors for being despotic and officious. Duhaut-Cilly later suffered some unpleasantness at his hands.

Don Ignacio Martínez had a large family, notably many young daughters of pleasing appearance, several of whom were already married. The husband of one of these young persons was an Englishman named Richardson, who appeared to be quite well acquainted with the harbor and the coast outside it.[7] He confirmed the Russian captain's opinion on the passage between the Farallons and Point Reyes and assured me that no danger existed there. He told me also that we had chosen a poor anchorage and offered to pilot the ship to that of Yerba Buena, situated in a cove farther inland and behind a large point that we could see a league away to the east.[8]

While we talked in Don Ignacio's drawing room, there was heard a salvo of seven guns from the *Héros,* which I had ordered for the moment when the crew supposed I had reached the presidio. I wished to see what effect this courtesy would have on the commandant of San Francisco. When I told him that the salute was addressed to him he seemed to grow a foot taller, and I noticed that several soldiers and civilians who had kept their hats on now respectfully removed them. He immediately ordered some of his daughters to bring cheese, others to bring tortillas and cakes, still others sweet wine from Mission San Luis Rey and brandy from San Luis Obispo. Their quick obedience could be translated like this: Papa must be a very great man if they shoot off seven cannons in his honor. All was confusion in the house, and in the midst of it he sent a corporal to the fort to return at least part of the salute, but of seven pieces loaded only three were heard to go off. At some small cost to the Mexican government, and with more excuses from Don Ignacio, the concussion blew two gun carriages to bits.

The loss of two old engines of war did not keep us from enjoying

---

7. The Englishman William A. Richardson left the whaler *Orion* at San Francisco in 1822, became a citizen, and in 1825 married María Antonia Martínez. Besides serving as pilot on the bay, he maintained a launch for hire and collected produce for sailing vessels.

8. The name Yerba Buena, perhaps first applied to North Beach, had by the late 1820s been transferred to a (now vanished) cove on the eastern shore of the peninsula south of Telegraph Hill, where Duhaut-Cilly moved the *Héros* from the official anchorage below the presidio.

the attentions of the pretty Californians. Their freshness and gaiety, only slightly restrained in the presence of strangers, delighted us and contributed not a little to our enjoyment of the delicious things they offered. The story we had just told of dangers run so close to the harbor had struck them with terror; one especially, sitting in front of me, went remarkably pale. "Do you think," I said to her, "that it was too high a price to pay for the tortillas prepared by your pretty hands?" She lowered her eyes, and the pallor receded before a richer tint.

Returning to the ship with Richardson, we found that the Russian brig had just arrived. We then hauled in the anchor cable, but before it was apeak saw the anchor-stock floating on the water; the force of the ebb tide, and a contrary wind from the west-northwest, had held the ship athwart and broken this off. If the accident had been limited to that, the repair might have been made easily enough, but when we raised the anchor we found that one fluke was gone. Since we had lost our third anchor in one of the moorings outside the bay, this new misfortune left us with only two, and with no knowledge of when or how we might procure another.

But we got under sail, and with the aid of a brisk breeze managed to advance slowly against the strong current. After sailing two miles to the east, running close to the shore, and then a mile east 15° south, we reached Yerba Buena Cove, where we anchored in five fathoms over a bottom of soft mud. The northern point of the cove hid completely the entrance to the harbor.

The next day, while the crew was occupied in setting up a tent at the most suitable place on shore and in unloading the materials I had obtained in Mazatlán for construction of a whaling boat,* we paid a visit to the superior of Mission San Francisco, two miles from Yerba Buena.

In order to plan our subsequent operations, I was eager to obtain as much information as possible on what success we might have in this part of California. Fray Tomás was expecting us and received us with

---

* Ordinary small boats are not suitable for disembarking on most parts of the coast where we would find ourselves.

a fine demonstration of friendship, a greeting that was never belied by his conduct in all my later dealings with this good friar.[9]

Hardly had we taken seats around the oak table, when they brought us *las once** and Fray Tomás asked me news of Spain in a tone that told me at once how much he regretted that California was no longer ruled by that country. He was delighted, he told me, to converse at last with a Christian stranger. All those heretics (meaning the English and Americans) opened their mouths only to lie and spout blasphemy.

In spite of this distinction and my wish to tell him something pleasing on matters that concerned him, I could not hide from him the poor state of his country at the time we left Europe. But had not the French gone into Spain to save Ferdinand and restore him to absolute power? How, after that, could I make him understand that the claim to absolute power was actually the cause of misery in Spain? It would have been a waste of time, and I had not come to California to rectify the political education of this honest missionary.

I found the San Francisco mission quite different from what it was when Vancouver visited here in 1794. At that time it consisted of a chapel and one house, forming two sides of a square. Not only was the square now completed but there was also a large church and a row of buildings that served as storehouses and dependencies.

Beyond this group of buildings, and separated from it by a large court where runs a stream of fresh water, are the habitations of the Indians attached to the mission. These are arranged in an orderly way and divided by straight streets at regular intervals. Some years ago this establishment had become one of the most considerable in California, both for the wealth of its products and for the number of its Indians. But in 1827 there remained of this splendor only the many structures that had once been needed, most of which were now falling into ruin.

When Roquefeuil visited in 1816 there were still seven hundred In-

---

9. Tomás Eleuterio Esténaga came to California in 1820 and was at San Francisco from 1821 to 1833. Though often ill, he was jovial in nature, and Beechey found his conversation in 1826 to be "no less palatable than his cheer."

* A light repast of cakes, cheese, and drinks, which precedes dinner and whets the appetite of the guests.

dians here; when I arrived there remained no more than two hundred sixty. The reduced work force produced proportionately less, and the mission became again one of the poorest on the coast. All that was needed to bring about the decline was the successive administrations of two missionaries without talent or energy. Fray Tomás succeeded them, and under him the establishment was not likely to recover. He was an excellent man, but poor health made him indifferent to the conduct of affairs, and he left the management to stewards while he enjoyed the peaceful life he needed.[10]

This worthy man gave me all the information I requested on the commerce of Alta California. After doing some figuring in the next few days, I decided that I could profit from the advantageous prices offered in this market. My plan, however, posed a serious problem that could be surmounted only by taking the ship back to Peru. The scarcity of money allowed no other means of exchange but cow hides and tallow; the second of these could be converted only in Lima, where it sold very well, I knew. As for the hides, it was easy to resell them to the American captains who were in California to obtain them.

There was then in port a schooner from that country engaged in this trade, and we made an agreement with the supercargo for all the hides we might acquire, to be paid in piasters or tallow. This ship had sold her cargo on the west coast of Mexico and now had only silver on board, but the padres* would exchange their goods only for things they needed, making it difficult for the supercargo to obtain the hides he wanted. The missionaries lived in constant fear that the government would extort their silver in taxes, as had happened several times—a potent motive for preferring merchandise to specie.

I learned also from Fray Tomás that the best season for buying hides

10. Mission San Francisco de Asís was dedicated in 1776 near the lagoon of Dolores (from which its popular name derived), the more permanent buildings described by Vancouver being erected between 1782 and 1791 and the present church probably between 1792 and 1810. Inclement weather, mediocre soil, and especially the polluted waters of the lagoon, which caused a high mortality rate among the neophytes, led to the transfer of many Indians to new sites north of the bay.

* Fathers. This is the name usually given to the superiors of the missions.

and tallow would not commence until May, the time when cattle could be butchered at the greatest profit, and if we waited we could do business with all the missions.

This circumstance suited us well since we then had no room to store anything on board and would soon have to return to Mazatlán to deliver to Don Ignacio Fletes the things we had sold him. So it was settled that, after trading with the missions on the bay of San Francisco, we would sail down the coast and visit the other establishments as far as the port of San Diego.

The immense harbor of San Francisco has two principal arms, one running to the north and the other to the east-southeast. Each of these two inland bays is nearly fifteen leagues in length, while the width varies from three to twelve miles. In this great expanse of water there are several islands, the largest of which is Los Angeles Island north of the presidio.[11]

Missions San Rafael and San Francisco Solano are situated on the northern bay; they are new and of little importance. On the eastern bay, in addition to San Francisco, already known to the reader, are the missions of San José and Santa Clara, the finest and richest in this part of California. Near Santa Clara there is the Pueblo de San José, merely a large village.

While we were in San Francisco Mr. R___ traveled by land to these missions, showing samples of our merchandise and selling what suited the padres, and I had them delivered in the long boat, which sometimes brought back local products. I myself dealt with the presidio and with the nearby establishments.

11. Now Angel Island.

Chapter 9

WE LEARN TO LIVE WITH danger when it is there all the time. If a resident of Holland should arrive off the coast of Naples when Vesuvius is spewing forth torrents of fire and clouds of ash, he might say to the Neapolitan, "How can you remain in a city where destruction threatens from so near? Have you forgotten the cruel fate of Pompeii and Herculaneum? Do you learn nothing from experience? Come with me . . . I will take you to a shore where volcanoes are unknown."

The Italian, carefree until now, says: "I have been living in ignorance, or have let myself become accustomed to danger, but you have opened my eyes. Let us go. My countrymen can dance on the fields that will open up under their feet."

When their ship reaches the flat shores of the Zuyder Zee, he asks: "Why are those men weaving willow branches together as if they were making baskets, and filling the meshes with clay? It is too much work and trouble. Let the land sink to its natural level."

"Heavens! What are you saying?" cries the Hollander. "Those are our dikes. They are the only thing that holds back the great ocean, which is higher than we are. If there is the slightest negligence in maintaining this thin barrier, millions of men and our fine cities will be engulfed by the water."

"And how can you sleep exposed to such a catastrophe? Farewell. I am going back to Naples. The lava of Vesuvius seems less threatening to me than the sea suspended over your land. If my homeland should suffer the fate of Catania,[1] at least I shall have lived my few days on this earth under the most beautiful skies in the world."

If I may compare small things to great, it is in this spirit that, in California, we grew accustomed to living with bears and rattlesnakes. But for a long time, before gaining a degree of confidence, we lived in terror of them, often quite needlessly. I have said that a tent had been set up on shore near where we were building a whaling boat. The master carpenter, together with an apprentice who helped with the work, slept on planks suspended from the roof, ten feet above the ground. They had provided themselves with guns, as much to ward off those who might be tempted to steal tools and materials as to secure themselves from the attacks of the wild beasts that abounded in the neighboring forest, we were told.

One night, about one o'clock in the morning, those on watch on the *Héros* heard a loud howling from the vicinity of the tent, and soon thereafter a gunshot raised the alarm. Apprised of what was going on, I promptly sent off a boat with an officer and four well-armed men. The frightened carpenters told them that three enormous bears, seen clearly in the moonlight, had been prowling around them for a long time. Nevertheless, the men did nothing until one of the animals put two paws on the canvas of the tent, as if to assault it. Only then did they shoot; they missed the beast, which moved off a ways but did not take flight. The officer and his four men searched the vicinity but found nothing. Following my orders, they then brought the two carpenters on board. These men would no longer sleep on shore, preferring to carry their tools back to the ship every evening.

When we told the story next day, the soldiers at the presidio conceived the idea of spending the following night in the tent in order to attack the bears and take them alive. Assembling four of the boldest and best horsemen, they prepared themselves for the hunt, to which

---

1. Destroyed several times by Mt. Etna, at whose foot it lies.

they were quite accustomed. But whether our carpenters had mistaken for bears some of the bulls from the hillside pastures, or whether the fire that the soldiers lit in the tent had scared the beasts away—although they are not afraid of this, it is said—the men waited in vain. No bears appeared.

As for me, I was inclined to believe that the fear inspired by such a formidable beast could easily metamorphose, in the eyes of the carpenters, an ox or a fox into some other animal. And if I may judge by the sound of the bellowing that reached my ear when on deck, I must believe that the adventure was set off by fear and illusion.

Be that as it may, bears are quite numerous in the vicinity. Without going farther than five or six leagues from San Francisco, one can often see troops of them in the forest and even on the plain. The Californians claim that they seldom attack passersby; only when a man happens to approach them closely or stirs up their ferocity by teasing them, do they make use of their terrible claws and their great strength.[2]

I cannot say whether the men fear the bears more than the bears fear the men, but I saw at that time a soldier who bore recent and unmistakable marks to show that the animals are not always of a peaceful disposition. Fray Tomás told me that he himself had saved the man's life when the bear had already sunk its claws into his right side and face. By the merest chance, when traveling an out-of-the-way road with some other men, he had heard the cries of the unfortunate fellow, whose horse was frozen with fear and could not run. They rushed up, making a deal of noise, and the ferocious beast left its prey and took flight.

At a narrow place in the road, the man reported, he had suddenly found himself face to face with the bear, only two steps away. Unprepared for a fight, he had attempted to get away by turning around, but the animal leaped on the horse's rump and held them fast.

2. The grizzly bear, now extinct in California, was quite common in the Spanish and Mexican periods. Bull and bear fights, one of which Duhaut-Cilly will describe, were a favorite entertainment of the people.

During our stay at Yerba Buena we spent most of our considerable leisure time hunting. Trading was desultory and often without result. The country abounds with hares, rabbits, and tufted partridges, and especially an astonishing variety of ducks and sea birds. All this for our table.

As for the collection that I was making with Dr. Botta, our efforts were equally successful: by the sea a multitude of beautiful shore birds; in the woods and on the hillsides, several fine species of hawks and other birds of prey; in the thickets, magpies, blackbirds, sparrows, and several fruit-eating birds quite different from ours; and finally, in the heath, a pretty species of hummingbird, perhaps the smallest that exists, with head and throat of glowing fire.

When this bewitching little creature lights for a moment on a dry branch, you might think it a ruby sphere or, rather, a little ball of red-hot iron, sending out rays of sparks. When several of them light on the same branch, the Arabian amateur of marvels might take it for a bough covered with precious stones, as in a dream from The Thousand and One Nights.

Early one Sunday, with two officers from the ship and a guide, I went to the mission, intending to make a hunting excursion to a place called Rancho San Bruno, where we expected to find a great quantity of game. But before going on we attended mass and listened to a sermon by Fray Tomás on the sixth commandment of God.[3]

He handled the subject with skill, but I have to say that his remarks sounded quite extraordinary to European ears, used to the circumlocutions commonly used for such matters. And although the good father had warned us in his first words that one must not fear to speak plainly of crimes that are committed with no sense of shame, it was only after he reminded us that he was speaking to half-savage Indians and to others almost as ignorant, that we could accustom ourselves to his naive language.

We then mounted our horses and followed for about three leagues

---

3. In the Roman Catholic Decalogue the sixth commandment forbids adultery.

one side of a long valley, with high verdant hills on both sides, where the mission herds were grazing. At every turn we observed those animals which I have described under the name of coyotes. The pelts of these are considerably less handsome than those of Baja California; their color is more of a dull gray, their tails less bushy, and their fur usually thinner.

At the southern end of the valley we crossed a ravine and soon found ourselves on a plain, through which ran a stream that formed small lakes here and there. Dismounting beside one of these ponds and tethering our horses, we went off, each in his own direction, to shoot ducks of several kinds and the wild geese that we found everywhere in great numbers. Some of us also shot a species of heron, here called *grulla,* considered a delicacy by the inhabitants.

After three hours of spreading terror and death among the not very wild hosts of air and water, we returned to the place where we had left our horses, all of us more or less successful and all with great appetites that we satisfied with the provisions we had taken care to bring with us.

We did not go back by the route of that morning but turned to the east and went around the hills that we had passed on our left. The slope is much steeper on this side of the hills, which rise almost vertically from the harbor. One needs experienced and sure-footed horses to venture on these *laderas* or narrow paths, barely marked on the side of the mountain and running close to frightful precipices, where the least slip would send rider and horse rolling to the edge of the cliff and from there, in a single bound, into the sea.

I don't know what sensations possessed my companions but admit that I heartily cursed our guide as I listened to him sing the *petenera**** and watched him striking a light for his *cigarita* just as if he had been riding down the middle of one of our royal roads. While not daring to let my eye wander over the immense and magnificent basin that began at my feet, I decided that the small, circular waves caused by my

* A California air.

falling body would make no more agitation on the shore than would the lighting of a fly on the great basin of the Tuilleries.[4]

On 4 February, when we were preparing to leave San Francisco and sail down the coast, I heard of the arrival at the mission of Padre Ramón Abella, whom Roquefeuil mentions in his account. I went at once to call on him, and he, learning that I was going to Monterey, requested passage there. This I granted with pleasure.[5]

In San Francisco our business was finished to our satisfaction, and it was agreed with the padres that we would return in June to collect the value of the goods they had bought from us. Our intention was now to carry on the same business with the other missions. The one at Santa Cruz, between San Francisco and Monterey, was one of those where foreigners were not welcome, but a happy circumstance allowed me to get permission to go there. The superior of that establishment informed me that he had a large quantity of grain for the commandant at Monterey, who had no way to fetch it by sea. I wrote to him that I would transport the grain if he would authorize me to anchor at Santa Cruz. Necessity pleaded my cause, and it was agreed that I would take the grain. So I had only to await favorable weather, but our last days at Yerba Buena were marked by continual high winds.

Bad weather was preceded by a violent earthquake. One night, about four o'clock in the morning, we were all awakened by an unusual noise and especially by a shock that made us think the vessel had been thrown on the rocks. The ship shivered and creaked all over, and the anchor chain gave out a frightful sound. When we ascertained that our position had not changed, it was not difficult to recognize the

---

4. The excursion took the party southward from the mission around the western flank of San Bruno Mountain into the plain lying between Sawyer Ridge and San Francisco Bay, perhaps as far as modern San Bruno. The return was by the eastern face of the mountain above the modern Bayshore Freeway (Highway 101). Rancho San Bruno was apparently a cattle range of the San Francisco presidio.

5. José Ramón Abella served at San Francisco from his arrival in California in 1798 until 1819, having met Roquefeuil there in 1817. He was at the Carmel mission near Monterey until 1833.

cause of the alarm. The noise and the shaking lasted for about eight seconds.

Next day the people at the presidio, still much frightened, told us that they had spent part of the night out of doors, that the shaking had been repeated several times, and that all their houses had been shaken and more or less damaged.

Fray Tomás also wrote to me that some parts of the mission buildings had been damaged, adding cheerily: "In the church the statue of San Emilio* fell from its niche and broke an arm, but San Isidro el Labrador (Saint Isidore the Farmer) had remained firmly in place, leaning on his spade."

On the eve of departure I received from Don Ignacio Martínez an official letter in which he asked me, in the name of the Mexican government, to convey to San Diego three bad Indian subjects whom he had to keep in irons to prevent them from escaping and robbing the people of the presidio and the mission. Since it was to my advantage to maintain good relations with the agents of the government, and in spite of my reluctance to support slavery, I consented to the commandant's request. I thought, moreover, that a stay on board would be for these unfortunates a momentary alleviation of their state, and hoped that a change of location and of masters might enable them to find a better way of life.

On the 7th we got under sail and left the harbor on the ebb tide. Greeted by a fine breeze from the northwest, we went swiftly along the coast, not far from shore. It is eighteen leagues from the entrance of San Francisco Bay to the roadstead at Santa Cruz, and the way is directly south-southeast and without peril.

All day we had telescopes in hand to examine the coast, whose aspect was altered every minute by the swift progress of the ship. The land is generally quite high in the interior and is everywhere crowned with conifers. It then slopes gently toward the shore but rises again to form a long line of hills, from which it descends at last to the sea,

---

* Saint Aemilius is invoked against earthquakes in California.

which here beats against vertical cliffs and there glides in sheets of white foam onto beaches of sand or shingle. Plains and hills were clothed in a splendid green, and everywhere we saw immense herds of cattle, sheep, and horses. Those belonging to Santa Cruz join those, less numerous, of San Francisco, so that this long strip of eighteen leagues is one continuous pasture.

On the morning of the 8th, after several hours of calm, we dropped anchor in eight fathoms in the roadstead of Santa Cruz. I went at once to the mission[6] with Padre Ramón Abella and there was received cordially by Fray Luís Taboada, the superior.[7] When I told him that I was ready to take on the grain for the commandant at Monterey, he ordered his Indian major-domos to get ready the carts to carry it to the shore from where we began putting it on board. While this was going on I did business with Fray Luís and with the people of the vicinity. That was the real purpose of my stop, the transporting of grain being a pretext.

I made a new friend at every mission visited. Hardly had I arrived when there sprang up a confidential relation between the missionary and myself, one that began with complaints about the government that had replaced the royal authority. After this beginning I was told of all the harassments that came naturally from this want of accord. He would then inform me in intimate detail about the people with whom I was to do business; in this way I learned how solvent was each one, evidence that I was happy to hear and that proved of the greatest value. During the entire course of our operations in California, I incurred only 800 piasters of bad debts.

Nearly all these fathers were men of great merit and of discretion; the advice they gave me came from no wish to denigrate but only with the purpose of serving me as a friend or a brother; they knew quite

6. Mission Santa Cruz, founded in 1791, was never very prosperous despite its pleasant setting, it being off the main road, the Indian population often in short supply, and the neighboring pueblo of Branciforte causing friction. Duhaut-Cilly probably saw it at its height.

7. Luís Gil y Taboada was at Santa Cruz from 1820 to 1827, having resided at several other missions since coming to California in 1801. In continuing ill health, he had asked for retirement in 1816 and again in 1821 but could not be replaced.

well that I would not abuse it and would receive it only as business information. This was true because they were happy to deal with a captain of their own faith. Never would they have discussed these matters with an American or an Englishman. Their good will and tolerance made them truly hospitable to everyone, but between simple courtesy and complete confidence there is a world of difference.

No location could be prettier than that of this mission. From the shore the ground rises in steps so regular that one might think them the terraces of a fortification. But I doubt whether the grass-covered revetment of an artificial work could ever attain to the beauty of this greensward, like a carpet of green velvet spread over the steps of a throne. The buildings sit on the third terrace, fronting the sea and with backs to a dense forest of great conifers, which contrast with the brilliant white walls.

To the right of the settlement the natural benches that support the land mass are abruptly cut by a little glen, at the bottom of which flows a quiet river of clear water, bordered by trees, whose dense foliage protects it from the heat of the sun. One would like to change places with the sky-blue kingfisher that, from its perch on a dry branch, peers through the shade at the fish below, betrayed by a ray of light on its golden scales. And one might envy the sweet life of the red duck, ambling peacefully under the galleries of verdure, or that of the white heron that here finds easy and abundant food. In truth the scene might not be like this if Dr. Botta were to repeat often his work of collecting bird skins from California. In the two days he spent in Santa Cruz he did much to disturb the habits of these poor creatures, and in justice I must admit that I took part in this cruel aggression.

On the 9th a storm threatened us from the south, and since the anchorage is protected only from the north, we were in haste to make ready to sail. Once more on this occasion we could congratulate ourselves on the energy and good will of our crew. When the danger arose, all our boats were on the beach, loading grain and hides. I had a cannon shot off to call them back, and also Dr. Botta, who had gone to the village to visit a sick man. We loaded the cargo, hoisted the boats, raised two anchors, and in less than half an hour were under way, just at the moment when a violent wind struck the bay.

No matter how fine the crew, it will not perform so well as this if it is not encouraged by the energy of skillful officers. The coolness and talent demonstrated on these occasions by Mr. Tréhouart, my second in command and my friend, maintained order and assured promptness.

The storm, however, did not last long, and the wind soon returned to the northwest, but nonetheless we kept on our course to Monterey, only seven leagues from Santa Cruz, where we dropped anchor at ten in the evening.

The next morning at sunrise I saluted the town with seven guns, which were returned with a single shot. Going at once to call on the commandant, Don Miguel González, captain of artillery, I begged him to explain, before doing any other business, why my salute had not been returned in full. He then opened a book, where he showed me that only a warship could expect its salute to be returned shot for shot.[8]

I also called on the commissioner of customs, Don José María Herrera, the administrator with whom I was to have regular dealings, not only during my stay at Monterey but also for the entire time I spent in California. He was something like a manager of accounts and finances for the entire province.[9]

He told me that Mexican laws were observed in California and that, strictly speaking, I should unload my entire cargo, but considering the lack of means at this one port for taking an entire shipload, I might unload only what I thought I could sell and reload afterwards without paying duty on what was left at my departure, adding that I might follow this procedure at all the other ports under his jurisdiction.

8. Miguel González de Avila was sent to California by the new Mexican republic in 1825 and by virtue of his rank became commandant at Monterey. Unpopular with the Californians, he was perceived as being ignorant and despotic, was charged with arbitrary acts, and the year after Duhaut-Cilly's departure was suspended by the government and ordered out of the country.

9. Herrera too was sent to California from Mexico in 1825 to take charge of the provincial finances and, like his friend and father-in-law Commandant González, became controversial. Though able, he claimed to be independent of the governor, was forced to resign in 1827, and was expelled in 1830.

A few days later I went to Mission San Carlos, situated about five miles to the south of the Monterey presidio. The road there is tortuous, winding between hills carpeted with green grass and shaded by great conifers and fine oaks. These trees are sometimes grouped so attractively that they might have been planted by a skilled designer. At times they form avenues, rows, or groves; at other times dense stands opening here and there to let the eye roam over green glades, set in the most picturesque way among the woods. Not even in the tropics are the climbing plants so draped from tree to tree like garlands; the different kinds are mixed, separated, mixed again in different ways, and the ground is so clean and fresh, so free of brush, that nothing could be more beautiful. While the forests of the torrid zone produce a more romantic effect, these appear more formal.[10]

The mission of San Carlos[11] is built on a small bay, open to the southwest, which offers neither shelter nor anchorage. It is poor and almost depopulated of Indians. Padre Ramón Abella, who was prevented by the bad weather from reembarking with us at Santa Cruz, had arrived by land, and here I found also Padre Altimira, a young missionary,[12] and Padre Sarría, prefect and chief of all the Franciscans in California, a man of great ability and fine character.

Sarría was at that time in utter disgrace with the Mexicans for having refused to swear to the constitution and for having prevented his

10. The author, generally careful in describing species, calls all the conifers of this region firs (*sapins*) even when writing of Point Pinos. Most of those seen here and earlier were surely pines (*pins*), with some wind-twisted cypresses. The well-known Monterey pine grows in patches along the coast south of San Francisco but is at its best near Monterey.

11. Mission San Carlos Borromeo (Carmel), established at the Monterey presidio in 1770, was in the following year moved a few miles south to a site overlooking Carmel Bay, where water and fertile soil were more plentiful and contact with the soldiers less close. Though the administrative headquarters of the mission system for much of its history, it was never notably prosperous or productive and by 1827 was in decline. A contemporary view by Beechey's artist, William Smyth, appears in Alexander Forbes, *California* (London, 1839) and, in color, in F. W. Beechey, *An Account of a Visit to California*, ed. E. M. Coulter (San Francisco, 1941).

12. José Altimira, three years older than Duhaut-Cilly, came to California in 1820 and served at San Francisco and at San Francisco Solano until replaced in 1826, when he went to Monterey. Independent in spirit, he had controversies with superiors and associates, and in January 1828, with Padre Antonio Ripoll, boarded an American brig as a fugitive, escaping both an order of expulsion and the country. He appears again in Chapter 14.

subordinates from doing so. Thus, he was a sort of prisoner at San Carlos, where they kept an eye on him. Since the agents of the government considered him the principal obstacle to the adherence of all the missionaries, they would have liked to send him back to Mexico. Commandant González had already sought to sound me out about taking him to Mazatlán, when I returned there. But I gave this officer to understand that, however much I might wish to perform a service to his government, I would never allow myself to be used as an instrument of violence toward whomever it might be, and that I would not take the padre prefecto on board unless he asked it himself. The good missionary, fearing that I might fall in with the commandant's designs, showed the most lively gratitude when I revealed my feelings about the matter.[13]

On the 24th, having sold all that was asked for and with no prospect of further business for the moment, I re-embarked everything that remained on the shore; but since the next day was a Sunday, I put off departure until the day after that.

That day we witnessed a spectacle quite new to us. The soldiers of the presidio, having captured a bear alive, offered it to me, and I bought it for a few piasters in order to watch a fight to the finish between this animal and a bull, which I also purchased. Both were brought into the courtyard of the presidio, where they were tied together with a long leather cord, which kept them from getting away from each other but allowed them to move freely. They were then left to all their ferocity.

The spectacle took place right after mass, and the watchers were many. When the combatants were left in the middle of the enclosure, the bull at first paid no attention to the bear and began to charge at the people around him; but soon, feeling himself held back by the leg,

13. Vicente Francisco de Sarría, arriving in California in 1808, was three years later appointed to the new office of commissary prefect, an administrative rank above that of father president. As a matter of conscience, he would not take the oath of loyalty to the 1824 Mexican constitution but permitted other friars to do so, and although under nominal arrest he was not deported because the governor considered him to be indispensable. After the order expelling all Spaniards (Chapter 18) Duhaut-Cilly offered him passage to Manila.

he turned quickly toward his more formidable enemy and with the first blow of his horns threw the bear over. The bear, unfortunately, had had one paw broken in his first fight with the soldiers and could not make use of his prodigious strength, but he bit the bull in the neck and made him bellow loudly. With fury redoubled, the bull charged like lightning on the wild beast, who in a few minutes was horribly gored and lay dead on the ground. So the bull was quite superior, but the issue might have been in doubt had the bear not been injured earlier.

I have since seen a number of fights between these animals in which fortune went the other way. The first part of the mortal combat always went in the bull's favor, but as soon as deep bites or fatigue forced him to thrust out his tongue, the bear never failed to seize this sensitive part with his great claws, not letting go his hold regardless of what his adversary did. The vanquished bull could only let out frightful bellows; lacerated in all parts, he fell down exhausted and bled to death. Thus the fierce wild bear is the terror of the herds of Alta California.

But the horsemen of the country master it by means of the noose. This noose or lasso, used in all the Spanish possessions of the two Americas, is a leather rope as big around as the little finger and fifteen or twenty fathoms in length.[14] While one end is fixed firmly to the saddle-bow, the other is tied in a running knot.

For anyone other than these skillful riders such a weapon would be quite useless; in their hands it is a powerful and formidable arm. With it they have been known to confront the lances and bayonets of regular troops. In the campaign of Buenos Aires they were so feared by the English army that invaded the city briefly in 1809 that no soldier would stray far from the fortifications. If he were surprised by a *gaucho** and missed his musket shot, he knew that his other weapons would not save him from a horrible death.

When a man wishes to use the lasso against an animal or another

---

14. The English fathom (six feet), like the French *brasse* (a little more than five feet), was meant to approximate the span of the two arms spread wide and was once commonly used as a measure of length, although both are now more commonly used for depth.

* A name given to the country people of the La Plata region.

man, he holds it coiled in one hand while he gallops within fifteen feet of the enemy, whirling the lethal loop over his head like a sling. And at just the right moment he casts it with such skill that he never fails to bind the neck or the body or the legs of the one he wants to catch, and whom he then drags cruelly along the ground as his horse gallops on.

In California bear hunting is considered a game of pleasure for three or four horsemen armed with their ropes. Putting down a dead animal as bait, they wait quietly. If the bear defends himself and tries to rush on one of the men, the others choose that moment to lasso him from behind. If the bear flees, as happens most often, the fastest rider tries to cut him off and make him fight. The first lasso that catches him allows him only to charge the man who threw it; but the others then come up quickly and snare him with theirs. Stretching the ropes in opposing directions, they hold him firmly while one of them dismounts and ties his four feet. They then roll him onto a cowhide and drag him where they wish.

These animals are also killed in a more expeditious and less dangerous way. In the branches of a tree there is built a *trapiste* (scaffolding) ten or fifteen feet above the ground, and several men wait there, armed with muskets, each of which is loaded with two balls. About twenty feet from the tree is placed a horse, dead for several days and beginning to putrefy. Bears, they say, have a keen sense of smell and are attracted from a distance; when they come they are easily shot by the hunters. Padre Viader, superior of the mission at Santa Clara, a wise and truthful man, assured me that he himself had killed a hundred in this manner.

Others dig a deep pit and cover it with a strong layer of branches, on which they place meat of a kind that will attract bears. Standing below, they shoot them or kill them with thrusts of the lance.

While the Californians make use of the lasso as an offensive weapon, they use it more frequently to manage their herds of mules, horses, and cattle. With it they throw them down, whether to kill or brand or geld them. Without the aid of this instrument, it would be impossible to control animals that live in liberty on vast lands and are almost as wild as if they had no masters. It is even imprudent for us

Europeans, unskillful horsemen, to ride among the enormous herds without being accompanied by some men of the country, who can at a distance recognize the fiercest bulls and who can, when necessary, save us from their fury by lassoing or harassing them.

South from the roadstead at Santa Cruz the coast curves inland and around to Monterey, where Point Pinos juts out for several miles to the north-northwest. Here in a small inner bay whose entrance faces north is the usual place of anchorage. From this point the most extended rocks of Point Pinos partially hide Point Año Nuevo and the mountains that rise behind Mission Santa Cruz and appear to be seven or eight leagues away. It is this little bay that is inappropriately called the harbor of Monterey even though a harbor should be protected from every wind.

Nevertheless, the local circumstances give to this place some of the advantages of a genuine harbor. On this coast the winds most to be feared are those from south-southeast to south-southwest, as I will explain later, and the anchorage is completely sheltered from these directions and is almost as well protected from the most common wind of all; this latter, blowing almost constantly from west to northwest, must first pass over Point Pinos. Thus it is only the winds ranging from north-1/4 northwest to north-northeast that can be harmful, and they are quite rare. One need only be passably well moored to have nothing to fear; no ship has been lost at Monterey since the settlement there of the Spaniards.

The best indicator for recognizing the entrance to Monterey is Point Pinos, which from a distance and from all directions appears to be a hill of medium height. Sloping down almost as much to the interior as to the sea, it has the appearance at first sight of an island. It is entirely covered with great pine trees, growing almost to the edge of the water. Some rocks, always quite visible, extend for about a mile out from its west-northwest flank.

To enter the bay at Monterey and quickly find the best spot to anchor, one should head for this point and, after passing outside the detached rocks just mentioned, sail parallel to the land and close in while steering for the head of the bay. The banks of seaweed growing around these rocks, the widest spaced of which are not less than eight fathoms

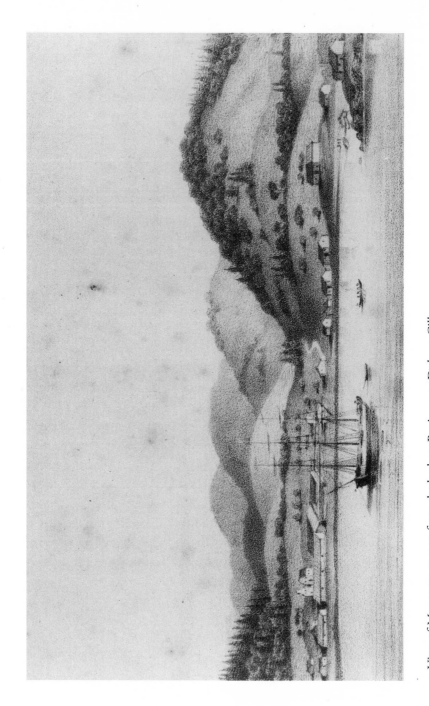

5. View of Monterey, as seen from the harbor. By Auguste Duhaut-Cilly.

apart, are a clear sign to keep a proper distance from the shore; skirting them at a cable's length will give the right heading. Arriving opposite a small hill where can be seen the remains of a fort, one will find a depth of eleven fathoms with a bottom of mud and sand; there one can drop anchor within hailing distance of the shore.

You must not expect to see a city of any size, or you will think you have not found the right anchorage. After doubling Point Pinos, the first buildings to be seen are those of the presidio, which form a square of two hundred meters on each side; having only the ground floor, they resemble nothing so much as a group of long storehouses roofed with tile. Then can be seen, to the right of the presidio and scattered here and there over a grassy area, about forty houses, also roofed with tile and quite attractive with their whitewashed exteriors. There you have, with an equal number of thatched huts, the whole of the capital of Alta California.[15]

Nevertheless, Monterey has grown considerably since 1794, when Vancouver stopped here on his return from the Northwest Coast of America. Then there existed only the presidio; all the houses that exist today, most of which belong to foreigners, were not built until after the independence of Mexico.

Beyond the houses there rises a line of lovely rounded hills, on which can be admired a picturesque medley of trees of several species, dominated as always by pines and oaks.

Landing is easily accomplished near a small guardhouse at the innermost part of the bay. A stream with but little water runs through a small ravine to the left of the old fort and is a convenient spot for filling water casks. It would be an excellent watering-place if the flow were a little more abundant, but is almost always sufficient for the needs of one or two ships.

15. Because Monterey was named and lavishly praised by Vizcaíno in 1602, it was sought by parties sent to occupy California in 1769 and became the province's capital city, chief port, and preeminent center of California life. Vancouver provides a description and view of the presidio as it was in 1792. Duhaut-Cilly's own sketch may be compared to the 1826 watercolor that appears in Beechey's *Account of a Visit to California,* op. cit.

Chapter 10

SANTA BARBARA AND SAN PEDRO

March—April 1827

HAPPY IS THE SAILOR WHO knows so well the land he is approaching that he can recognize his position through a brief opening in the fog and can thus reach a safe haven before nightfall instead of passing the night, uncertain and fearful, at the entrance to the harbor, unable to enter. Happy also is the one who, in the middle of a storm, can profit from a brief flash of lightning to make out the round summit of a hill, the whitish face of a well-known rock, or the steep profile of a cape. In less than half a second his practiced eye recognizes these shapes, and he orders the steersman to weather the helm; the wind fills the great trapezia of his topsails; the ship surges forward, and the waves that were breaking on her sides now produce only a loud murmur in the wake. A headland is passed to starboard, a small island to port. The distant roar of the sea dies down, and soon the lighted windows of the port are beacons guiding the ship to the anchorage.

The appearance of the coast is thus an essential study for the mariner wherever he goes; observations of this kind have always been given the most assiduous care by those who have done the most for the safety of navigation. I am not unaware how meaningless these matters may be for most readers, but they are so intimately bound to the purpose of this work that I must on all occasions take care to include my observations of this kind.

After Monterey our next visit was to be at Santa Barbara, about sixty-five leagues distant to the southeast. Between these two places there are several missions, among others the very rich one of San Luis Obispo, with a rather good anchoring spot not far away. It would have been profitable for us to stop there, but since this establishment was not on the list of ports open to foreigners, it was for Santa Barbara that we set sail on the morning of 27 March.[1]

On the 28th we were in sight at once of the islands that form the passage known as the Santa Barbara channel and of Point Conception. This point, beyond which the coast turns to the east, is quite remarkable in its form. It rises from the sea looking like a great wedge; then, after falling toward the interior and stretching out a long tail, it rises again, gently, to the mountain tops.

As soon as we had passed this cape the sea, until then quite rough, became smooth and calm, but there was little wind and we proceeded slowly, having on our right the islands of San Miguel, Santa Rosa, and Santa Cruz.

This coast, which we skirted at a distance of two miles, is dominated by a chain of mountains parallel to the shore and six or seven hundred meters in height. From their base extends a plain that ends in a line of vertical cliffs, and between these and the sea a narrow beach of sand and shingle. This pleasant country, grazed by great herds of horses and cattle, is cut at almost equal intervals by narrow valleys. In these grow thick stands of splendid oaks, whose crowded and bushy tops seem to even off the terrain. Streams run through the valleys, providing water for the cattle feeding all about.

At certain hours of the day, watching from the ship, you can see these animals leave the pasture and troop in long files to quench their thirst and then return in the same order, but with slower steps, to the

---

1. Mission San Luis Obispo de Tolosa, founded in 1772, was in decline by 1827, but if Duhaut-Cilly had arrived in July instead of March he would have been permitted a visit because of changes in government regulations about that time.

fields where plenty and repose await them. But from time to time men on horseback come to disturb this happy indolence. Then they all flee, seeking to evade the deadly lasso. But in vain. Misfortune is the lot of those chosen by the Californians for the bridle or the knife. They will not escape slavery or death.

Free horses know not how to make use of their speed. They dash off without plan and often, when seeking to get away from danger, they circle back to it. But when guided by an intelligent rider, flanks bloodied by the huge spurs, the tamed steed will make good use of the terrain and go by the shortest route. The bull too, better armed but slower, turns in vain against his pursuer; at the very moment when he charges one of his enemies, thinking to pierce him with his horns, another snares him from behind, and he is garroted without pity.

The naked mountainsides, burned to a violet color, make a charming contrast to this beautiful landscape, where nothing is lacking but a few fine châteaux to make a magnificent picture. But California is still far removed from the time when a richer and more numerous people will adorn it with such structures. However that may be, this slope of mixed fields and groves is one of the most pleasant along the coast.

As we ran along the coast, we found the sea covered almost everywhere with bitumen, sometimes formed into round plaques of some thickness and sometimes spread on the water in large patches, reflecting yellow or bluish.[2] The odor of this stuff was strong enough to be annoying and to make breathing sharp and difficult. For a time I did not know whether this natural tar, spread so widely over all the channel, flowed from some location on the coast or whether it welled up from a source under the sea; but on another visit to Santa Barbara I learned that there exists, halfway from the presidio to Point Conception, and between the ranchos of Los Ortegas and Los Dos Pueblos, a great pool of asphalt that bubbles up constantly and whose overflow runs into the sea, not far away.[3]

2. Natural deposits of asphalt, formed by the evaporation of oil, appear at several places along the California coast, and were noted near Santa Barbara by the Portolá party in 1769.
3. The well-known Ortega rancho, Nuestra Señora del Refugio, extending for some

On the evening of the 29th we dropped anchor in the roadstead at Santa Barbara and in a fog that allowed us to see little of our surroundings, but on the morning of the 30th we had a full view of the place where we were moored. As far as the eye can see to the east there is no change in the appearance of the land except that the cliffs are broken to form the quite shallow bay of Santa Barbara, and the chain of mountains, a little lower here, is cut by a deep gorge. The harbor, open to half the horizon, is sheltered only from west to east-by-north. Facing it, four leagues away, is the high and rather large island of Santa Cruz and to the left of this, toward the southeast, the Anacapa group (Indian name), composed of four small islands.

I went ashore with Mr. R——— and we went to see the commandant, Don José Noriega. He was living in the presidio while awaiting completion of quite a fine house he was having built outside it and for which I was bringing some beams taken on board at Monterey. In Don José we found an educated and respected man, with a numerous and charming family, who gave us an open and courteous welcome. His considerable fortune and fine character gave him great influence in the country and, although he was a Spaniard, he had just been named a delegate to the Mexican congress.[4]

The presidio of Santa Barbara, like that of Monterey, is a square enclosure surrounded by houses and other structures, all of one story. Near the northeast corner is a building somewhat different from the others and surmounted by a small tower; this is the residence of the commandant. In the opposite corner, turned toward the shore road, it is apparent that the California engineers have tried to construct a defensive bastion, but one would have to be endowed with much charity to call it a success. The presidio is constructed on a plain between two ravines in which flow two small streams of water. Around

---

twenty miles eastward of Point Conception, was occupied by the Ortega family in 1794. Los Dos Pueblos, between it and Santa Barbara, was named for two Indian rancherías in 1769.

4. José de la Guerra y Noriega, son of two distinguished Spanish families, came to California in 1801 and in 1815 became commandant at Santa Barbara. A candidate for governor in 1822 and elected to the Mexican congress in 1827, he was deprived of both these honors because of his Spanish birth.

this fort are clustered, in no particular order, from sixty to eighty houses inhabited by the *gente de razón* and by the Indian servants of these rational people. Each of these dwellings possesses a small garden surrounded by a picket fence.[5]

We then went on foot to the mission, situated at the upper end of the plain about half a league from the presidio. The road rises slightly while traversing a fine meadow where graze saddle horses and the cows that furnish daily milk to the presidio. As we approached, the mission building took on a handsomer aspect. From the harbor we might have taken it for a medieval château, with its tall windows and its tower, but as we draw closer the structure seems to become larger and, without losing any of its beauty, gradually takes on a religious air. The turret becomes a belfry, and the bells, instead of heralding the arrival of a knight, sound the office or the angelus. The illusion is no more, the castle has become a convent.

In front of the building and in the middle of a wide plaza is a gushing fountain. Although imperfect in workmanship, it was a great surprise to us, who never thought to encounter in this country so far from European refinement, a kind of luxury that among us is reserved for the most opulent dwellings. The clear and bright water, after being raised to more than eight feet above the ground, falls in broad sprays over a descending series of stone basins that together form a sort of octagonal pyramid. The water fills to the brim a reservoir of the same form, whence, issuing from the jaws of a stone bear, it falls into a fine laundry basin of stucco, around which some Indian women and Californian girls were washing clothes. The latter looked at us from under their splendid chestnut hair, and I expect that their examination of the two strangers was as complete as it was swift.

In all lands only the fair sex has the ability to size up a person with a furtive look and in the twinkling of an eye, and especially to note

5. Santa Barbara was in 1782 the last of California's four presidios to be established. Described by Vancouver in 1793 as "excelling all the others in neatness, cleanliness, and other comforts," it had subsequently deteriorated, in part from earthquake shocks in 1812 and 1821. *Gente de razón* were defined by Miguel Costansó in 1793 as European Spaniards, creoles, and people of mixed blood to differentiate them from the native Indians.

what is ridiculous about him. I saw one of the young girls smile in an almost imperceptible way and thought that I myself might be the reason for her malicious mirth; but the quite grotesque appearance of my companion—his teeth blackened by an excessive use of tobacco, and his monkey head surmounting a meager body of four feet eight—did much to restore my self-esteem.

We went up a flight of several steps, leading us under a long peristyle or cloister, supported by fifteen square pillars forming fourteen arches, which, from a distance gave the mission the noble look that had struck us at first sight. Here was seated an old and feeble padre, whom age and infirmity had made so insensible to everything around him that he scarcely knew us for strangers when we greeted him and inquired of his health. It would take strong means to get his attention, I could see, and I leaned over him and said, in a tone to vanquish his deafness: "I am French; I have come from Paris and I can give you recent news of Spain."[6]

No talisman ever produced a more magical effect than these few words, whose power to gain the friendly interest of these good fathers I had already experienced. Most Spaniards are strongly attached to their country; they love its land, its customs, everything, even the abuses of its government. No sooner had I pronounced the words than the old man, starting out of his lethargy, so overwhelmed me with gratitude and with urgent questions that I could scarcely find an instant to reply. He had regained some of his lost vigor in speaking of the native land that he would never see again.

The events that had brought about the invasion of Spain by a French army were known to him; he looked on Ferdinand VII as a quasi-martyr and on the French as liberators. Our attitudes and our backgrounds often cause us to view an event in quite different ways; while the poor friar rejoiced to learn that our troops were still in the peninsula, I could not hold back a painful recollection of my own, remembering how impatiently we once put up with the presence of foreigners and in what ill humor we counted the days until they would

6. The old padre was Antonio Jayme, who retired there from Mission Soledad in 1821.

leave, no matter what obligations some people thought were owed to them. It is quite rare, impossibly rare, that an invasion has as an objective or result the well-being of the occupied country.[7]

This old man was not the superior of the mission, nor did he perform any function; he merely lived here while waiting for God to bring his half-existence to an end. The administrator was Fray Antonio Ripoll. Since the latter was busy at that moment, we put the time to good use by visiting his garden, which we found large, well planted, and well tended. Its paths, laid out in an ordered way, were shaded by fine olive trees, and there we could see at the same time fruits from temperate climes and those from the torrid zone. Bananas spread their great leaves between apple and pear trees; mixed with ruby red cherries were golden oranges.[8]

Fray Antonio, a man of good countenance and high intelligence, put to me some of the same questions already asked by his aged comrade, only with more discretion and understanding; and when I had satisfied his curiosity, or rather his concern, he offered to show us the mission buildings and church.

The facade of the chapel is embellished with six half-columns that support a triangular pediment bearing several statues of saints. The interior of the church is only a nave with a flat ceiling and without side aisles. The edifice would excite no surprise had it been built by Europeans, but when we consider that it is the work of poor Indians taught by an ecclesiastic, that it was erected in a country that, although it contains all the needed materials, provides them only as they are found in nature, then we cannot help admiring the patience of this friar, the talent he has demonstrated, and the great care he must have given to the work of construction.

7. Ferdinand VII was forced by a revolt in 1820 to reinstate the 1812 constitution he had abolished, whereupon French troops, representing the Holy Alliance, intervened in 1822 and restored the king's power. Duhaut-Cilly's memories of foreign intervention in France were of the Allied army of occupation after Napoleon's final defeat.

8. Padre Antonio Ripoll came to California in 1812 and served at Santa Barbara from 1815 to 1828. Capable and devoted, he learned the Chumash language, built the church which still remains, then, as Duhaut-Cilly later tells, fearing expulsion as a Spaniard under a Mexican law of 1827, secretly left the country.

At home, how do we go about erecting a building of this sort? Ten architects arrive with plans and estimates; one has only to choose the most suitable. Contracts are made with suppliers; all the materials, ready to be put in place, are brought to the designated spot so that one has only to verify the quality and give them the finishing touches; and finally, the best workmen compete with one another to be chosen.

Here, on the contrary, everything is unformed, including the men, and the first care of the builder was to train the workers. Out of raw earth he had to make bricks and tile; he had to fell great trees at a distance and transport them by physical effort over new roads built past ravines and precipices; to gather from the shore and with great effort seashells for the making of lime; in sum, even the smallest elements of the building cost much preliminary work, thus adding greatly to the difficulties. One is astonished both by the boldness of the plan and by the perseverance in carrying it out; only a boundless zeal for the spread of his religion could have led Padre Ripoll to victory over so many obstacles. Nevertheless, he took little more time to complete the building than would have been needed in Spain; the church was commenced in 1820 and finished in 1824.[9]

The nave, altar, and sacristy are embellished with paintings, the best of which are from Mexico; the others were done by the Indians themselves. The pillars, friezes, borders, and plinths are tastefully marbled and decorated with arabesques passably well done. What distinguishes the whole and suggests indulgence in regard to the faults of architecture is an extreme cleanliness, not found in our churches of the third order or even of the second order.

The talent and concern of Fray Antonio were not expended solely on the construction of his church; while giving himself to this good work, he also took care to nourish and clothe his Indians. We went to visit his woolen shops. In the buildings devoted to this work two

9. After the earthquake of 1812 the Santa Barbara mission church was rebuilt between 1815 and 1820. Planned by Padre Antonio Ripoll, it was of hewn stone, based on classical models, and because of its setting and graceful proportions was known as the Queen of the Missions. There was in 1827 only one tower, as described by Duhaut-Cilly; the second tower was finished in 1833.

hundred individuals of both sexes were occupied in various tasks. The women and children carded and spun the wool while the men were warping and weaving blankets, sackcloth, and especially a coarse flannel resembling cloth before fulling. The work of the several crafts and the machines for it were also planned by the padre and carried out by the Indians, from whose ranks he has trained carpenters, masons, blacksmiths, and indeed all the kinds of workers needed in such a large establishment.

At that time he was giving full attention to a water mill he was having built at the base of a hill to the right of the mission. The water, brought from more than two leagues away by a ditch that followed the side of the mountains, was to fall from a height of about twenty feet onto the buckets of the wheel. The fall was not perpendicular but at a pitch of about 35°, and the wheel was horizontal rather than vertical; it was a full circle on whose plane were disposed, in the manner of spokes, objects like great spoons, slightly concave, which were to receive the force, one after the other, and thus impart movement.

At first glance I was surprised that a man of judgment like the padre had preferred an inclined flow when it would have been quite easy to cut back the hill and obtain a more direct fall; although no expert in hydraulics I could see that his device would lose power to the extent that the fall departed from the vertical. But before expressing my opinion, a little reflection brought me back to that of the inventor, and I could see that if he lost power in one way, he would gain it in another by avoiding the friction of two gears, since the turning grindstone would be attached directly to the shaft of the wheel.

Another objection can be made in regard to the speed of rotation; in this system it is equal for the wheel and the millstone, while in our ordinary arrangement the speed of the stone increases as the radius of the wheel differs from the radius of the hub. But since Fray Antonio's workers were little versed in mechanics, he was avoiding many mistakes by simplifying the mechanism, and I did not doubt the entire success of his undertaking. Nevertheless, I pointed out to him that the material being used for grindstones was not suitable. Having been taken from a single piece of stone and thus nearly homogeneous and of an equal hardness, the two stones would wear down too quickly. After dinner the padre went to his siesta and we returned on board.

While we transacted our business with the padres of the Santa Barbara, Purísima, and Santa Inés missions,[10] it was learned that the general had just arrived at that of San Buenaventura, seven or eight leagues from Santa Barbara. At once all was in an uproar at the presidio, and a cavalry escort was sent to meet him.

Don José María Echeandía was only a colonel of artillery, but since he possessed the title and authority of commandant-general, civil and military chief of the two Californias (*comandante-general, jefe político y militar de ambas Californias*), he was given the title of general in the country and addressed as Your Lordship (*Vuestra señoría*).[11] He enjoyed extensive power and often misused it. The state of mind of the Californians was well suited to give him despotic ideas, which he did not, perhaps, bring with him from Mexico. Already accustomed to Spanish ways and manners, they loved whatever was then in power, justifying their regard for it by granting it exaggerated qualities. Like the sculptor in the fable, they adored what they had themselves created.[12]

With this kind of people, as we can see, it would have been difficult not to let himself be carried away by the sweet use of power. What could the assembly do, which met once a year and was called the provincial legislature (*ayuntamiento de provincia*)? All twenty members had been chosen under his influence, and they gathered only to applaud the views of the civil and military chief, most of which were not in the best interest of California. In order to present claims I sometimes attended these meetings and learned how they were conducted. The general would make a proposal, based often on the most specious

10. La Purísima Concepción, founded in 1787 near present-day Lompoc, was administered by Marcos Antonio Vitoria from 1824 to 1835. Santa Inés Virgen y Mártir, some twenty miles east of Purísima, was in 1804 the third and last of the Santa Barbara channel missions to be established. Father Blas Ordaz was alone there from 1824 to 1833.

11. Governor José María Echeandía arrived at San Diego in October 1825 and resided there—except for intervals at Santa Barbara and Monterey—until March 1829, when he returned with the capital to Monterey. The provincial legislature, as Duhaut-Cilly notes, may often have been compliant, but, notwithstanding this impression, they were in 1829 dismissed by the governor for being unmanageable.

12. Perhaps a reference to Pygmalion, who fell in love with the statue he had made and who, much later, inspired Shaw's play of that name, which, still later, was made into the musical *My Fair Lady*.

grounds. If some member tried to speak, he stopped him short by speaking again himself, and he was verbose. If, when it came to a vote, he perceived the least hesitation on the part of a member, this irresolution was met by a menacing stare, and the negative vote was metamorphosed at once into a vote in favor. For show only, one or two of the faithful would play a comedy of arranged opposition, which, after a few weak arguments were refuted, always left him with the honor of victory.

But it must be admitted that the position of this officer was a prickly one. On the one hand, the Mexican government demanded strict enforcement of the articles of the constitution and the excessive customs duties; on the other hand, it made no provision of money or supplies to the commandant-general. The latter, in order to provide for the expenses of his troops and his administration, was obliged to disregard some of his government's orders in relation to commerce with foreign vessels. Since the duties they paid were almost his only source of income, he softened as much as he could the severity of the Mexican laws. To hold these ships to a system that was difficult in Mexico and quite impracticable in California would have been to send them away not to return. To the continued reproofs of his government, he replied with observations, quite true, about the difficulty of his position. The slowness of correspondence rendered these administrative questions interminable, and at that time the matter remained *in statu quo*.

The second resource of the commandant-general was the supply of food contributed by the missions for the subsistence of his soldiers. The missions had always provided in this way for the maintenance of the garrisons, but the missionaries regarded this aid in one way under the Spanish government and in another under the Mexican constitution. The padres could never, in truth, count on reimbursement for what was provided to the Spanish authorities, but they considered this a duty and, moreover, one in their interest. No one at that time questioned their right to the missions, and they were not unaware that to refuse the assistance might leave them exposed to the mercy of the Indians. But things are quite different today. They know that the government, in regarding the missions as property of the republic, looks on the missionaries as no more than farmers, and that if it keeps them at the head of their establishments this is because they alone can administer and maintain them. They have been informed that Mexican friars—of their order but devoted to the cause of independence—will gradually replace them as old age and infirmity render them unable to exercise their functions.

This knowledge of the government's attitude to the Spanish friars was beginning to inspire in them a great indifference to the prosperity of the missions; they demonstrated their disgust by a reluctance to provide the troops with the provisions needed.

Nevertheless, the commandant-general preferred to act with moderation, more effective than harsh measures that would inevitably have broken the bonds that still existed between him and the padres. A violent rupture would have produced in California a disastrous effect. Pushed to the limit, the missionaries had only to give freedom to the Indians, and at once the missions would have been abandoned and given up to the flames. These people would have gone back to their savage ways, and Mexico would have lost the province, because the creole population, too lazy and too proud to devote itself to agriculture, would have fallen into total misery. It is only the work of the Indians that supports them.

These difficulties were not the only ones faced by the administration of Commandant Echeandía. I have reason to believe that his powers were quite broad and even in some ways discretionary, but there was one person who claimed to be outside his control: this was the commissioner in Monterey, of whom I have already spoken. The touchy rivalry that we often see at home between the several civil offices and the military authorities was present here in all its force and was even more troublesome because there was no higher jurisdiction to settle matters on the spot.

The bureaucrat who collected duties and taxes never turned over all the funds demanded of him. The Pactolus from his strongbox flowed only drop by drop,[13] and if the man of the sword wished to cast an inquisitive eye on the accounts of the man of the pen, the latter, redder

13. A gold-bearing river in ancient Lydia, source of wealth for Croesus.

than an angry turkey and more puffed up, would refuse, saying that he was accountable only to the government in Mexico. I will not set myself up as judge between these two rivals, but I presume that the commandant-general was acting within his rights. Had he not been, he could not have suspended the commissioner from his duties, as he later did.

Admirably situated to observe these intrigues, I decided early on to conduct myself as a neutral. I received and spoke to all parties alike; that was the proper role for a foreign merchant. My dealings, however, were more frequent with the missionaries and with the commissioner than with the commandant-general and his supporters; each spoke to me in confidence, and I listened most often without expressing an opinion, except perhaps to the padres. In this way I lost none of the few opportunities there were for trade.[14]

Early on 5 April we learned that the commandant-general was on his way, and at noon we could make out in the distance on the beach road from San Buenaventura the large cavalcade that accompanied him. An hour later he entered the presidio to a salute of seven guns from the land and an equal number that, on invitation of Don José Noriega, I had fired from the ship. At once I went to pay my courtesy call and easily obtained permission to unload at San Diego the merchandise that I wished to leave there before returning to Mazatlán.

On the 8th, Palm Sunday, I settled my accounts with the commissioner's deputy and paid the import duty on what I had sold in Santa Barbara. I then went to the mission to take leave of Fray Antonio, of the commandant-general, and of Don José Noriega. I attended the day's ceremonies, which took place with extraordinary pomp. Palm branches, elegantly decorated with flowers and with braids made from the leaves themselves, were distributed to all the gente de razón, and the Indians had simple olive branches. The solemnity of the Lenten season did not permit the padre to perform all of his music inside the church, but outside it his Indians rendered some songs with much

14. Just before leaving California in September 1828 (Chapter 19) Duhaut-Cilly has uneasy relations with Echeandía during the affair of the *Franklin* in San Diego.

taste and a delightful harmony, singing Spanish and Latin words to pretty Italian airs.

After mass we retired to the padre's drawing room, and there heard a serenade to the commandant-general. The musicians were many and all in uniform. Although they rendered passably well several French and Italian pieces, I judged that they had succeeded better with the earlier songs. I then went back on board and we at once got under sail.

We made for the bay of San Pedro, which serves the mission of San Fernando, the pueblo of Los Angeles, and the mission of San Gabriel, one of the richest in California. That harbor is twenty-six leagues from the one we were leaving. We set a course that would take us between the islands of Anacapa and Point Conversion at the extreme eastern end of the Santa Barbara channel.[15] Before reaching that point we passed directly in front of the mission of San Buenaventura, a poor establishment with a bad anchorage. We did not stop. Before Point Conversion the mountains retreat toward the interior and the land near the coast is low and the water sown with rocks, making the approach dangerous; it is best to stay well away, especially at night.[16]

The bay of San Pedro, with its opening to the south, forms three sides of a square and is sheltered to the west by Point San Vicente. About six leagues in front of it lies the island of Santa Catalina. On the morning of the 9th we caught sight of Point San Vicente, which, to one coming from the west, can be mistaken for an island of moderate elevation; but as one comes nearer the low land joining it to the mountains of the interior comes into view. We skirted it at a distance of half a mile and dropped anchor in seven fathoms, bottom of sand.[17]

The bay of San Pedro is quite deserted, the closest habitation being

15. Point Conversion, named by Vizcaîno in 1603, is now identified as Point Mugu.

16. San Buenaventura, founded in 1782, was in decline in the 1820s but had earlier been one of the large producers of cattle and grain. Father José Altimira was in charge in 1827.

17. The fairly open bay of San Pedro was the most important of the minor embarcaderos along the California coast, and most of the trading vessels stopped there. The nearby rancho was that of San Pedro, granted to Cristóbal Domínguez in 1822.

a rancho that can be seen four leagues away on the road to the pueblo of Los Angeles. It is possible to spend several days here before anyone at the pueblo knows that a ship has arrived in the roadstead. One can send a man on foot to the rancho to ask for horses but ordinarily one fires a gun in order to be noticed. In the calm of the evening, especially, the sound easily carries that far and even as far as the pueblo. At sundown we employed this method with success. As we did not yet know the range of our carronade eights, we loaded two of them with balls with the double intention of learning their power and of making a louder noise. The detonation was first heard against the cliffs of the bay, then it crossed the plain that extends to the north, rolling like distant thunder, and as soon as the sound had died down an echo from the mountains reached us from more than ten leagues away, a faint cannon shot but clear and distinct, as if our salute had been returned by the inhabitants of Los Angeles. We calculated that the ball had carried 450 *toises* [about 1,000 yards] but did not reach to the shore.[18]

The next morning some men appeared on the point, bringing a number of horses. Since I was little inclined to leave the ship in a roadstead that was still dangerous in that season, it was agreed that Mr. R_____ would go alone to the mission of San Gabriel and that, on word from him, I would send the things that he sold there. With matters thus settled, we went on shore and he set off, accompanied by a guide.[19]

One of my officers and I had brought our guns, intending to hunt, the only diversion that could be hoped for in this desert, but we were deprived of the sport by an unexpected difficulty. What we had taken from a distance to be a slope of grass and heather turned out to be a

18. As noted in Chapter 1, the carronade was a short, large-bore naval gun, named for Carron, the place in Scotland where it was first made. Falconer's *Marine Dictionary* (1815) says that the 8.05-inch bore used a ball weighing 68 pounds. Duhaut-Cilly tells us that the *Héros* was armed with twelve carronades but does not say whether they were all eights (*de huit*).

19. Mission San Gabriel Arcángel, founded in 1771, became the wealthiest in the Franciscan chain, and it was with the mission rather than the nearby pueblo that the bulk of the coast trade was carried on. Pedro José Bernardo Sánchez was in charge when Duhaut-Cilly called there in the following August.

thick growth of mustard, already higher than the head of a man.[20] Wishing nevertheless to go as far as a knoll where it appeared to be less dense, we made our way into this veritable forest and soon repented having done so. At every step among the dry stalks of the past year, covered over by the new growth, we could hear the sound of rattlesnakes, crawling here in such great numbers that a young man who accompanied us killed two of them in a quarter of an hour.

In vain did we try to walk cautiously and in silence; the sound of our treading on the dry plants was confused, in our imagination, with the sounds that we feared to hear. Beneath this natural growth we could not see the ground, covered over by several layers of detritus, which crackled and gave way under our feet. We expected at every moment to step on the tail of one of these dangerous reptiles, and we shuddered involuntarily, thinking that its head, when it reared up, would be at least on a level with our own.

O Lemaout! Sole apothecary who knew how to concoct something appetizing. We might never have tasted your *moutarde celtique* if you had had to harvest the precious seeds on the plains of San Pedro, even had California lain at your doorstep.

We finally reached a hillock where we found only sparse grass and some bushes. We shot several rabbits as well as a kind of owl that has its nest in the ground and lives there in families. After spending a few minutes on this high ground, from where we had a wide view of the horizon, we were ready to return to the shore, and managed this by following the route that we had already broken through the mustard.

Before regaining the ship we visited a small islet, to which we had allowed ourselves, on first arrival, to give the name of Anniversary Island. When we entered the bay of San Pedro and noticed this nameless rock, it had been just a year since we left France.[21] On its highest

---

20. This was perhaps fennel, an introduced plant that grows as described here and is still a weed in parts of California. The mustard that now grows on cultivated fields and hillsides is much smaller.

21. Perhaps Dead Man's Island as identified in J. H. Kemble's edition of Dana's *Two Years before the Mast* (1964, p. 106).

point we found the eyrie of a sea eagle with two eaglets sitting among the disgusting remains of fish, while the father and mother circled around us as if to defend them. We had no wish to deprive them of their repugnant family, but by firing several times with small shot that bounced off their thick plumage without doing much harm, we delivered ourselves from their loud cries. These powerful birds are black with the under part of the tail and the top of the head a yellowish white.

Chapter 11

INDIAN CAPTIVES, SAN DIEGO, & MAZATLÁN

April–May 1827

FREEDOM! FREEDOM! FOR the past half a century we do nothing but repeat this word, so that one might think the tongues pronouncing it belong to heads that know not its meaning, or rather that it has no meaning. For as soon as one person says he is free, ten others cry out that they are oppressed. One who discerned too much freedom a few years ago, now demands more of it. Each one sees freedom in his own light, and it is quite impossible to create it to please everyone. Freedom to dip both hands into the public coffers? Freedom to seize the land one wants? Freedom to hold sinecures, to be paid large sums for imaginary services? Freedom to calumniate, to revile, to vilify the most worthy things? Is this to enjoy freedom? Rather, it is to abuse it and profane it.

It is thus clear that there can be no agreement on what is political freedom, but that is not what I wish to write about. There is a kind of freedom understood not only by all men but by all living creatures, the one demanded imperiously by our nature, the one that, indeed, society must take from the criminal. But it is also the one that injustice and force tear away from the unhappy slave and that had been lost by the poor Indians that Don Ignacio Martínez entrusted to me to convey to San Diego.

For six weeks they had been on board a French ship and thus on the soil of France, where there is no slavery.[1] Furthermore, they had enjoyed the same liberty as all others on the *Héros* and had never shown any but the best conduct. But they could not ignore that in a few days they would go back to their fetters and their tyrants, and they must have wished to escape such an unhappy future. On the night of the 15th they were clever enough to steal the only boat lying alongside the ship and, after first letting themselves drift noiselessly away, they disappeared without being noticed by the two seamen of the watch. As soon as I was informed of the matter I sent two boats in search of the one they had taken, and it was found abandoned on the rocks of Point San Vicente but without damage.

Since I had consented to take charge of these unfortunates, I would certainly have prevented their escape had I known of their intentions in time to act. But I was happy that they had with so much adroitness reclaimed the liberty that had, perhaps with injustice, been taken from them. I made no effort to recapture them, contenting myself at the first opportunity with passing word of their flight to the alcalde of the pueblo, while making a wish, not to be fulfilled, that they might escape his pursuit.

I learned later that after wandering for several months in these deserted hills they had finally been recaptured by a ranchero of the neighborhood, well known for exploits of this kind. He made the poor Indians pay dearly for the several cows they had killed for food; catching them by surprise one day, he succeeded in garroting two of them and put a bullet between the shoulders of the third, who was fleeing.

Among the Indians, most of whom appear to be quite submissive, there are some who put a great value on freedom and seek to get it by fleeing. They get away easily enough but are often recaptured by the

---

1. Here and elsewhere Duhaut-Cilly uses the word "slavery" in a loose and general sense, confusing chattel slavery, which includes ownership and the right to buy and sell, with other forms of enforced labor. So also Richard Henry Dana, when he writes in Chapter 15 of *Two Years before the Mast* of slavery aboard ship. And Duhaut-Cilly, sometimes without evidence, tends to make the assumption, not unknown a century and a half later, that criminals are victims of society.

parties sent after them by the missionaries and the military commandants. And with no thought that these men have only exercised the most natural of rights, they are usually treated as criminals and pitilessly put in irons.

One of these unfortunates, after having tried several times to flee his oppressors, was finally condemned by the commandant at San Francisco to die in irons. It is true that Pomponio—for that was his name—had added to the crime of desertion several robberies and even murders of those who were detailed to return him to prison. On each leg he wore a huge iron ring, riveted in such a way that he had no hope of getting away. Nevertheless, endowed with the strength and courage to withstand frightful torments, this man made one more plan to free himself and carried it out. While his guards were deep in sleep, he sharpened a knife, cut off one of his heels, and thus slipped off one of the irons; it was without uttering a murmur that he mutilated himself in a most sensitive part. Can one conceive the strength of soul that it required to repeat the cruel operation, for he had gained only half his liberty? He never hesitated; cutting off the other heel, he took flight, without fearing the sharp pains that each step added to his suffering. It was the trail of blood that revealed his escape the next morning.

Untouched by a deed that the ancients might have deified, the tyrants were only more inflamed against their victim and pursued him relentlessly. Pomponio lived in the woods among the bears that he feared less than he feared men, and for three years he raided the mission and presidio of San Francisco. Finally, a picket of cavalry surprised him asleep, and, to put an end to the matter, he was shot.[2]

Two months before we came to Santa Barbara there was played out a scene there that seemed to show that republicans of all times and all countries, not to speak of Rome and Sparta, have always needed helots, that is to say, wretches, who can be reduced to a brutish condition and killed for sport.

2. Pomponio, a native of the San Rafael region and a refugee from Mission San Francisco de Asís, was, after several years of depredations, tried by court-martial in February 1824 and executed in December.

For some time an Indian named Valerio, endowed with great courage and prodigious strength, pushed to the limit by the bad treatment inflicted on him—for his shoulders had often been furrowed by the rod—had deserted the mission. His hiding place was not known, but every day his depredations revealed his presence in the vicinity. When necessity arose he came by night to the huts of his former companions and took what he needed to sustain life. They let it happen; woe to anyone who might stand in his way. He crushed with his knee the head of a woman who quarreled with him about a common utensil.

Valerio should have remained content with what he got from the Indian huts; none of his compatriots would have betrayed him; but he wanted revenge on the *mayordomo* (major-domo, a kind of steward) of the mission, a base and cruel man and author of all his wrongs. One night the Indian appeared like a shadow in the man's room. The mayordomo, remembering things that made him tremble, was frozen with fright by the glittering eyes. But Valerio did not want his life; he merely seized a box of papers valuable to his enemy and went away.

The danger was past. The mayordomo's blood, suspended by terror, began to circulate once more; it flowed again to his heart but with it entered rage. He did not dare, however, to follow Valerio himself; he entrusted this to a vile creature, who discovered the hiding place of the Indian. This was half a league from Santa Barbara, in the depths of a spacious cave protected on one side by an inaccessible mountain gorge and on the other by a dense wood, whose entrances were known only to him. He took such great care that he never walked on the sand or the bare ground near his dwelling place so as not to betray himself by the imprint of his feet. Before entering the protective forest, he would leap over the bushes, bounding like a deer, in order not to disturb their tops.

Hardly had the dawn come when the mayordomo went to denounce Valerio, first to the padre and then to the commandant of the presidio. He heaped on the poor wretch all sorts of calumnies, painting him as a wild man, and finished by exhibiting a long knife that he had, he said, torn from the hand of the savage at the very moment when he would have plunged it into his entrails. In this infamous way he transferred his own fury to the hearts of the officers and soldiers. The assembled Mexicans agreed that the Indian must be shot like a dog. But who was to carry out this barbarous sentence? It was Rodrigo Pliego, a young officer who had always on his tongue the words liberty and justice and whose scarlet coat covered imperfectly the tattered garment of a coward like fancy dress over a dirty shirt.

He needed four soldiers armed with guns and four archers to accomplish the perilous adventure. At the head of this troop the warlike republican, brandishing his saber, advances cautiously toward Valerio's sheltering cavern. Crouched by a small fire, Valerio is quietly preparing his cheeses,[3] when, at a signal from Pliego, one of the archers lets fly an arrow that buries itself under the shoulder of the unfortunate wretch. The cheese is overturned; the bleeding man rises to his full height, shoots a terrible look at his executioners, pulls the arrow from his breast to throw it back at them. But they don't give him time; three other arrows and two bullets strike him and he falls to the ground.

The convoy returns; on the back of a horse reposes a red and brown object, the body of Valerio. In the front row of the onlookers is the mayordomo; now triumphant and relieved, he shouts: "All honor to Don Rodrigo!"

"Look," says Don Rodrigo, "*¡cuan gordo era el indigno, y cuan amarilla le sale la manteca!* (See how plump the dog was, and how yellow the fat that shows in his wounds!)."

Later, when speaking of the executioner of the Sandwich Islands, I will reveal the nationality of the mayordomo.*

On the 17th we departed the bay of San Pedro for San Diego. The

3. Perhaps some kind of gruel. Cheese would have been difficult to make in a primitive cave.

* This account was related to Mr. A. Bourdas, my brother-in-law, by Pliego himself, who boasted of having led the expedition. [This emotional story, told at third hand and embroidered not a little, is difficult to check. Duhaut-Cilly says it took place in early 1827, but he may have picked it up on one of his later visits since Valerio was, according to contemporary records, still being sought in February 1828, and since Rodrigo del Pliego, an officer at Monterey from 1825, was not transferred to Santa Barbara until August 1827. In 1828 he was declared incompetent and ordered back to Mexico.]

distance between these two ports is twenty-eight leagues and the direction is southeast 9° south, corrected. At three o'clock the next morning we came in view of some land whose small extent and form caused us to take it at once for the Coronados, a group of small islands five leagues to the south-southwest of the entrance to San Diego. Nevertheless, we wished to make sure that it was not an island that Vancouver places at seven leagues to the west-northwest of that harbor. But having obtained 32° 34′ of north latitude by the meridian height of the moon, we were confirmed in our first opinion and at break of day found ourselves in the best position to enter the port.*

I had obtained such good information about this place that we experienced no difficulty in entering without the need of a pilot. The harbor of San Diego is without doubt the finest in all California, much preferable for the safety of a ship to the immense bay of San Francisco, whose very size leaves it much too exposed to wind and wave. That of San Diego does not have this drawback; it is a narrow passage from one to two miles wide, running first to the north-northeast and then turning to the east and southeast, thus forming an arc five leagues in length. On the west it is sheltered by a long and narrow hill called Point Loma, quite steep and stretching out to the south-southwest. Two miles inside this point there projects a perpendicular tongue of earth and pebbles like an artificial mole, ending in a perfectly rounded bank. A deep and narrow strait, about two hundred fathoms wide, separates this natural causeway from a sandy peninsula that, following the curvature of the channel, gives protection on the side of the sea for the length of the bay.

The depth is not everywhere the same; as one advances toward the interior the channel in the center of the bay is made narrow by the shallows on both sides. The most suitable mooring spot is a mile past the narrow strait, facing a pretty beach of yellow sand. The anchor is

---

* It was not difficult for me to determine later that this supposed island of San Juan does not exist. [Vancouver placed such an island on his 1798 chart of the Northwest Coast with its situation marked as "doubtful." It had been pointed out to him by officers at the San Diego presidio who said it was new and not yet found on their charts (it being probably the tip of San Clemente Island). The four Coronados are off the coast of Baja California.]

dropped in twelve fathoms and within hailing distance of the western shore.

From the outer extremity of Point Loma stretches a long patch of seaweed, which extends more than a league to the south-southwest. It lies so thick on the water that if one attempts to pass through in a light breeze it is possible to be held up by this obstacle; but there is no other danger because the depth is everywhere from fifteen to twenty fathoms. The long ropes of this species of fucus rise from the bottom and spread out on the sea their broad, brown leaves. Some of the slender stalks bear globes of the form and size of a number-24 cannon ball, hollowed like a grenade or an artillery shell and doubtless intended by nature to support the branches of kelp when they become too heavy to float.

To avoid passing through this floating prairie we brought Point Loma to the north-northeast of us, then steered in that direction, and went in rapidly with a good breeze from the west-northwest, skirting first the kelp and then the point at a distance of half a mile. Following this direction one avoids a bank with only a few feet of water and where the sea does not always break. This shallow begins on the sandy point that forms the right side of the entrance to the harbor and extends about a mile and a half on a line to the south.

The soundings, which had gradually diminished, gave no more than three fathoms when we came athwart the extremity of Point Loma, but on coming half a point to starboard, they soon showed five fathoms. As we came opposite the shallow mentioned above, where the waves were breaking in several places, we steered by the end of the natural mole, passing it at two ship-lengths with a depth of ten fathoms.

A low fortification with twelve guns is built where this tongue of land is attached to Point Loma. As we approached they raised the Mexican flag and called attention to it with a cannon shot; at once we hoisted our own flag and returned the salute. Whenever we saw unfurled the colors of Mexico, they produced in us a sensation akin to joy and made our hearts beat faster for a moment. Those of us who served under the Empire always took that banner at first sight for the flag that once guided us to victory; the Mexican flag differs from the

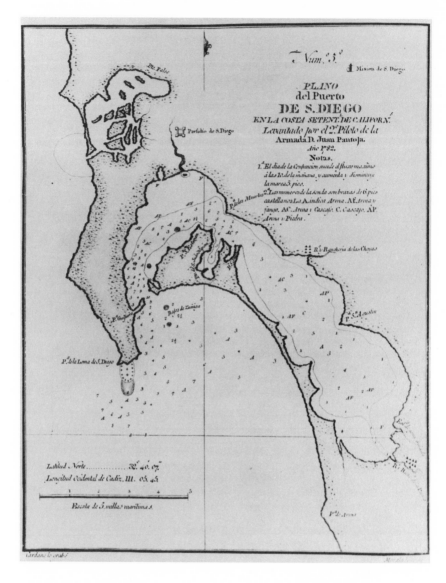

6. Map of San Diego Harbor as it was in the early nineteenth century.
(The Bancroft Library.)

tricolor only in having green for blue; all else is the same and arranged in the same way.

Once past the fort we had only to steer for the sandy beach to the north and anchor in front of it in eleven or twelve fathoms. Of all the places we had visited during our stay in California, except San Pedro, which is quite desolate, the presidio of San Diego was the most bleak. It is built on the barren slope of a hill and has no regular shape but is a mere jumble of houses rendered more gloomy by the dark brown color of the crude bricks of which they are made.

Nevertheless it was then the seat of government. A very mild climate, more congenial to the poor health of the commandant-general than that of Monterey, had perhaps led him to prefer this place, but some uncharitable persons claimed that the company of a certain lady of San Diego had embellished in his eyes a spot so unattractive in itself.

Spread out on a sandy plain below the presidio are thirty or forty houses of poor appearance and a few badly kept gardens. A stream, which dries up during the summer, runs past the foot of the hill and empties into the sea to the west of Point Loma.[4]

The mission of San Diego can be seen two leagues to the north of the presidio; there I went on the morning after our arrival. For most of the way the road ran along the side of the stream, and when it moved away it passed through a long field of mustard, whose fine yellow flowers, open at that time, dazzled the eye with brilliant gold. In the distance we could see some high mountains, whose summits are sometimes covered with snow. At the base of one of these, eighteen leagues from San Diego, is the mission of San Luis Rey, one of the most considerable in the country.

That of San Diego, administered at that time by the padres Vicente and Fernando, is not anywhere near so wealthy, although it numbers a thousand Indians and owns twelve thousand cattle, nineteen thou-

---

4. The presidio was established in 1769 near the San Diego River, several miles from the harbor's mouth. By 1827 it was in a dilapidated state, although the governor had his official residence in the commandant's quarters from 1825 to 1829. The town that Duhaut-Cilly observed began to be settled outside the presidio in the mid-1820s.

sand sheep, two thousand pigs, and a proportionate number of horses and mules.

The fine appearance of this establishment loses much as one draws near; the buildings, although well arranged, have deteriorated and are poorly maintained. A distasteful air of uncleanliness reigned in the dwelling of Fray Vicente and Fray Fernando, who appeared to be so accustomed to this state of affairs that they scarcely noticed what lay around them. Their greeting, however, was as kindly as their house was dirty.

The good fathers were about to sit down to eat and they invited me to join them. Nothing that they offered me could stir the appetite, and as Fray Vicente pressed me vainly to partake, Fray Fernando exclaimed: "How singular! The mission air must not agree with strangers. I notice that none of them do honor to our table." While uttering these words he was preparing a salad of cold mutton with onions, peppers, and an oil from the mission whose odor turned the stomach. And not having a knife, he broke up this mixture with his fingers and even his teeth, stirring the whole thing with his fist in a nicked platter, where could be seen the remnants of last night's supper.

Only disgust could conquer the desire to laugh that might easily have overcome me, but my traveling companion, a young Californian, devoured in a manner to please everything that was set in front of him. "*Eso si, es gana* (That is what you call an appetite!)," said Fray Fernando.[5]

At the end of several days we prepared to leave San Diego and go to Mazatlán to deliver the merchandise that we had sold there in the previous December, hoping that Don Ignacio Fletes would be successful this time in getting permission for us to unload it. For this short trip we had intended to retain on board only that part of the cargo, but in San Diego we were offered no storehouse suitable for everything else

5. Mission San Diego de Alcalá, first at the presidio site, was moved to a more favorable agricultural setting up the river in 1774. The padres in 1827 were Fernando Martín, who arrived in San Diego in 1811, and Vicente Pascual Oliva, who came in 1823, both serving there many years.

and especially for three hundred barrels of powder that they did not wish to take into the fort. So we decided to put on shore only what we thought might be sold during our absence, and it was agreed that Mr. R____ should stay in California while we made the short voyage to the coast of Mexico.

While the things were being landed and our carpenters were preparing a small storehouse, we frequently amused ourselves by hunting on Point Loma. The abundance of game there is such that I speak of it with some reluctance, fearing that the reader who can make comparisons may accuse me of exaggeration.

"The truth is not always believable."[6]

But I will not draw back before the truth. Hardly had we put foot on shore when on all sides, to the right and to the left, we stirred up great bevies of quail, a species of crested partridge that I have mentioned elsewhere and that has an excellent flavor. Hares and rabbits moved in bands across the fragrant and flowering fields that carpeted the slope of the hill. In the midst of such great numbers there was no need for a hunting dog. A hare that in France would cost the hunter and his pursuing pack several hours of toil and fatigue requires here only a little silence and care. Moving step by step through heather and bushes, we never went thirty meters without seeing the chance to kill one of these animals, and several times it happened that we killed two with one shot. The mere difficulty of choosing a victim can be troublesome. In the end such easy sport became tedious, and some of us made it more difficult by shooting single balls.

The California hare is as swift as ours, and in such great numbers that when one flees another is caught unawares. In size, form, and flavor this quadruped is quite like the one in Europe, but its fur has less black and more yellow. In respect to this game Point Loma is a more favored spot than the surrounding country, which is much less populated.

The California creoles are little given to hunting, but Point Loma sometimes becomes the theater for bloody forays by the Indians. Two

---

6. *Le vrai peut quelquefois n'être pas vraisemblable*—From *L'Art poétique, III*, by Nicolas Boileau (1636–1711).

or three times a year those from Mission San Diego obtain permission from the padres for expeditions there. The hunters, to the number of two or three hundred, form themselves into a line of battle stretching from the steep face of the mountain to the shore of the bay, and they move forward abreast, driving before them the long-eared band. The Indians are armed with *macanas,* curved and polished sticks that they throw with great skill. As they advance the number of fugitives, added to at each step, grows larger and brings on the excited cries of the hunters. At first the agile object of these maneuvers attaches little importance to them, thinking there is sufficient room to flee, if need be.

> ". . . he browses, he takes his ease,
> He looks about for things that please . . ."[7]

But there must soon be an end to this drama. Having come to a narrow place, where the slope of the hill ends in a cliff, the hares, seeing themselves cut off on the left by the precipice, on the right by the unscalable escarpment of La Loma, and in front by impenetrable thickets, begin to recognize the imminence of danger. They are panic-stricken, and in their terror they dart here and there to find a way out. Some try vainly to scale the wall to the right; others cast themselves into the bay; there are some, and only these have a chance to escape, who attempt to penetrate the enemy front. There is a general massacre, a veritable Saint Bartholomew, in which many perish before the others can cross the battle line, opened up at last, by the Indians.

There is also found in the vicinity of the anchorage that running bird that I have described before under the name of *churay,* to which is attributed the power to kill snakes for food. The churay is a little larger than a magpie and in form much resembles that bird of our own country. Like the latter, it has a long tail that it often raises to a perpendicular position. It is tawny in color, with some feathers that

---

7. . . . *il broute, il se repose, / il s'amuse à toute autre chose . . .* From La Fontaine's fable of the hare and the tortoise.

reflect green. Seldom does it fly and only for short distances, but it can run almost as fast as a horse. When it finds a sleeping snake, they tell us, it builds a high wall around it of spiny cactus branches; this accomplished, it wakens the snake with loud cries. The snake, seeking to flee, is impaled on the long points of its prison, and the bird finishes it off with its beak.[8]

Early on the 30th we made preparations to sail, waiting for the wind to come up, and at nine in the morning got under way and left the harbor. We passed between the Coronados and the coast. These small islands, of which the two principal ones lie southeast to northwest, form a small group, quite high and shaped like the roofs of houses. Viewed lengthwise, they take on a pyramidal aspect. There are no trees, only moss and a coarse grass, which at that time bore yellow flowers.

On 5 May we reached the bay of San José del Cabo, where I needed to take care of some business and land a passenger. Dropping anchor at five in the evening, I went on shore at once, and having found a horse, brought to the beach for me, rode to the mission. It was a great pleasure to see once more Fray Tomás and Pedrin. At such a great distance from our country and deprived for so long of all communication with our families, these good people became for us relatives rather than friends.

My business was soon finished, and after two hours we raised the anchor and were under way again. Because of light winds we were slow in crossing the Gulf of Cortés, and it was only on the 8th, at two in the afternoon, that we anchored near the island of Venado. A boat from the ship *Rosa* came alongside. We learned that this vessel was still moored at Creston. Captain Thérèse was waiting there not only for payment for the sale of his cargo but also for funds belonging to some

---

8. The churay or roadrunner or paisano is a large ground-dwelling desert cuckoo, which feeds on insects, lizards, and rodents as well as small snakes. Lawrence Klauber, in his great book *Rattlesnakes* (2nd ed., 1972, pp. 1283–84), cites many written accounts from 1859 to the present day, of this cactus-corral story, concocted for the astonishment of visitors. Rattlesnakes go easily through and over cactus.

Spaniards who, realizing the gravity of what was happening in Mexico, were taking precautions to preserve what they owned.[9] I went at once on shore in order to profit from the rest of the day and from the coolness of the hour to reach the presidio that evening. With Mr. Tréhouart, my second in command, I left written instructions on how he should deal with the local authorities during my absence, for our position there was quite delicate, and I was taking with me Dr. Botta, who wished to see the presidio.[10]

We set out at five in the evening. The weather was most beautiful, and the moon, soon taking the place abandoned by the sun, illuminated with a grayish light the vast forests that border the route almost the entire way. In this solitude there was no sound but the song of the cicadas and the cries of night birds. The hooves of our horses resounded in the deserted woods, and everything around us took on shapes indistinct and fantastic. We stayed silent so that we might better enjoy the situation and were distracted from our reverie only when a bright firefly passed before our eyes or when our guide, several steps in front of us, stopped to strike tinder and light his cigarita.

Don Ignacio Fletes was not at the presidio of Mazatlán, where he stayed but seldom, but was at that moment in Rosario with his family. In the morning I prepared to go there to find him, but when I presented myself to obtain a passport, the commissioner of customs informed me in the most precise terms not only that he refused permission to make the trip but also that I should depart at once for the harbor and set sail without unloading anything. Although I had fully expected to encounter some obstacles in delivering the merchandise that I was bringing to Don Ignacio, I had hoped that this merchant, who enjoyed some influence in the country, would succeed in removing them.

9. On the previous 20 November this vessel, identified by Duhaut-Cilly as a Genoese ship coming from China, dropped anchor under Venado Island just ahead of the *Héros*.

10. The position of the Spanish population in Mexico during and after the war of independence was precarious; a few days after Duhaut-Cilly's visit they were debarred from holding office and, on 20 December of that year, were made subject (with some exceptions) to expulsion. In Chapter 18 Duhaut-Cilly is present when the order of expulsion is read in San Gabriel.

I asked the commissioner the reason for such great severity, and he replied that our previous stay in the port of Mazatlán had been too long and had compromised the administration. And indeed he showed me several letters in which the sharpest reproaches had been addressed to him on this subject—criticizing me and threatening him with the loss of his position. It was inconceivable, they said, that a vessel which, because of its cargo and its declarations, could not be allowed to unload, should stay so long in a port where it could do no business; that there had been more than enough time to replenish water and provisions; that so much delay had been only a pretext; and finally that the government suspected the vessel of smuggling and the customs employees of allowing this.

I contested these accusations, pointing out that I had not stayed without authorization and, consequently, that they could not accuse me of disregarding the law. Nevertheless, given such suspicions, I had no trust in what measures they might take against me and realized at once that the most prudent course would be to renounce the project that had brought me there. During my stay at the presidio I feared to learn at any moment that they had made an effort to arrest the ship in the harbor, and although the instructions I had left on board were such as to calm my fears, the consequences of such an attempt would have been disastrous for the rest of our operation. I knew of several events that showed how little justice often went into the proceedings of Mexican administrations and how difficult it could then be to restore one's rights. I obtained, however, a long enough delay to write to Don Ignacio and ask that he tell his office in Mazatlán to settle our account.*

While awaiting the return of my courier I called on several acquaintances I had made in the country. Without surprise I learned of

---

* Not long before this a foreign ship had suffered at Acapulco a great violation of human rights. The manifest included some merchandise that the captain did not know to be prohibited. After several days of consultation the customs made a ruling that he could unload all his cargo into the government warehouses on condition that he re-embark the forbidden goods when he departed. No sooner was the cargo on shore than the whole of it was seized on the pretext of contraband. Only at the end of a year was the captain acquitted, but without reimbursement. It was the fable of the wolf and the stork.

the agitation that was disturbing men's minds in all parts of this vast republic. The entire nation was split into two parties, the Escoseses and the Yorkinos. The latter were a terrorist group, which claimed to see conspiracies or stirred them up in order to promote harsh and bloody measures against the Spaniards and even against all Europeans. Unfortunately, some members of the government, seeing them at first as inspired merely by an excess of patriotism, shared their views and subscribed in part to their principles. But it was not long before they raised the veil covering the ugly designs of these ardent patriots, and they then tried to quiet the storm. It was not difficult to see that, in expelling the rich Spaniards from Mexico or in cutting off their heads, the real purpose was to get hold of their fortunes. Have mass proscriptions ever had any other motive? Modern first consuls and tribunes drive beggars from their tables and their houses. The rich cross the sea or die.[11]

Those who, like us, were born in the midst of revolution, only we know how difficult it is to construct dams strong enough to hold back such torrents. Moreover, in the intoxication of a newly gained freedom, the people are easily alarmed, fearing always that it may be taken from them and, at the least suspicion, they throw themselves into the most cruel fits of rage. Nothing is easier than to make them see as traitors and enemies those whom one would like to destroy. So those in power managed to slow but not to stop the course of events. At Guadalajara the treasure of the cathedral was pillaged; a monk named Arena had just been executed for having participated, it was said, in a plot against the republic. In the end there was discontent, fear, and aggravation everywhere.

The government had no confidence at all in its officials, especially in its financial employees. The latter, always on the point of being denounced by those who sought a pretext to ruin them and take their places, justified the distrust they inspired by feathering their nests while they could. I have seen in Mexico some almost unbelievable examples of corruption.

11. The Escoseses and Yorkinos were political factions organized around the Scottish and York rites of Freemasonry, the former embracing conservatives and royalists, the latter chiefly creoles and mestizos.

An event happier for the country had just taken place in the state of Sonora. The Yaqui Indians, in revolt for almost two years, made peace with the republic. I could not learn the terms of the treaty but have reason to believe that the expression *indultados* (the pardoned), which the Mexicans used to designate the pacified Yaquis, is hardly appropriate for men who, after defeating part of the republican army, held the remainder besieged in the city of Pitic for a year and who had so terrorized the commercial city of Guaymas that it was abandoned by all its inhabitants.[12]

On the 10th, in the evening, I received a letter from Don Ignacio Fletes, in which he advised me to push my affairs no further. At the same time he authorized his office in Mazatlán to settle our account. I therefore completed the business, and next morning we returned to the port.

Leaving Mazatlán to return to San Diego, we had a close look at Cabo San Lucas, passing at a distance of two leagues. When this extremity of the peninsula of California lay eight miles to the northwest of us, we took two series of lunar distances from the sun, one of which gave us 112° 23′ and the other 112° 21′ of longitude west, adjusted to the meridian of the cape, an observation 3′ less than the single one we had been able to make on our first visit to San Lucas. The mean of the three observations would place the cape at 112° 21′.

---

12. The Yaquis of Sonora, the most war-like of the Mexican tribes, had challenged Spanish authority since the early seventeenth century, nor would the revolt noted by Duhaut-Cilly be their last. Pitic was the former name of Hermosillo.

Chapter 12

A VISIT TO SAN LUIS REY

June–July 1827

THE PASSAGE BETWEEN MAZATLÁN and San Diego was not made as easily returning as it was going. We had to struggle against weak and contrary winds that obliged us to tack about slowly for twenty-eight days, and it was only on 10 June that we reached this port.

On our arrival we learned that Mr. R_____ was at San Luis Rey, and with the view of doing some business with the head of that mission, I got ready to go there. At the presidio I found a dozen persons preparing to go to the same place in order to attend a double celebration of the consecration day of the mission and the patron saint's day of Padre Antonio Peyrí.

To avoid the heat and take advantage of a fine moon, we set out at ten o'clock in the evening just as that luminary, now in her third quarter, was rising above the hills to the east. At the end of an hour the road dived between two chains of mountains, and the light of the moon was blocked by the high ridge to the right, so that darkness reigned at the bottom of the valley. This trip was far from being as silent as the one I had recently made in quite similar circumstances, traveling by night to the presidio of Mazatlán.

The anticipated pleasure of the festivals of San Luis inspired a gaiety in my companions of the road, which they stoked with glasses of brandy whenever they stopped to light their cigaritas. After the songs of the country came scandalous stories recounted by each man in turn, and if these anecdotes added to the hilarity of the company, they struck home against the reputation of one's fellows. Complete abandon soon reigned among the party; it was a time for confidences but also for low jests tossed off by all and without restraint.

One person in particular was for some time the target of all their shafts, but I will not say to which group he belonged. He defended himself with well-sustained retorts, and an impediment of speech lent a most sardonic tone to his raillery. But the situation did not allow anyone to become angry, and this man was less in a position than any other to take offense at the rather sharp jests aimed in his direction, for his conduct, all too public, condemned him to these consequences. In the end he outdid his adversaries, surpassing the boldest of them in the liberty of his language. Although I laughed at all his sarcasms, the feeling that remained with me was an invincible distaste for this individual. I was, moreover, the only neutral in this war of tongues, and I gained profit from it in learning the manners of the land.

After following this defile for three leagues we came to the edge of the sea, and the tide was low enough to permit us a route much more pleasant that night than the inland road. We sped along at full tilt on a beach of hard and level sand, shut in between the water and a vertical cliff. At times the way was so narrow that the foaming waves, as they came rolling in, washed the feet of our horses, then retreated forty or fifty paces.[1]

At a place where the waves came up to the foot of the cliff, an Indian, deprived by wine of half his wits and equilibrium, tried to take the narrow passage at full gallop and fell with his horse at the deepest spot, one leg pinned under his steed. As the first to reach him, I was about to dismount to help him up when in the bright moonlight I

---

1. The party proceeded from San Diego up Rose Canyon to a junction with Soledad Canyon and down the latter to the sea. Going north along the beach, they crossed the mouths of several creeks until reaching the San Luis River, which they followed a few miles up to the mission.

saw that he, in that position, was peacefully smoking his paper cigar. This he continued until a wave came up to extinguish it in his mouth and then, as though he had nothing better to do, he struck the horse's head with the end of the reins, and the animal at once arose with its rider and resumed its course, with no word at all being uttered by the Indian.

Unaware whether the tide was going out or coming in, I was reminded of an interesting incident in *The Antiquary* of Walter Scott. If the narrow strip of beach that we were traveling had suddenly been invaded by a flood tide, it is certain that we could have found no way to climb that vertical wall of cliff, and on that deserted shore no itinerant peddler would have come along to rescue us. But fortunately the sea does not rise so rapidly on the coast of California as it does on that of Scotland, and we would have had sufficient time, I think, to reach one of the ravines that cut the cliff from time to time.

Seven leagues from San Diego we came to a large stream called the Estero de San Dieguito, which rushed into the sea with great force, forming a turbulent bar where it met with the waves. With no hesitation the Californians boldly rode into the torrent, and I, under pain of being left behind, had perforce to follow them, and it was not without difficulty that we reached the other side. Although we took the precaution of heading our horses up into the current, we were carried downstream and came out well below our starting point and quite close to the bar, breaking only two fathoms away and almost over our heads like a fearsome arch above us. When all had crossed without mishap, we took up again our fast run along the beach for another seven leagues.

We then turned inland once more, and after an hour and a half of riding and from the top of a small hill we descried ahead of us the splendid buildings of the mission of San Luis Rey, their dazzling whiteness revealed in the first light of day.

At that distance and in the uncertain light of dawn, the edifice, of a splendid design and supported by its numerous pillars, had the look of a palace; from afar the architectural faults were not seen, the eye taking in only the elegant mass of the building. The verdant valley where the mission stood, populated by great herds that now appeared only as red and white dots, extended as far as the eye could see to the north, where it ended in a range of high mountains whose contours and summits were softly outlined in the light morning mist. Instinctively, I pulled up my horse in order to observe the beauty of the scene for a few minutes by myself, while my California friends, little observant by nature, rode on down the hill. I did not rejoin them until a quarter of an hour later just as we entered the mission.[2]

The padre being in church, we waited for him under the gallery, where he soon came to receive us with the courtesy and urbanity that he possessed to such a high degree. He had us served at once with chocolate and ordered beds prepared in order that we might rest until the dinner hour.

We came together again at noon and enjoyed the lively and pleasant conversation of this excellent man. The mission was all astir with preparations for the two festivals, the first of which, that of San Antonio, was to be celebrated on the morrow, the 13th of June. Although these were religious occasions, the superior of the mission, wishing to attract the greatest number of people, was accustomed to keep open house and to provide all the spectacles, games, and amusements so dear to the Californians. Few inhabitants of the surrounding country failed to attend such a captivating convocation, and the vast buildings of San Luis Rey hardly sufficed to lodge the number of men and women who assembled there.

By a rare chance it happened that the patronal day of the padre fell this year on the same day as the 29th anniversary of the founding of the mission. He told me how he had come to this then deserted plain at four o'clock in the afternoon of 13 June 1798 with the commandant from San Diego, a detachment of troops, and some workmen. "Our first care," he told me, "was to build a number of huts—like those of

2. Mission San Luis Rey de Francia, founded by Father Peyrí in 1798, became, because of his uncommon energy and skill, his long tenure, and his even-handed treatment of the Indians, the largest and one of the most impressive of the California establishments. Both imposing and extensive, its domed church, arched corridors, numerous adjacent structures, populous Indian village, and handsome setting were well remembered by all visitors. Near its height at the time of Duhaut-Cilly's visit, it declined rapidly after the departure of Peyrí in early 1832.

the savages of this country—to serve as shelter while the mission was being constructed; but before marking out the foundations the next morning, we improvised an outdoor altar on the grassy sward, and there under the arch of the open sky I celebrated the first mass ever offered to the Eternal in this valley which He has since heaped with so many blessings."[3]

The buildings, as conceived by the padre, were laid out on a wide and grand scale. He also directed the execution of the plan, in which he was assisted by a quite ingenious man who had also helped with the design of the buildings at Santa Barbara. Although the ones here are more magnificent, I could recognize the work of the same hand.[4]

The edifice forms an immense square, five hundred feet on each side. The principal facade is a long peristyle borne on thirty-two square pillars that support vaulted arches. Although the structure is of only one story, its elevation and fine proportions give it both grace and nobility. The flat roof is of tile, and around it there runs on the outside as well as within the square a portico with an elegant balustrade that adds to the impression of height. The interior comprises a huge courtyard, clean and level, around which are placed pillars and arches similar to those of the peristyle and supporting a long cloister that communicates with all the dependent buildings of the mission.

On the right of the exterior is the church, with its bell tower ringed by two galleries, one above the other. The facade is simple and without pilasters, but the interior is rich and well decorated. A spigot brings water to the sacristy.

The dwelling rooms of the main building are occupied by the padre

3. The feast day was that of St. Anthony of Padua. Father Engelhardt, in his book on this mission (1921), gives a much more elaborate account of the founding, with the chief role being played by Padre Lasuén, president of all the missions at that time. Regardless of who did what in those first days, it seems clear that Peyrí was the true founder and creator of the mission where he spent nearly 34 years.

4. In a document found in the cornerstone of the present church, constructed from 1811 to 1815, Peyrí named as master mason José Antonio Ramírez. The latter, who was one of the artisans sent from Mexico in the 1790s to teach trades to Indian and white apprentices, also helped in the design of the new stone church in Santa Barbara, 1815–1820.

Vue de la mission de San-Luis-Rey en Californie

7. View of the mission of San Luis Rey. By Auguste Duhaut-Cilly.

and by visitors to the mission. Those off the courtyard are for the young girls who, until marriage, do not live with the other Indians. There too are storerooms for food and utensils, and the workshops where are made the woolen and cotton stuffs for the Indians' garments; and finally, an infirmary with its private chapel, since everything has been planned for the convenience of the sick. They could go to the church under shelter of the arcades; this is a refinement. Nothing could be more elegant than the beautiful vault over this small temple, where Fray Antonio has made brilliant use of his talent for ornamentation.

In addition to the immense block of living quarters just described, there are two much smaller buildings, one for the use of the mayordomos and the other for the garrison of the mission, comprising a sergeant and eleven soldiers. The latter has a flat roof and a guardhouse with barbicans and slit windows.

Two large and well-planted gardens provide an abundance of vegetables and fruits of all kinds. The wide flight of stairs down which one goes to the southeast garden reminded me of that in the orangery at Versailles; not that the materials are equally rich or the architecture as splendid, but there was something similar in the disposition, in the number and size of the steps. At the bottom of the stairs are two fine washing basins of stucco, one a pool where the Indian women bathe every morning and the other used for washing clothes on Saturdays. Part of the water runs afterward to the garden, where the numerous water channels maintain a constant humidity and freshness. The second garden, located on higher ground, can be watered only by mechanical means; a chain pump, worked by two men, is set in motion twice a day to accomplish this. These gardens produce the best olives and the best wine in all California.*

To the north and two hundred paces from the mission begins the ranchería or village of the Indians. It consists of thatched huts of different shapes but most of them conical, scattered or grouped in no

---

* I brought back some of this wine and still have a part of it. After seven years it has the taste of paxarete [Spanish compound wine, also known as pascarete and pajarete] and the color of white port.

planned order over a large expanse of ground. Each holds one family, and all of them together contained at that time a population of more than two thousand people. At first they built stone houses for the Indians and placed them in a regular order, and this practice is still followed at several missions. But it was recognized later that this kind of dwelling was not well suited to the health of the Indians, who were accustomed to their own huts, and many of the padres decided to let them build these in their own way. But why seek in the style of the houses the cause of Indian mortality? This lies entirely in slavery, which withers the faculties and weakens the body. I cannot believe that free savages in more comfortable houses would live less long.[5]

The mission dependencies are not limited to its various buildings. Fray Antonio has established within a radius of ten leagues four ranchos, each composed of an Indian village, a house for the mayordomo who acts as manager, suitable storehouses for the harvests, and a fine chapel. Every Sunday these stewards come to the mission to report to the padre on the week's work and on the condition of the rancho. Fray Antonio was able to instill in them a rivalry that he could use to great advantage for the general welfare of the mission. It is principally on the lands of these ranchos that are found the great herds of San Luis Rey. The number of cattle possessed by the establishment comes to about thirty thousand and of sheep to more than twenty thousand; the other products will be shown on the large table of mission holdings that accompanies this narrative.[6]

On the 12th, in the evening, volleys of musket shots and fires lighted on the plaza proclaimed the festival of the following day. This began

5. Like others of his time, Duhaut-Cilly could not know that the American Indians had little resistance to European diseases.

6. Bancroft presents a list of San Luis Rey mission establishments as identified by Peyrí: a stock farm, unnamed, west 3 leagues from the mission; San Antonio de Pala, northeast 7 leagues; Rancho de Temécula, southeast 9 leagues, used for wheat and pasturage; Santa Margarita, north 1.5 leagues, with house, garden, vineyard, and land fit for all crops; Rancho de San Pedro or Las Flores, 3 leagues farther north, with chapel, houses, and granaries; a stock ranch, one league (from San Pedro?); Rancho San Jacinto, 12 leagues northeast in the mountains, stock ranch with a house; good timber 2 leagues east of Pala and 9 leagues from the mission. (*History of California* 2, 555, note 21.)

with a high mass chanted by Indian musicians. These were as numerous as the ones in Santa Barbara but were far from equaling them; and it has to be said also that most of the instruments, made in the mission, were of an inferior quality. Immediately after mass came the bullfights, which lasted for much of the day.

The performance, which took place in the interior courtyard, offered nothing remarkable. The riders all tormented the bull, which put its head down and rushed now at one and then at another. But such is the skill of these men and their horses that they are almost never struck, although the horns of the bull appear to touch them at every moment.

At first I was placed with several others on the balcony of the padre's house, overlooking the entire arena, but I and my curious companions were soon pursued by the young Indian girls who had been relegated to the same place to avoid any accident. There were more than two hundred of them, aged from eight to seventeen, and they were all dressed in the same way, with petticoat of red flannel and white chemise. Their black hair, half as long as themselves, floated about their shoulders. They came in crowds about us, demanding copper rings or pieces of money, and at first we amused ourselves by throwing out reales and watching them rush together and tumble over each other in a way that was wonderfully funny. But little by little they grew bolder and so familiar with us that they threw themselves upon us and even tried to dig into our pockets. Their bursts of laughter and their squalling cries, drowning out the bellowing of the bull, reminded me of the critical position I once found myself in on the island of Java, when I was attacked, quite unarmed, by a troop of monkeys. I should say, of course, that these malicious Indian girls did not bite, but they tore at our clothes and scratched us and intended to leave us no more money in our pockets than the monkeys of Pulo-Marack had in theirs.*

The moment had come, we decided, to effect an honorable retreat. To accomplish this we used a stratagem; taking all the small coins that

* Peacock Island, an islet off the coast of Java.

remained to us, we threw them as far as we could, and as soon as the pack left us to run after the quarry, we took advantage of this short respite to make our escape. Going down to the lodging of the padre, we took shelter behind a barricade that had been set up in front of his door.

They do not kill the bull, as in Spain. After they had taunted, tormented, and tired him out for half an hour, a carriage gate was opened onto the plain, and as soon as the animal saw this exit, he ran out as fast as he could go. The horsemen sped like arrows in pursuit, and when the fastest one caught up with the bull, he seized him by the tail and, spurring his horse at that moment, overturned him and sent him rolling in the dust. Only after this humiliation was the animal allowed to regain the pasture. This exercise, which requires as much agility as strength on the part of the horseman, is known in the country as *colear el toro,* tailing the bull.

Toward evening the *ginetes* [horsemen], having changed their mounts, staged on the esplanade of the mission the *carrera del gallo* (cock racing), less dangerous and more interesting than the bullfight. They bury a cock up to the neck in the ground and line themselves up two hundred paces away. Then, taking off like shafts from a bow, one hand on the saddle horn, they bend down and, as they pass, pull the cock out by the head. So great is their speed that they often need more than one pass before succeeding. This is not all; when one of them seizes the cock, the others all run at him to take it from him; he tries to get away by running and turning; they block his way and press upon him; the horses mix together, bump each other, rear up; the cock is torn to pieces, and some of the riders are thrown head over heels and become the butt of laughter and sarcasm from their comrades and from the pretty spectators.

The last game, also on horseback, was that of Four Corners. The players, armed with stout willow branches, struck at each other without mercy whenever they came within reach, and the game did not end until the branches were broken off up to the stumps; all this did not take place without some good blows over the head and to the face. The young Californian females seemed to take as much delight in these various combats as the great ladies of the fifteenth century did in the brilliant tournaments where their knights broke lances in their honor.

While the gente de razón amused themselves in various ways, the Indians were engaged in their own favorite games. The one that seems to please them most consists of rolling along the ground an osier hoop or ring three inches in diameter; while it rolls two of them try to spear it with sticks four feet long. If one of the sticks or both together go through the ring or if the ring comes to rest on one or both, a certain number of points is counted depending on the difficulty. When one pair of contestants has played, another pair begins, and then alternately until the game is completed. According to La Pérouse, this game is known in the Indian language as *takersié.*[7]

Other Indians, in the manner of Lower Brittany, divided themselves into two large teams, and the players of each, armed with curved sticks, attempted to propel a wooden ball toward the goal, while those of the opposing team strove to drive it in the contrary direction. This game appears to appeal equally to both sexes. It happened that the married women challenged the young girls and the latter lost. They came crying to complain to the padre that the stronger women had taken unfair advantage, holding their arms when they tried to hit the ball. Fray Antònio, with the judgmental gravity of Solomon, required a complete account of the affair.

During the explanation the good missionary was seated gravely under the arcade with eyes half closed, the index finger of his right hand resting on his brow while the middle finger, passing under his nose, formed a sort of t-square, a pose that gave him an air of profound meditation. When the Indian girl had finished pleading her cause, he raised his head and declared the game null and void. But he could not prevent himself from smiling in his cowl, and he said to me in a low voice: "Poor little dears! We have to do something for them. (*Las pobrecitas! Es menester de hacer algo para ellas.*) It is in this and in similar ways that I have managed to gain the trust of these Indians."

---

7. This game seems to have been played by a number of Indian tribes and was described by La Pérouse, who called it *takersia,* and by other travelers. The illustration of the game as played by the Mojave Indians is from Bernard Möllhausen, *Diary of a Journey from the Mississippi to the Coasts of the Pacific,* London, 1858.

And indeed, of all the missions in California, his is the one in which these people are the best treated. Not only are they well fed and well clothed, but he even gives them money on festival days. On Saturdays he always distributes soap to the women. On these occasions they all pass in front of him and, while two men dip into huge baskets and give to each her portion, the padre speaks to them one after the other. He is acquainted with all of them, giving praise to one and gentle criticism to another, to one a little joke befitting the occasion, to another a fatherly admonition, and they all go away satisfied or touched.

When night was come I went with Fray Antonio to watch the Indian dances, which to me were as interesting as they were strange. These were illuminated by torches, which, by contrast, seemed to spread a somber veil over the starry vault of the sky. A dozen men, wearing only thongs, heads bedecked with tall feather plumes, danced together with admirable rhythm. Their pantomime, always representing some scene or another, was performed mainly by stamping the feet in unison and by making with eyes and arms gestures of love, anger, fear, and the like. They held the head erect, the body arched, the knees a little bent, and the sweat, running down their bodies, reflected like a burnished mirror the light of the torches. When the sweat bothered them they scraped it off with wooden blades.

The orchestra, arranged in a semi-circle, like an amphitheater, was composed of women, children, and old men, behind whom one or two rows of connoisseurs could enjoy the spectacle. The harmony of the chants that governed the action was at once plaintive and wild; it appeared to act on the nerves rather than on the soul, like the sounds of an Aeolian harp during a hurricane. The actors rested from time to time, and when the chanting ceased everyone let out breath at the same time and with a loud noise, either as a kind of applause or, as I was assured, to drive away the Evil Spirit. For although they may all be Christians, they retain many of their former beliefs, which the padres, as a matter of policy, pretend not to notice.

The next day, after the ceremonies and the procession, the games recommenced as before, but this time the bull baiting was marred by an accident. One of the Indian girls, playing on the balcony of the mission, fell over the balustrade to the paved courtyard from a height of twenty feet and broke her head.

8. The game of takersia or takersié as played by the Mojave Indians.

X

I had not found Mr. R____ at San Luis Rey. He wrote to me from San Juan Capistrano, another mission farther to the west, that he would, if I judged it advisable, continue by land to Santa Barbara, where he begged me to rejoin him with the ship. I agreed with this plan, which could only be favorable to our business and, after settling accounts with Fray Antonio, set out once more for San Diego with only two or three companions and arrived there on the evening of the 15th.

While the bull baiting was going on at the mission, the people at the presidio had staged the same kind of entertainment, and this almost cost the life of a young man from my ship, whom I had left at the storehouse. He was near-sighted, and instead of staying well back at a respectful distance from the bull, he had imprudently come near just when they were releasing the ropes that held it. He was cruelly tossed by the animal and was quite unconscious when rescued but fortunately was not injured.

This scene, commencing in a tragic way, was then enlivened by a singular incident. The presidio church, forming one side of the interior court, is built on a steep hillside in such a way that one end of the roof rests on the ground while the other is raised nearly forty feet above it. The bull, more disposed to flight than to combat and frightened by the cries of the spectators, threatened by the noose and seeing no route of escape, was cornered near the spot where the roof of the church came against the hillside. There was no way to retreat, and a leap of two feet up put him on the flat roof of the chapel. As he continued to advance, one could surmise that he would make a sudden entrance into the sanctuary through the tiles, as one foot and then the other broke through them. Stumbling along in this way, he reached the highest part of the roof before recognizing with a new fright the danger in front of him. He then tried to turn around and retrace his steps but slipped and fell into the courtyard along with a heap of debris and in a cloud of dust. Can one conceive how the cruel death of this poor animal brought cries of joy to the descendants of the Spaniards?

On the morning of 22 June we got under sail and left the harbor just as the northwest wind came up. En route to Santa Barbara we were obliged to tack to windward and did not arrive until the 29th. There I found Mr. R——— and after exchanging accounts on our activities we agreed that he would travel by land to San Francisco, visiting the missions found along the way, while I would go by sea to the same port and start loading the tallow for Peru.

Leaving the roadstead at Santa Barbara, we sailed through the group of islands that form the southern border of the channel and we had occasion to reconnoiter one that is not shown on any map but is well known to navigators who frequent these waters; this is San Nicolas. It lies seven leagues to the west of Santa Barbara Island and twelve leagues south of Santa Cruz Island. Its northernmost point is at 33° 25′ north latitude and 121° 33′ longitude west of the Paris meridian, and may be five or six leagues in circumference. It is less elevated than its neighbors, the highest part being to the north. Four leagues northwest is a dangerous rock, which we passed less than a league away; at this distance it resembled a launch with sails set. While in sight of this island we could see all the others, and we took some positions that do not accord well with those given by Vancouver. One may be justified in deeming these latter inexact since his omission of the island of San Nicolas seems to indicate that he did not examine with care this part of the California coast.[8]

On the afternoon of 17 July we arrived near the entrance to San Francisco Bay and we took note of the southernmost of the Farallons, passing at a distance of two miles and recalling the troubles that this region had caused us six months earlier. Although the weather was foggy, we could make out the crude dwellings of about a hundred Kodiaks stationed there by the Russians of Bodega to hunt seals despite the displeasure of the Mexican government. We noticed a man standing in front of his hut and saw the *baidarkas* pulled up on the rocks.*

8. San Nicolas Island, the most remote of the Channel Islands, was shown on a 1602 chart of the Vizcaíno expedition and appeared on a dozen maps earlier than Vancouver's although not noted by him. Duhaut-Cilly's latitude is within nine minutes of a modern reading.

* Kodiak boats. I shall have occasion to speak of them again later. Roquefeuil calls them *boyedarques,* Kotzebue *baydares,* Corney *bodaries* and *bodarkis;* the Californians call them *kayoukès.* [Baidarkas or kayaks were, according to Adele Ogden in *California Sea Otter Trade*

If these hunters killed only the seals that abound on the Farallons, the Mexicans would have little reason to complain, since they themselves do not hunt them; but the Kodiaks, in their light boats, slip into San Francisco Bay by night, moving along the coast opposite the fort, and once inside this great basin they station themselves temporarily on some of the inner islands, from where they catch the sea otter without hindrance. In this way they have nearly taken away this small source of wealth from the Californians, who have no way to prevent it, since the government possesses no boats suitable for stopping this kind of depredation. Moreover, it happens only too often that the commandants in San Francisco reach an understanding with the Russians to allow this contraband, receiving, at the discretion of the hunters, a modest portion of the proceeds.[9]

The sea otter or Saricovian otter was formerly quite common on this coast from San Francisco to San Diego, but today one can find but few. During the whole time that we spent in the country we purchased nearly all those that were taken, a catch amounting to no more than one hundred fifty. The pelt, moreover, so fine in the higher latitudes of the Northwest Coast, is here of an inferior quality.[10]

From the south Farallon we steered in a rather dense fog to the northeast 1/4 east, a bearing that brought us a little to the right of the harbor entrance. Supposing that this small deviation was not caused by a side current carrying us to the south during this passage of six leagues, we had to conclude that a course of northeast 1/2 east would have put us directly into the channel. When we arrived in front of the

_____

(1941), small, light craft made of strips of wood or whale bone over which skins were stretched. One to three holes were left on top, each large enough for a skin-clad rower whose jacket fastened snugly to a ring around the opening. From twelve to twenty feet long, narrow, shallow, and sharp at both ends, they were propelled by double-bladed paddles and traveled about ten miles an hour. Duhaut-Cilly will later have an opportunity to enter one.]

9. The natives of Kodiak Island on the Alaskan peninsula were used in large numbers by the Russians for seal and otter hunting on the Northwest Coast. They were stationed on the Farallons from 1812 to 1840, in the later years chiefly to obtain seals, gulls, and eggs to provision their posts at Ross, north of Bodega Bay, and at Sitka.

10. The pelt of the sea otter, more valuable in the Chinese market than fox, sable, or marten, was taken in quantity on the Northwest Coast from the late eighteenth century. The catch in California was at its height before 1815.

presidio, the breeze was light; fearing that we could not reach Yerba Buena, our anchorage on the first visit, before nightfall, we were ready to drop anchor when the wind suddenly shifted to the southwest, blowing with some force. Profiting from this change, we reset the topsails, which had already been taken in, and quickly reached our berth, where we moored close to a Spanish ship under an English flag, named the *Solitude*.[11]

11. The ship *Solitude,* 268 tons, Captain Charles Anderson, first reached Monterey in September 1826. In 1827, according to Adele Ogden, she was bound from Acapulco to Honolulu and arrived at San Francisco on July 17.

Chapter 13

A VISIT TO SANTA CLARA & SAN JOSÉ

July 1827

IN ALL COUNTRIES AND at all times military officers have lacked a just appreciation of commerce. Whatever the circumstances that allow these proud defenders of territory and of national honor to exercise temporary power over commercial affairs, they appear to make a point of obstructing and discouraging all activity. One need not be clairvoyant to discern the origin of this unfriendly attitude; it is the daughter of jealousy. It is as if the hornet and the firefly were given the right to reproach the bee for the honey that it collects from the flowers they disdain and scorn. So, gentlemen, enjoy your honors, parade under your gold epaulettes, and allow us to emulate without hindrance the foresight of the ant.* It is particularly to Don Ignacio Martínez, commandant at San Francisco, that I address these words, and I wish to Heaven that they applied only to him!

Hardly had we dropped anchor when I received a letter from this officer, who, acting on a new decree of the general, informed me that I should at once leave Yerba Buena and move to the anchorage at the

---

* It is not to the officers of our brave navy that I address these reproaches. From them I have never, in all my maritime career, experienced anything but good and loyal conduct.

presidio, adding that I would not be allowed to do any business until I had obeyed this order.

I replied at once that no matter how well disposed I was to conform to the laws of the land, I could do so only if they were not such as to compromise the safety of my ship; that he should be aware that the anchorage proposed to me was not safe, for I had already lost an anchor there during my earlier stay and while he was present; that if such a mishap occurred once more, I would have no replacement; and that, moreover, it would be most unjust to force a captain to moor in dangerous waters while requiring him to pay the exorbitant duty of twenty reales the ton; and that consequently, I would not change position until the general had replied to a letter I was writing on this subject.*

While awaiting a reply to this protest, I decided to visit the missions of Santa Clara and San José in order to find out whether the padres had collected the goods they were to deliver to us and at the same time try to increase the quantity with new sales. I wished also to wait there for Mr. R___ and learn the results of his trip.**

I set out on the evening of the 19th, accompanied by Mr. Richardson and a servant. We first passed by Mission San Francisco, where we did not find Fray Tomás, who had gone to inspect his grain harvest several leagues away. We next followed the road we had taken earlier on our hunting trip to the valley of San Bruno, arriving that night at a ranch where we found a son-in-law of Don Ignacio with his wife and children; he was tending a garden that furnished fruit and vegetables to the entire family.[1]

Introduced by Mr. Richardson, their brother-in-law, I was greeted graciously by husband and wife, who provided one of the best meals I had had for a long time. While it was composed only of vegetables,

---

* The tonnage duty for the *Héros* amounted to 925 piasters, about 4,625 francs.
** Mission Santa Clara is about twenty leagues from Yerba Buena.
1. From San Bruno Valley the author continued down the plain paralleling the bay, stopping for the night at the Buri Buri rancho, then going on to Santa Clara, the pueblo of San José, and Mission San José. Beechey's officers had made a rest stop at Buri Buri a few months before, and Vancouver in November 1792 had almost certainly dined on San Francisquito Creek, a "favorite luncheon spot with early-day wayfarers."

we seldom ate these on board, so that the excellent green peas and French beans were not for me a poor feast, especially when followed by a fine basket of strawberries gathered in the mountains by the Indians; their taste and fragrance were not inferior to those of our best European berries. But the sleeping was less excellent than the eating, since all of us, guests, husband, wife, and children, were obliged to stow ourselves away on one huge leathern bed where, devoured by fleas and but little protected from the cold of the evening, we passed a rather bad night.

On the morning of the 20th we took early leave of our friends and continued on our way, the same way that Vancouver had followed in 1793. I did not pass without a feeling of respect through the charming grove where the celebrated navigator had dined with his officers and which I recognized from the description in his narrative. The stream where he quenched his thirst and the grassy sward were now dry in the heat of summer. The water and greenery, I said to myself, will renew themselves every year at the same time, but they will not bring back the famous mariner; only his memory remains with us.

After leaving the rancho where we spent the night we experienced a notable change in temperature. In the vicinity of the anchorage at Yerba Buena the air was always cold and penetrating, but when we had gone a few leagues into the interior the heat, mounting steadily, soon became uncomfortable. Looking back toward San Francisco we could see what appeared like a wall of fog, which seemed to be and indeed was halted at that point on the horizon, while the rest of the sky was free of clouds. This double phenomenon, this abrupt change in heat and in the clarity of the atmosphere, although quite singular, seemed explainable enough to me.

The port of San Francisco is situated in a reflex angle of the coast, exposed directly to the northwest wind, which gains in strength as it is forced into a kind of funnel. It brings with it a dense fog and a mass of cold air from the sea and from more northern lands. The coastal mountains arrest a part of this column of air, but the part that goes over them or passes through the strait encounters at once a large open space, spreads out, and loses its force; then the heat increases in inverse proportion to the diminution of the wind, thinning out the mist, which is dissipated as it rises to the upper regions of the atmosphere, leaving the earth to be acted on by the sun in an almost perpetual calm.

As we advanced, the mountains on our right, which began at the entrance to San Francisco Bay and were at first barren and sandy, became covered to their summits with forests of conifers. Soon we came to an immense grove of splendid oaks mixed with several other mature trees, into which we rode along a wide and level path. This magnificent wood, planted by nature, is not encumbered with lianas or brush; the trees are disposed in thick and leafy clusters or scattered here and there but with no considerable clearings. A sward of tender green is spread everywhere like a carpet, and the traveler regrets that such a beautiful place is inhabited only by coyotes and bears. However, we never saw any animal of the latter kind. They seldom attack passersby, but since the sight and smell of them are enough to frighten horses and make them unmanageable, I felt all the sense of danger that a rider of mediocre skill can feel.

I noticed that most of the oaks in this wood were covered with mistletoe. If this parasitic plant had been as common in ancient Gaul, our ancestors might not have chosen it as a symbol of their cult. The trunks and branches of these trees, draped with this foreign vegetation, showed us that the beautiful priestesses of Teutatès had never strolled here with their golden sickles.

Turning to thoughts more modern, I reflected ruefully that such fine materials were destined to rot away uselessly alongside one of the most magnificent harbors in the world. Every knee that I saw in passing, this piece of wood so difficult to find at home, caused me to suffer the torments of Tantalus.[2] I would like to have transformed the forest into a huge fleet, whose masts I could now see, still bearing their foliage, waving on the nearby mountains.

Leaving this great wood, we entered a plain that extends from the foot of the mountains to the shore of the bay, about five leagues in

2. A ship's knee, a section of a tree trunk where it turns into a large flat root forming almost a right angle, was used as a brace in building and repairing wooden ships.

width and considerably more in length. No more shade sheltered us from the burning sun; no breath of air cooled the heated atmosphere. Soon we caught sight of Mission Santa Clara, but the effect of a mirage was to make it appear to be placed in the middle of a large lake, and the surrounding trees seemed to rise from the water as from a great flood. But as the imaginary waters retreated before us, keeping the same distance, the parts of the scene became clear, one after the other, and we saw the establishment in its true situation, in the center of the plain.[3] It was just such an illusion that, during the Egyptian campaign, lulled our soldiers, dying of thirst, with the treacherous hope of refreshing themselves in the clear waters of those phantasmal and delusive lakes.

I was cordially welcomed by Padre José Viader, superior of this mission. He was finishing his dinner and was about to retire to his siesta, but he stayed up until we had been served and beds had been prepared for us. The buildings of Santa Clara are not so handsomely constructed as those of San Luis Rey, but this mission is not, for all that, less wealthy or less productive. I stayed here five days, awaiting Mr. R____, and accomplished some business.[4]

It was the time of the grain harvest, a time of joy and gaiety in the fields of France, but no sentiment of this kind was visible on the faces of the Indians occupied in this work. It is very simple: whether they harvested little or much, they would have only their daily pittance, and it meant nothing to them that there might be something left over. This interesting sight brought back to me, nonetheless, some pleasant memories, and I did not fail to be on hand, especially when they gathered up the grain.

The threshing floor of the padres is round, about sixty feet in di-

3. Because of a scarcity of native workers, Mission Santa Clara de Asís, established in 1777, started slowly but became more prosperous after its move to higher and more fertile ground above the Guadalupe River in 1781. Its population was at its highest in 1827, but crops had declined.

4. José Viader came to California in 1796 and was promptly assigned to Santa Clara, where he remained until his retirement in 1833. Although not the superior until 1830, he was an able manager and was in charge of temporalities for much of his career.

ameter, and enclosed by a low wall. When it has been filled to a certain height with heads of grain without the stalks, a band of mares is brought in and made to run in a circle for two hours; this band is relieved by another, and so on until no grain remains on the heads. They do not use horses for this work as it ruins the animals; the mares, never used for riding, are still quite able to produce colts although their legs are bad because of this exercise.

Each threshing produced 300 *fanegas;* in a very approximate calculation Padre Viader estimated a total of 4,000 fanegas of 125 Spanish pounds each or about 56 kilograms. Thus, his entire harvest would come to 224,000 kilograms.

This quantity, which at first seems enormous, is still only sufficient to feed the twelve hundred Indians of the mission along with the visitors who come throughout the year. In order to obtain these four thousand fanegas, the padre had sown two hundred. Thus the land yielded only twenty for one, much less than the hundred for one that La Pérouse attributed to the soil of this country, and yet the harvest had been a good one. Doubtless, however, the production would be greater if the land were fertilized; until now the missionaries have sown with no other preparation than one shallow plowing.

Barley, peas, beans, green beans produce about the same result. In addition to these food sources Mission Santa Clara possesses at least twelve thousand cattle and fifteen thousand sheep. During the time when I was there the padre was killing one hundred fifty steers and cows every week for hides and tallow. Part of the meat was dried and made into *tasajo* or jerked beef but most was wasted, although the Indians ate much of it every day.

About half a league to the southeast of Santa Clara lies the village of San José, inhabited by free Californians and some foreigners. This hamlet, honored with the title of *pueblo* (small city), was established several years after the mission and continued to grow for a time. There we saw fine gardens. The inhabitants owned herds and harvested grains, but the natural indolence of the creoles and other causes that I will speak of later have held back development and led to a decadent community that today comprises eighty houses and eight hundred people, of whom one-sixth are Indian servants. The road from the mission to the pueblo is shaded by two splendid rows of trees planted by the hand of man. This is the only promenade of its kind in California.[5]

During my stay at Santa Clara I went also to Mission San José, situated four leagues to the north, and there I spent twenty-four hours with Padre Narciso, who managed it. Together we arranged for the delivery of the hides and tallow that he owed me on account of his purchases during my earlier trip to San Francisco and of the purchases he now made.[6]

This missionary was an educated man who read much. But whether he chose the most melancholy books or had eyes only for the most lugubrious passages, he seemed no longer to perceive the world except through a funereal mist; no soul ever held less joy than that of Fray Narciso. At that time he was perusing the lucubrations of Abbé Barruel, and without accepting the conjectures of the latter, he thought, he told me, that he recognized in the Masonic societies the fulfillment of the revelations of the Apocalypse. The spirit of agitation and revolution that was then disturbing almost all countries was nothing else, according to him, but the Antichrist. And our conversations on the political situation in Mexico were not such as to give rise to more cheerful thoughts. What I told him about the plans of the Yorkinos was too much akin to his habitual thinking not to renew in him the fits of sadness that I was trying in vain to dispel; the more efforts I made to do this, the more reasons he found to moan about the evils that were about to descend on the universe, and he ended by predicting the imminent end of the world. Although his discourse did not persuade me, it enveloped my imagination in a dark cloud. When I

5. The pueblo of San José de Guadalupe, California's first civil rather than military or religious community, was founded in 1777 to provide supplies for the presidios and as a way to people the land with Spaniards. Beechey's officers, who passed through a few months before Duhaut-Cilly, judged the population to be about five hundred, living in "mud houses" that they did not count. The shaded road to the mission, or *alameda*, was planted by the padres for the comfort of those attending mass.

6. Misión del Gloriósimo Patriarco San Josef, or Mission San José, founded in 1797, with a church of undistinguished appearance, dedicated in 1809, was, because of its excellent land, large herds, abundant water, and continuing good management, one of the most prosperous, particularly in its later years.

had passed out of sight of his dismal abode, I felt as if I were awakening from a frightful nightmare.[7]

While I was on this little trip Mr. R——— arrived at Santa Clara and there we were reunited. We made known to each other the results of our operations, and we agreed that he would remain at the mission in order to load with hides and tallow the boats that I would send from San Francisco.

Returning on board the *Héros,* I found a favorable reply from the general, authorizing me to remain in the anchorage at Yerba Buena, and I at once began doing business with the local people. But Don Ignacio, vexed no doubt at the success of my move, made some difficulty over embarking the goods brought by a number of individuals for sale or barter, and I found myself obliged to write him a stern letter, telling him that he had no reason to interfere either with the collection of duties or with my commercial affairs, the commissioner of customs being the only person I need deal with on such matters, and that henceforth I would obey no order from the military commandants concerning the affairs of the commissioner. After that I experienced no further difficulties.

I dispatched to Santa Clara a large launch belonging to Mr. Richardson, which was quite useful to me during the rest of my operations in this port. The ship's longboat was used in the same service, but was rather small for this trip, which could not be made in less than three days. When the wind blows in a direction opposing the current in this inland sea, the waves are quite high and there is some danger to heavily laden vessels.

7. Padre Narciso Durán was assigned to Mission San José in 1806 and served there for twenty-seven years and after that in Santa Barbara. It seems likely that Duhaut-Cilly found him in one of his brief periods of despondency, since other visitors remembered him as generally jovial in nature and fond of a joke. He was one of the most practical and successful of the padres and served terms as president and as prefect to the California missions. Although strongly opposed to secularization, he acted as an administrator during the period of change. It is also worthy of note that he did more than anyone else to adapt European music to mission use and to train Indian singers and instrumentalists. Augustin de Barruel (1741–1820), whose polemical and anti-revolutionary writings prompted the gloom of the occasion, was a French Jesuit.

Chapter 14

─────────✧─────────

SAN FRANCISCO SOLANO

August 1827

WHILE THE TRANSPORT OF goods from Santa Clara and San José was proceeding, I undertook an expedition to Mission San Francisco Solano, the last established of five missions around San Francisco Bay.

I had been informed that there was a quantity of deer tallow there and did not want to let it be purchased by someone else. On 4 August at four o'clock in the morning I left in the ship's launch, being well armed and having with me eight seamen, the second mate of the ship, Dr. Botta, and Mr. Richardson, who acted as our guide. We profited from what remained of the ebb tide and from a light northwest breeze to cross the bay, running past Alcatraces (Pelicans) Island. This name had been bestowed with justice, we saw; the island was covered with a countless number of these birds. A gun fired over the feathered legions caused them to fly up in a great cloud and with a noise like a hurricane.[1]

─────────────

1. From Yerba Buena Cove Duhaut-Cilly passed west of Alcatraces (now Yerba Buena) Island, then eastward of Angel Island and along the shore of Tiburon Peninsula beyond San Quentin Point. Crossing San Rafael Bay (from where that mission could be seen), he sailed between points San Pedro and San Pablo into the "new sea," San Pablo Bay. Noting Carquinez Strait far to the right, the party continued northward to Sonoma Creek, which meandered through low tidal channels to near Sonoma.

We then passed between the right shore of the harbor and the island of Los Angeles (the Angels), where the flood began to favor us. The coast that we were skirting is formed of mountains of moderate height, covered with grass that was rather parched at the time. In the ravines we could see clumps of oaks. From time to time we noticed great numbers of deer, wandering in bands over this inclined pasture, and we watched them run, browse, fling themselves across the hillsides, sometimes so steep that we had difficulty imagining how they could avoid falling.

Many bears also live in these wooded spots, but since they seldom come out except at night, we did not see any. However, a man named Cibriano,[2] who was with us in the launch, told me that several months earlier, when he was passing through this channel, one of these ferocious beasts, swimming to Los Angeles Island, approached the boat and tried to climb into it; soldiers in the boat fired four balls point blank just as the bear got his claws on the gunwale and killed it stone dead.

When we had made about five leagues we found ourselves opposite Mission San Rafael, situated at the head of a cove on the north shore of the harbor. This mission is quite poor and possesses no goods for trade; we did not stop there. The east side of this little bay forms with an opposing peninsula a strait of one league in width and is closed in by four small islands, of which the two principal ones are called San Pedro and San Pablo; the name of San Pedro is given also to a ranch occupying the isthmus that joins the peninsula to the mainland.[3]

Coming out from this strait we saw opening in front of us a new sea, whose distant shores we could barely discern, and soon our attention

2. Blas Cibrian, a soldier at the San Francisco compound, 1827–33.
3. Missions San Rafael Arcángel (founded in 1817) and San Francisco Solano (1823) were established north of the bay as branches of San Francisco de Asís in order to provide healthier places for the neophyte Indians and to attract converts. Neither proved to be notably successful. Points San Pedro and San Pablo are the northwest and southeast termini of San Pablo Strait, which leads from San Francisco Bay into San Pablo Bay and thence through Suisun Bay to a confluence of the Sacramento and San Joaquin rivers and into the interior of California. Rancho San Pablo (not San Pedro) was on the mainland in the vicinity of present-day Richmond.

was called to another passage, which served as outlet for the great river known as the Sacramento, coming from the north, and also for a less considerable stream flowing from the southeast.

Propelled by oars and by the current, we directed ourselves to the north-northwest toward a group of mountains at the foot of which is built Mission San Francisco Solano. I reckoned that we had made thirteen leagues from Yerba Buena when we reached the mouth of a small channel, which meanders through a marsh covered with reeds, and into which we steered. This stream makes a thousand turns as it advances into the interior; although the distance from its mouth to the place where we disembarked is no more than three leagues in a straight line, we traveled at least double that in following its windings.

The distance cannot be shortened by traveling on land because there is no solid ground until you reach the landing spot. The borders of the channel are indicated only by the rushes and reeds that grow in the water, or rather in a kind of mud. Reaching solid ground, we still had a league to go to the mission, but Padre Buenaventura Fortuny— that was the name of the superior—had been apprised of our coming and had sent horses; we lost no time in going there.[4]

Since leaving the ship, we had gone, by my reckoning, about seventeen leagues in a direction that was almost north, a figure that corresponds well with the difference in latitude, since Yerba Buena lies on the parallel of 37° 48′ and San Francisco Solano on 38° 39′.

This establishment, the northernmost of those possessed by the Spaniards on this coast, was founded on 25 August 1823 by Padre Altimira, who located it in the middle of a plain of great extent, bounded on the north by mountains and hills and on the south by the bay, and everywhere crossed by streams of fresh water. There are few happier sites, and this mission could become quite important in a short time, but was still of small account at the time of my visit.[5] Although poor

4. Fortuny, after twenty years with Padre Durán at San José, reestablished Mission San Francisco Solano in 1826, after its brief abandonment because of Indian raids, and remained there until 1833.

5. Although when Padre José Altimira was assigned to Mission Dolores in San Francisco in 1820 a branch had already been established across the bay at San Rafael, he advocated a still

Father Buenaventura Fortuny desired to treat us well, he could offer us only cakes of Indian cornmeal and dried beef. This destitution did not encourage us to prolong our stay with him; having quickly bought all the tallow available at the mission, I set our departure for the morrow.

I said above that the tallow was deer tallow, and since this term may sound strange, it is well that I describe the manner of procuring it. The hills in this part of California and the plains lying between them support an immense number of deer of prodigious strength and size. So abundant is the pasturage that by the month of July they have become quite fat and have lost much of their lightness of foot, and it is then that the Californians choose to hunt them.

Mounted on the fastest horses and armed with hunting knives and the fatal lassos, they ride to the places where deer are numerous and race after them at full speed. Although these denizens of the plains have lost a part of their speed, they retain enough so as not to fear an ordinary horseman, but these men, born in the saddle, so to speak, seldom fail to catch them and snare them with incredible skill. As soon as the deer is noosed, it is thrown down, and often enough is pierced by its own weapons, rolling on the sharp points of its antlers. This accident is not rare, but when it does not occur, the horseman dismounts and with the aid of his companions cuts the deer's hamstrings, then leaves it lying there while he rides in pursuit of others. They do not always use the rope; when they can get within arm's length they use the hunting knife to sever the tendons of the leg.

This kind of hunting requires some tactical skill. The hunter must know how to keep the animals from getting into the woods or onto the mountain sides and how to make them run in the direction of the wind; in this way the deer, which run with open mouths for better breathing and cooling, will more quickly lose breath and be caught. If the game requires great skill, it also presents great danger. Sometimes the horseman, carried away by excitement, cannot avoid being thrown

---

more northern location and, without permission, erected mission buildings in the fertile Sonoma Valley (see Chapter 9, note 12). He was at Monterey in 1826 and 1827, where he met Duhaut-Cilly.

with his horse by the cracks and holes in the ground; sometimes, going too fast, he cannot turn his horse in time to keep from being thrown against the branches or trunks of trees that stand in his way. Even when the deer is lassoed and thrown down the hunter has to approach with great caution for the kill. He must respect both the sharp horns that sprout from the animal's head and the sharp points of its hooves. I once saw what appeared to be a saber cut on the leg of a horse; this was only a wound from the cutting foot of a deer.

Once the fat has been taken from the animals, the flesh is abandoned on the hunting ground, and bears, attracted by the scent, come from all sides to feed on it. Often the hunters must dispute the terrain with these dangerous beasts, which sometimes lose their lives on the field of battle.

They pointed out to me a youngster of sixteen, who had taken twenty-three deer in one day. Assuming that each one produced three *arrobas*[6] of tallow, this young man had earned for his day's work one hundred thirty-eight piasters, about seven hundred francs. From the soldiers of the mission garrison I purchased four thousand francs worth of this product, garnered from their hunt.

Before leaving, I went with the padre to his garden, which I found in a most deplorable state. Coarse grass and marshes had invaded part of it, and the rest was poorly planted and poorly maintained. He showed me the place where, several days before, some wild Indians of the vicinity had killed two men of the mission, shooting them with arrows while they were asleep. The murder was attributed to the hatred borne by *los gentiles* for all Christian Indians, but it appears on this occasion that it was a matter of revenge and reprisal.

The Spanish government of California has always followed the atrocious practice of sending expeditions from time to time against the tribes of the interior, either to recapture Indians who have escaped from the missions or to keep the gentiles at a distance by inspiring them with fear. These expeditions have cost the lives of several soldiers and many Indians and have served only to nourish hatred. The last

6. An arroba is equal to twenty-five pounds.

and most ridiculous of these little campaigns took place in 1826 under the command of Alférez (second lieutenant) Sánchez; this is how it came about.[7]

After the harvest the padre at San Francisco Solano had given permission to eighty of his Christian Indians to visit their former homes, and they were on their way in a great long boat, going up the San Sacramento River, when the wild Indians attacked unexpectedly at a narrow spot where they could neither flee nor defend themselves, killing more than forty of them. So an expedition was decided on and entrusted to the fiery spirit of Sánchez, who set out at the head of twenty or thirty mounted soldiers. At their approach the defending Indians hid in ambush in the woods, from where they shot arrows at the soldiers, who could not get at them or even see them. Exasperated, the latter took vengeance on the Indian women and children, who could not flee. They massacred about thirty of them and returned in shameful triumph with two young girls and a child as prisoners and token of their victory.[8]

When one inquires of these imitators and descendants of the Spaniards whether there is not some other way to make peace with these men, imbued with the ideas of their fathers, they ascribe to the Indians a character so barbarous that, to hear them speak, it is not possible to deal with them in any other way. "They live," it is said, "in separate

7. José Antonio Sánchez, whose military service began at the San Francisco presidio in 1791, was an aggressive and courageous fighter who, though never promoted beyond the rank of alférez, carried out more than a score of Indian campaigns by 1827. The expedition of November 1826 described by Duhaut-Cilly was also reported by Captain Beechey, apparently the only other source relating to the affair.

8. An accurate and honest observer of things he himself saw, Duhaut-Cilly was sometimes credulous or confused about what was told to him. Beechey, who was in San Francisco and San José at the time of the reprisal expedition and who quotes the official report of Sánchez, gives quite a different account of what was clearly the same affair. The mission was San José, not Solano, and the skirmishes were up the San Joaquin River rather than the Sacramento or San Sacramento, as stated here. The first excursion party, armed with muskets and a cannon, seems to have been less than innocent; the second party was composed largely of vengeful Christian Indians from the mission. They and the soldiers killed a number of wild Indians, recovered the cannon, and returned with forty captives, women and children. In San José Beechey says he saw the captives being taught to recite the names of the trinity and of saints. (F. W. Beechey, *Narrative of a Voyage to the Pacific . . . London,* 1831, quarto edition, 361–66.)

villages, and if you make peace with one village, the neighboring groups regard those as traitors and join together to destroy them." But when one considers that the missions are populated by these same peoples and that the padres, alternating kindness with severity, have been able to gain over them the great ascendancy that keeps these establishments stable, one cannot help thinking that the commandants of the presidios are pursuing a bad policy as well as acting against humanity.

I myself observed a practice that seems to show that resentment of such a deplorable system has not gone so far as to make the natives intractable. At harvest time the missionaries at San Rafael and San Francisco Solano obtain as many gentiles as they wish to help bring in the grain. They come to the missions with their wives and children, build their temporary huts, and work in the harvest in return for a small quantity of wheat or corn given to them by the padres. We saw two or three hundred of them who had been at Solano for several weeks.

No people could be more wretched than those in the little camp set up in front of the padre's house. The men are almost naked, and the women wear only a cloak made of rabbit skin twisted into strips and sewn together. This garment is very warm but, being quite thick, it serves as a haven for a prodigious number of those parasitic insects so disgusting to us. For them, on the contrary, this becomes a kind of portable farmyard where, during moments of leisure, each may select his favorite viands. While the young men are letting fly their arrows at beaver or stag, their sweethearts are engaged in another kind of hunt. The succulent results of this are presented on a mussel shell to those who return, quite as a dandy may proffer a bon-bon box of mints to his lady.

We were able to transport in the launch only a part of the tallow I had bought, and even then it was quite heavily laden for the long run we had to make. We departed at two o'clock in the afternoon and rejoined the ship at two in the morning.

A few days later we went to visit Rancho San Pedro [San Pablo], situated, as I have said, on the isthmus of the peninsula that projects into the strait of the same name. I had already had an opportunity to make the acquaintance of the worthy man who was living there: Francisco Castro was descended from a Frenchman who has left in California a numerous and well-regarded family. At eleven o'clock we arrived on the beach nearest the farm, where two sons of Castro were awaiting us with horses, and we found a most friendly welcome at this truly patriarchal house. A man of sixty years, Francisco Castro was perfectly preserved, with noble face and figure. His entire family, ten children and two daughters-in-law, resided under the same roof in perfect harmony. Among her brothers and sisters one young girl of fifteen was noticeable for her interesting face and charming deportment.[9]

After an excellent dinner we mounted our horses to visit the property, which covers four square leagues. There were a number of fields where wheat had recently been harvested, but all the rest is pasture land where graze from fifteen hundred to two thousand cattle and several hundred horses.

Returning to the house, we found that two of the young men were getting ready to set out after a bear that they had seen that morning at some distance from the farm. Politely they proposed that we join them; but however appealing the invitation, we did not feel ourselves good enough horsemen to take part in the combat, and we let them go off alone. At the end of three-quarters of an hour we saw them returning, each with a young bear cub fixed to his rope.

They had gone to the place where they had seen the bear, a thicket of hazel trees mixed with oaks. Encountering nothing at first, they were picking hazel nuts from horseback when the two cubs appeared close by. Without thinking that the two young ones would not be alone, they caught them with their lassos; but at the first cry of her cubs the mother, eating acorns in a nearby oak, dropped quickly from her tree and ran to the rescue with all the rage of a mother's love. Recognizing their imprudence in employing their weapons against a weak enemy, the young men had recourse to flight. But one of them ran a great danger because the furious bear threw herself at him and seized

---

9. Francisco María Castro, born in Sinaloa in 1775, was alcalde at San Francisco in 1800, a member of California's first *diputación* in 1822, and grantee of the San Pablo rancho the following year. Concerning his reputed French descent Bancroft found no further evidence.

the tail of his horse; only by a sharp turn of his steed did he make her let loose, and only his great speed enabled him to get away from the ferocious beast.

These men were so accustomed to exposing themselves to this kind of danger that they merely made jokes about the fruitless efforts of the bear, and Castro, who loved his children to distraction, hardly seemed to notice that they had almost been torn apart by the claws of this terrible adversary. He merely said that he expected them to provide themselves with a firearm next time for use in an emergency.

The bear cubs, which they had not let go, could have been about three months old and were already the size of a large mastiff. Like their mother they were of a dirty white mixed with gray and brown. All the bears of the country are of this color; there are few black ones. I had them skinned, saving the skulls and the paws, and carried the spoils off to the ship.

By the 19th everything we were to take from San Francisco had been loaded, and we prepared ourselves to leave this port and continue loading at other points along the coast. On our previous stay at Yerba Buena we had found quite enough water to fill our casks, but that was in the winter; this time we could procure only enough for our daily use, and it was not very good. We had, then, to look for it in another spot. Learning of a watering place on the other side of the harbor, I decided to take the ship there in order not to lose time in transporting water in the boats. The right bank of the harbor entrance, after one gets inside the narrow channel, turns sharply to the north and provides at once a sheltered spot with a copious and convenient spring, opposite which we cast anchor a gunshot from the shore, and there we obtained all our water in a few hours and with great ease.[10]

10. Springs and an abundance of wood at Sausalito made it a favorite shelter for foreign vessels, which, while there, also enjoyed greater freedom from governmental restraints than when at the official anchorage below the presidio.

Chapter 15

THE PUEBLO OF LOS ANGELES &
MISSION SAN GABRIEL

August — October 1827

ON 20 AUGUST WE SAILED from San Francisco and moored on the next day in the roadstead at Santa Cruz. There we took on the things owed to us and on the 26th got under sail once more for Monterey, reaching that place several hours later.

On entering the harbor we were not a little surprised to see the French flag flying over a ship at anchor there. This vessel was the *Comète* of Bordeaux, coming lately from the Sandwich Islands. I shall not go into particulars about this strange expedition and will say only that Mr. R_____ was the instigator and that it had been fitted out by the head of an office in the Ministry of the Interior, who knew all our plans and had taken advantage of his knowledge.* This operation made manifest the irresponsibility and bad faith of Mr. R_____, and if it had succeeded, it would have utterly ruined the business of the *Héros.* But although no harmful competition was possible from this time on, I nevertheless felt constrained to forbid any business relations between the captain of the *Comète* and Mr. R_____, who garnered

---

* The official died before we returned. [This was Catineau-Laroche, head of the Bureau of Commerce.]

only shame as a reward for his duplicity. So nothing further will be said about this ship, which several days later we left in the harbor and in the utmost difficulty, the captain not knowing what to do with the remaining part of his cargo.[1]

During our stay in Monterey we were busy transferring to a storehouse all the merchandise that would not be needed on our coming trip to Peru and that, while taking up uselessly part of the cargo space of the ship, would also have been exposed to the insects that feed upon the *surons** of tallow. Mr. R_____ and two trusted persons were to be charged with guarding these things and with making sales.

Besides the articles that might be sold in California during my coming absence, I arranged with Mr. R_____ that if we could charter a suitable ship, he would betake himself to the Northwest Coast of America with the goods intended for that trade and would sell them at the Russian settlement of Sitka. In that way we would avoid the need to go there with the *Héros,* whose voyage had already become only too long.

We took action accordingly and, having finished our business at Monterey, made our way to Santa Barbara, where we arrived on 13 September, after having anchored briefly at a place called Cojo, a league to the east of Point Conception, in order to take on some tallow owed us by the mission of La Purísima.[2]

We remained in Santa Barbara only long enough to load the goods from that mission and from those nearby. There we encountered a schooner under the Sandwich Island flag and commanded by an American. To the supercargo we proposed that he charter the ship to

---

1. The *Comète,* a ship of 500 tons with a crew of forty-three, Antoine Plassiard, master, had left France after the *Héros* and, in addition to her trading cargo, had carried to the Sandwich Islands three Catholic missionaries and a few agricultural workers. She was now on her way down the American coast and was subsequently sold at Valparaíso as unseaworthy. The relation of the two voyages to each other is discussed in the editors' introduction.

* Packing bags made of cattle hide.

2. Cojo Bay, under a bluff just east of Point Conception, was known as a better anchorage than the open roadstead at Santa Barbara. The landing place for La Purísima mission, some miles over the Santa Inez range to the north, it had been opened to foreign trade the previous July.

us for the intended trip to the Northwest Coast, and after several days the deal was concluded. It was agreed that the *Waverly* (that was the name of the schooner) would come to join us in San Diego in order that Mr. R____ might go on board.[3]

We put to sea and continued our descent of the coast, dropping anchor on 21 September in the bay of San Pedro. Since the first word received there from San Gabriel led me to fear a delay in sending the tallow we had come to fetch, I decided to go there myself in order to expedite its dispatch, and I departed at once, accompanied by Dr. Botta and a guide.

For the first four leagues the way goes north across an arid plain, but after passing the ranch of which I have already spoken it traverses vast pasture lands stocked with great herds owned by the inhabitants of the pueblo of Los Angeles. Through this multitude of animals we were obliged to clear a passage, but often enough the hostile attitude of the bulls suggested prudence, and we described a circle around them at a reasonable distance.

Leaving this plain, we came to nothing less than a forest of mustard [fennel?] whose great stalks stood higher than the head of a horseman and formed something like a thick wall on each side of the route. In recent years this plant has become a terrible scourge in parts of California, invading the finest pasture lands and threatening to spread over the entire country. In the beginning the people could have fought off this enemy by eradicating the first troublesome plants, but their negligence has allowed the evil weed to increase in such a way that it may no longer be controllable by such a small population. Fire has been tried but without success. When the stalks are dry enough to burn they have already spread most of their seeds, and fire only renders the soil more suitable to reproduction of the plant they wish to destroy.

The pueblo of Los Angeles is built at the base of a chain of hills of moderate elevation and on the banks of a small river that does not dry

3. The *Waverly* was a Hawaiian brig of 142 tons, which spent much time on the coast. Thomas M. Robbins was master, 1827–1828.

up in the summer. This little town lies twenty-six miles north of the bay of San Pedro, and there we lodged at the house of a man whom I had met earlier in San Diego. Before sunset we ascended a high point from where we could see, like a mere dot, the *Héros* at anchor to the right of the small Anniversary Island. There, we said to ourselves, is the atom that carries all our hopes and of which each of us occupies only about one four-thousandth part. How little is man! And how little also is one of his greatest creations![4]

From the same spot I counted eighty-two houses comprising the pueblo, from which I concluded that it might contain one thousand inhabitants, including two hundred Indian domestics and laborers. The land around the village and the low ground separating the two channels of the river appeared to me to be cultivated with some care, the principal crops being corn and grapes. The vines grow well here, but the wine and brandy that come from them are quite inferior in taste to the exquisite fruit from which they are made, and I believe that this inferiority must derive from the making rather than from the vintage.

Entering this village, I was struck chiefly by the air of liveliness, ease, and neatness that seemed to characterize the inhabitants, something that I had not observed in any of the presidios: so true is it that agriculture, for the free man, breeds much happiness, while in a military establishment, on the contrary, all is unease and constraint. To provide the benefits of civilization there was wanting in this budding town only an upright and independent court of law that could mediate the differences that arise between individuals. The authority of an *alcalde,* who brings together the functions of mayor and justice of the peace, is not sufficient to assure the security of property, especially

4. The pueblo of Los Angeles, like San José in the north a civil community, was founded in 1781 and, by contemporary accounts, then had a population of about 700, Indians excluded. Its flat-roofed, single-story adobes about a public plaza and the patterned arrangement of its agricultural lands toward the river imparted a sense of order, while its informality, as the author suggests, was manifest not only in the well-being of the people but in delinquency and dissension. Distant from the coast, the pueblo was visited only by occasional traders; Duhaut-Cilly's account of it is one of the best.

when titles to it are so uncertain that they constantly bring on disputes and sometimes unjust expropriations, as I will point out in a moment.

Since it was in the pueblo of Los Angeles that I remarked the greatest care in the appearance of the inhabitants, this is the best place to say something about the way they dress; since this has much in common with that of Baja California, I am led necessarily into some repetition that I would prefer to avoid by treating the subject only once.[5]

Only the men have what might be called a national costume and one that is entirely suitable to their manner of life, which is to be almost always on horseback. They wear short breeches of wool or velvet of a dark color, decorated with gold or silver braid, but they never button them at the knee although they seem designed for that. Below the open knees can be seen the legs of white drawers, descending to mid-calf and partly covering white stockings, always worn loose. A Californian with stockings pulled up neatly would invite a burst of sarcastic remarks. Their jacket is usually of the same material as the breeches; it has no collar and is trimmed with piping and with red ornaments. The rows of metal buttons are not meant to close it since the two sides are not full enough to meet over the breast. As they do not wear braces, the white shirt always shows between jacket and breeches. Instead of braces they wear a red sash wound several times around the waist and called a *faja*.

Their boot is a kind of leather buskin, laced up on the outside. The upper part is divided in two lengthwise, one part yellow and the other brown, and the whole is adorned to good effect with a kind of embroidery. At the heel of the boot is an edging of fringed leather that sustains the weight of the monstrous spurs they use. When on horseback their legs are enveloped in *gamuza* [chamois], as also in Baja California; it is in this part of their costume that they show the greatest vanity; the manner of wrapping it around the calf of the leg is the touchstone of California fashion; woe to him whose *bota* reveals the shape of his leg. The best-attired young man must appear to be held

5. At the beginning of Chapter 5 there is a description of the costume of the horsemen of San José del Cabo.

up by two fat sausages, and as if to add to the illusion, the bota is bound tightly around the middle of the calf by a ribbon of silk and gold, woven by the cavalier's lady-love.

Their hat of choice is made of felt, flat in shape and with a wide brim. To protect themselves against the cold, they carry a cloak, which is nothing more than a piece of material with a hole for the head to pass through, a garment found in all the Spanish colonies of America and called sometimes a *poncho* and sometimes a *manga.* The ensemble of this costume is far from lacking grace or brilliance but its chief advantage is in allowing complete freedom of movement.

The women are ridiculously attired, their dress a bizarre mixture of foreign and California fashions; and the effect is especially extravagant when they borrow something from the Mexican women. The latter (at least those who are found in California) are so ludicrously costumed that one must have a large measure of gravity to preserve a serious mien when viewing their toilette.

I can still remember the hilarity that overcame us at the sight of the headdresses adorning on a festival day the two daughters of Miguel González, commandant at Monterey. I do not know which of us had given them to believe that those melon-shaped bandboxes, used for some time by our ladies to carry their things about, were in fact hats in the latest Parisian fashion, needing only ribbons and feathers to complete the design. The young ladies purchased these eagerly and, having decorated them according to instructions, they expected to produce a great sensation and cause the California women to perish with vexation. But we had, charitably, let the whole company into the secret, and they were greeted with a great explosion of laughter, and the name of *cabeza-melones* (melon heads) remained with them.

One sees very few California women who hold strictly to the extremely simple costume of the country, a petticoat that is white in the upper part and red below: the *naguas* that I have mentioned elsewhere. It hangs from the hips, where it forms a great round pad. A white shirt, similar to that of the men, a *rebozo* of white and blue cotton, white stockings, and black shoes: that is all their finery. In general they have beautiful hair, which they let fall behind in thick braids, as do the men. Those who from coquetry would be more refined try to make themselves elegant and succeed in being grotesque. We always preferred the indigenous costume to the potpourri of borrowed elements.

The day after our arrival at the pueblo we made our way to Mission San Gabriel, distant three leagues to the east-northeast. It is situated in a fertile plain at the base of some very high mountains and has abundant running water. Although this mission is, without doubt, the richest in all of California, its buildings are far from equaling in beauty those at San Luis Rey. The church had been brought down two years before by an earthquake, and they were then occupied in building another.[6] The wealth of San Gabriel lies in its immense herds and its splendid vines, which produce some very good wine. At that time they were loaded with ripe grapes, the purple and succulent clusters hanging down to the ground.

The warm greeting of Padre Sánchez, superior of the mission,[7] might have made me consent to prolong my stay there, but being unable to convince him that my consignment should take precedence over that of the *Solitude*, which had preceded us by several days at San Pedro, I was so vexed at the delay that I decided to stay no longer at San Gabriel. In spite of the entreaties of the padre, I returned to the pueblo for the night in order to go on to the harbor the next day.

About eight o'clock that evening we were taking tea with Don José Carrillo (that was the name of my host) and his family when we felt a strong earthquake shock. Their first move was to rush into the courtyard, where I followed them; almost at once, however, I remembered that the young son of Carrillo, a child of eight years confined to bed by a burn on the foot, was still asleep in the drawing room, and I ran to look for him. I carried him in my arms to his family, who had not yet noticed his absence; and it was only after a new shock that his mother came crying to thank me for what I had done. Her fright had

6. There is no other record of an earthquake in 1825, but the church at San Gabriel was severely damaged by the quake of 1812 and may have been repaired over a period of years by Padre José María Zalvidea, a practical and industrious man who was stationed there from 1806 to 1827.

7. Padre José Bernardo Sánchez was at Mission San Gabriel from 1821 until his death in 1833, being its superior from 1827 and president of the California missions from 1827 to 1831.

been so great that she had been able to think of nothing but saving herself.[8]

So tremendous a phenomenon is an earthquake that I was not surprised at the oversight of this tender mother who passionately loved her only child. This terrible scourge is so fearsome and comes upon us so suddenly and without warning that it sometimes suspends all our faculties and even deprives some people of the will to flee; they have been seen to remain as if petrified, exposed to the collapse of a building and unable to take one step to escape being buried in the ruins. In Lima, when an earthquake occurs at night, it often happens that the streets and squares are suddenly filled with naked men and women. Thisbes[9] are rare in Peru, I know, and we must agree that only an inescapable terror could cause these women to forget their sense of modesty. It is not surprising then, when all vital instincts are in some way arrested, that the functions of the heart, even those of a mother, may be momentarily suspended.

On the 1st of October we still had some things to bring on board, and I found myself unwillingly detained in this dangerous roadstead, where the lateness of the season made me fear being surprised by a sudden storm. Only too soon were these fears proved genuine; on the morning of the 4th I almost lost the ship.

During the night of October 3rd to 4th the weather became threatening; when the wind blew briefly from the southeast, I at once had the small bower anchor raised and made preparations to get under way; but the threatening signs diminished and I awaited daylight to better judge the weather. At sunrise everything foretold a stiff blow from the open sea, and while it was still almost calm, I sent a boat to the shore to bring some surons of tallow and some other things that were still there in order that we might be ready to set sail when the boat returned. During that time the wind freshened, and there was

---

8. José Antonio Carrillo, then alcalde at Los Angeles, had, at thirty-one, already been a member of the *diputación* and the governor's secretary and would become one of California's foremost citizens.

9. Thisbe, a maiden in Babylon, is said to have dropped her mantle when frightened by a lion.

not a minute to lose. As soon as the boat was back we hauled in the cable. We were moored quite near the rocks of the coast in five fathoms of water, and as the wind was blowing directly from the sea, we experienced a most ticklish time getting ready to sail. One circumstance made it even more difficult; we had, as I have said, raised the small bower during the night, and the ship, on a single anchor for several hours, had veered around and fouled the stock, so that we still had more than twenty fathoms of cable out when the anchor began to drag.* The prompt setting of sails while at the same time we continued working the capstan, that is what saved us. The ship began to move, still dragging the anchor while we finished hauling it in, and we managed to double Anniversary Island at the distance of a pistol shot, brushing the bottom at three fathoms and a half. This danger once passed, we tacked about and got out of the bay. On this occasion we again owed the safety of the ship to the size and the quick work of the crew. Had we remained at our mooring, the fouled anchor would not have held, and, since we were too close to the rocks to have time to drop another successfully, it is likely that we would have run onto the coast.

Hardly were we away from the roadstead when the wind became violent, but we were no longer concerned and passed tranquilly through this small hurricane between San Pedro and the island of Santa Catalina. On the next day the weather was once more calm, and the wind resumed its usual direction from the northwest. We returned to the bay, where, without anchoring, we sent the longboat to fetch the tallow that had arrived during our short absence, and as soon as the boat returned we set sail for San Diego, where we would finish our loading while sheltered from alarms of this kind.

In that harbor we found the *Waverly,* which had arrived a few days ahead of us. There we occupied ourselves making provision of wood and water. The first of these is easy enough and costs nothing; one obtains it on the uninhabited peninsula that forms the southern shore of

* I shall not try to define these terms; no definition would be sufficient to make the situation clear to those not acquainted with the sea.

the harbor, cutting the small trees and bushes that grow there. As for water, this is quite scarce in the summer; we had to buy it at the presidio and have it delivered in carts.

On the evening of the 12th, while returning to the harbor, my horse went down, entangling me in its fall, and I felt a sharp pain in my right shoulder. I remounted and rode for more than a league before reaching the ship, which I boarded without assistance, but at the first inspection Dr. Botta told me that I had broken my collarbone. This accident could not have come at a more awkward time. I still had many things to do on shore, and on board needed to complete my accounts, to give instructions to those I was leaving in charge of the storehouse in Monterey, and finally to put in writing my agreement with Mr. R____ regarding the trip he was to make to the Northwest Coast.

It was arranged with him that during my absence of five or six months he would return to Monterey on the *Waverly,* and would load on that schooner the merchandise he judged suitable; that he would then go first to the American establishment on the Columbia River, and if he did not succeed there in bartering for all the cargo, he would go on to the Russian colony of Sitka on Norfolk Sound, where we hoped he could deal the rest advantageously in exchange for sea otter and fur sealskins. He would then return to Monterey, where we would meet after my return from Peru. With everything thus settled and arranged, I set sail on 20 October for Lima, leaving the *Waverly* ready to depart the next day for Monterey.

Chapter 16

GENERAL DESCRIPTION OF THE CALIFORNIAS, I

October 1827

DESCRIBING THE CUSTOMS of a people is of real interest in only two circumstances: first, when the people depicted are very little known and their ways, compared to our own, are bizarre or unusual. Art is of no use here; the attraction of the account arises from the contrast presented to our imagination; the plain observation of facts provides the charm of the story. And it is this aspect of travel accounts that has always been given the greatest attention.

These matters may also be of compelling interest when they concern a civilized nation, especially a rival in power or wealth or manners. But in that case it is not the busy navigator who should undertake the task, but the historian. The traveler may well be as erudite as Humboldt, as interesting as Cook, as light and amusing as Arago, but he can hardly be a historian comparable to Rollin, an enlightened critic like Addison or Jouy, nor will he write as poetically as Chateaubriand.[1]

---

1. Most of these names will, perhaps, be sufficiently well known to the reader, but it may be of interest that the last mentioned, the great romantic writer François-René de Chateaubriand (1768–1848), was from Saint-Malo and personally known to Duhaut-Cilly.

Their customs and habits, even the most intimate details of daily existence, these are what interest us among a primitive people. For a civilized nation, it is otherwise; the ways of the people concern us less than their laws, their government, their political tendencies, matters important in our dealings with them. If an author wishes to delve into their private affairs, he will need for success a critical mind along with great skill.

But if advanced nations and purely primitive peoples are equally worthy of study, the same is not true of a population whose customs are debased and no longer original. This is the case with California: a confusion of Spanish, English, Mexican, Indian, and other ways, a dull mosaic without life or character. This lack of an individual quality would have held me back from a portrayal if the natives of the land had not been on hand to cast some color onto the faded canvas.

Until now I have been speaking of California, of its presidios and missions, without providing the information needed to understand what has been said and what remains to say about these things. I shall now consider this country in a more general way and will then say something about the native peoples.

This part of America, now subject to the rule of Mexico, is divided into Alta and Baja California. The latter, the part that I know least, is properly speaking a long and narrow peninsula, bordered on one side by the great ocean and on the other by the Gulf of Cortés, also known as the Vermilion Sea, and lying between the twenty-second and thirty-second parallels of north latitude.

The settlement of Baja California, which goes back about one hundred twenty years, was made by the order of Dominicans, who still have charge of the missions of that province.[2] But although it has been

---

The influence of his fellow Breton's writings on the noble savage, as in *Atala* (1801), may be noted in Chapter 11.

2. The first permanent European settlement in the Californias, at Loreto in 1697, was made by the Jesuits. Upon their expulsion in 1768, they surrendered their missions to the Franciscans, who in turn left them to the Dominicans when they departed for Alta California in 1769. Loreto remained the civil and military seat of the lower province until 1839, when the capital was transferred to La Paz, the chief port.

settled for a longer time than Alta California, possesses gold and silver mines, and produces other things of great value, it is far from being as prosperous as the other province; this must be attributed to the nature of the soil, much less fertile and less susceptible to cultivation. It is separated from the coast of Sonora by the Gulf of Cortés and by the Rio Colorado (Red River), which flows into this little sea precisely at its northern extremity. The principal presidios of Baja California are those of Real San Antonio, which I have spoken of, La Paz, and Loreto, the most northern one. On the coast bathed by the Vermilion Sea they take tortoises for their shells and oysters for pearls. The latter are abundant and often quite large and pear-shaped. I have seen some that would have commanded enormous prices had they been of a better color, what the people of the country call *buen oriente,* but nearly all are spotted or shaded a deep olive in some parts. The shells themselves are usually edged with a rim of this color, so that the mother-of-pearl is of inferior quality.

At the time I visited the country an English company had sent a ship there to fish for pearls. This expedition, whose shares must have commanded a high price in London, was not a success. Their diving apparatus was good, but the paying out and hauling back required too much time in relation to the area covered; when dropped in a place where the oysters were few, the day was taken up with fruitless tries, expensive and without return.[3]

There are no more free Indians in Baja California, and the number of those subject to the missions or the government or to private individuals is not large and grows smaller every day. The Dominicans who administer the missions of Baja California are quite inferior to the Franciscans in talent and in discretion. I met only one of exemplary conduct, the father at San José del Cabo; the public behavior of all the others was more or less scandalous.[4]

3. In 1827 the General Pearl and Coral Fishery Association of London sent two vessels to the Gulf but obtained only a small number of pearls of inferior quality and no coral.

4. The priest at San José del Cabo was Tomás de Ahumada, as described in Chapter 5. Near the end of Chapter 18 Duhaut-Cilly observes the different reactions of Dominicans and Franciscans to the government's expulsion of the Spaniards.

Alta California is a prolongation of the peninsula and is part of the American continent. In length it extends from the port of San Diego in 32.5° north latitude to that of San Francisco in 37.75°. It comprises the southern part of the stretch of coast called New Albion by the English.[5]

In 1769 the first mission was founded in San Diego; since then twenty others have been established between the two extreme points, a stretch of one hundred fifty leagues in length with a width never more than twenty leagues; beyond that are no settlements in a country inhabited only by savages.

The founding of these missions was accomplished in agreement with the Spanish government, and although persuasion was the first means employed by the Franciscans, it was considered necessary to provide some military support, not with the avowed intention of attacking the natives or of conquering the country, but to protect the newly founded establishments from aggression by the Indians. For this reason there were set up at the same time the four presidios of San Diego, Santa Barbara, Monterey, and San Francisco. These are a kind of fortress where are stationed the troops assigned to guard each mission.

The following list [next page] will show the state of the missions of Alta California in 1827, with their geographical positions, their distances from each other, and the number of their Indians.

The table shows that the number of Christian Indians in the several missions of Alta California amounted in 1827 to 20,153. According to Roquefeuil there were 22,000 in 1817; thus, there has been a reduction of 2,000 in ten years.[6]

But while this part of the population has decreased, the number of creoles, whom I call Californians because they will one day be the sole

5. Vancouver, who renewed the claim made by Francis Drake in 1579, defined New Albion as extending from latitude 39° 20′, where he first reached the coast of present-day Mendocino County in April 1792, to the Strait of Georgia. H. R. Wagner made it include the area from 35° to 45°.

6. If Duhaut-Cilly's figures were printed correctly, as reproduced here without change, the number of Indians was 21,052 and the decrease was 1,000 instead of 2,000.

Missions	Founded in	Latitude North	Indians	Leagues to prec.
San Diego	16 June 1769	32° 48'	1,829	
San Luis Rey	13 June 1798	33° 3'	2,767	13 leagues ½
San Juan Capistrano	1 Nov. 1776	33° 26'	1,060	12 " ½
San Gabriel	8 Sept. 1771	34° 10'	1,644	18 "
San Fernando	8 Sept. 1797	34° 16'	957	9 "
San Buenaventura	31 Mar. 1782	34° 26'	908	22 "
Santa Barbara	4 Dec. 1786	34° 30'	923	10 "
Santa Ynes	12 Sept. 1804	34° 52'	516	12 "
Purisima Concepcion	8 Dec. 1782	35°	662	8 "
San Luis Obispo	1 Sept. 1772	35° 36'	424	18 "
San Miguel	25 July 1797	35° 48'	904	13 "
San Antonio	14 July 1771	36° 50'	806	13 "
Soledad	9 Oct. 1791	36° 38'	512	11 "
San Carlos	3 June 1770	36° 44'	306	15 "
San Juan Bautista	24 June 1797	36° 48'	1,221	12 "
Santa Cruz	28 Aug. 1791	37°	461	13 "
Santa Clara	18 Jan. 1777	37° 20'	1,450	11 "
San José	11 June 1797	37° 30'	1,806	5 "
San Francisco	9 Oct. 1776	37° 46'	265	20 "
San Rafael	18 Dec. 1817	38° 1'	939	8 "
San Francisco Solano	23 Aug. 1823	38° 39'	692	9 "
			20,153	

inhabitants of the country, has increased by the same amount during these ten years. The traveler just cited accounted them in the same year of 1817 to number thirteen hundred, while in 1827 that figure had risen to three thousand five hundred. As in Baja California these people owe their origin to the first Spaniards, who married Indian women. Little by little the group has increased sufficiently so that the men no longer have to seek out such women, and their skin color, olive at first, has lightened more and more. Today the inhabitants have the complexion of Spaniards. A great number of marriages between California women and foreigners, contracted since the independence of Mexico, is helping to make the population fully white.

Nearly all the men are tall and well formed; they have handsome masculine features, and their thick, black beards proclaim their Spanish origin. But they do not make a good show of their height; the habit of being always on horseback gives them an awkward posture. So little accustomed to the use of their legs are they that they walk with the weight of the body shifting from side to side as if they were crippled. Californians are indolent; the only work they have a taste for is taking care of the herds, since this must be done on a horse. They excel in everything that has to do with riding; their only skills besides that of the horseman are those of the butcher and the ostler.

Agriculture is quite neglected by the Californians. The work of this kind performed by some of them consists in cultivating a few vines and small gardens planted indiscriminately with several kinds of fruit trees and vegetables that they do not know how to graft or to improve. It is true that the lack of laws in the country does not encourage husbandry. To feel the wish to better himself a man must own property, but no piece of land here has a clear title. Neither government nor missionary has ever ceded the smallest piece of land to the inhabitants either by grant or by sale. Only they can own and transmit the right of ownership. I have spoken of ranchos and large farms worked by private individuals and have mentioned cultivated fields in the pueblos of San José and Los Angeles; these people can be stripped of them without consideration; even the ground on which their houses are built does not belong to them. All grants so far made to the Californians are revocable. After more than half a century of occupation by the same family it still has no legal rights. Lawsuits among the heirs of such a property have sometimes ended in seizure in the name of the government, which, in order to bring the claimants together, concedes it temporarily to a person with no rights to it at all. These are then only a kind of fief that can be withdrawn at the whim or the pleasure of the seigneur.[7]

This system cannot long endure; if the Mexican government becomes firmly established, the lands not belonging to the missions will surely need to be distributed to the Californians, but until that happy

7. Mexican land laws were changing even as Duhaut-Cilly wrote. Under colonization acts of 1824 and 1828 grantees fulfilling designated procedures received full rights of land ownership, although the effect of these acts was not immediately felt in California.

revolution takes place there is nothing to reassure those who cultivate, and agriculture will remain in discredit.

One can object that the present resources of California suffice for the inhabitants. I agree, but it is her future prosperity that concerns me; what California lacks is workers. Everyone knows that a population can grow rapidly only as the means of subsistence increases. The kings of Spain had an interest in keeping the creoles dependent and, without feeling shame for the great injustices and favoritism thus brought about, they looked on their ownership of the land as a means of control. The republican government of Mexico must consider these things in quite a different way; it must look with favor on anything that tends to make for an increase in the population, because strength lies in numbers, in the multitude.

Very few Californians live at the missions; they are found in the two pueblos mentioned above and in the four presidios. It is not entirely clear how these latter support themselves; many of them become soldiers and thus manage a sort of existence. Military service among the Californians, active enough since they are employed as express messengers and stewards, in no way resembles that of the European soldier. There are never any drills; they are merely expected to mount guard at the presidios and the missions. Their most usual and regular function is as customs guards; those charged with this surveillance know how to profit themselves by the encouragement of smuggling.

The troops, although divided into artillery, cavalry, and infantry, are all mounted. Each soldier must own several horses, which are pastured on government land. They have no uniform, properly speaking; the national costume described above takes its place. In society these men are on quite a different level from that of our European soldiers; in this respect they resemble Turkish janizaries more than any other body of troops. They have been known to ask the hand of their commander's daughter, and to receive it. They attend all the ceremonies of their officers, returning courtesy for courtesy, and go everywhere in equality with them. Their pay would be excellent if they could get what is due them, but that has never happened under either the Spanish or the Mexican government, and there are those who are owed more than twenty years' pay. Only rations do they receive with some regularity, and clothing from time to time, woolens, linens, and boots provided by foreign ships as payment of duties.

The people of the pueblos and the ranchos are more sure at least of the means of survival. Their herds, vines, and gardens supply abundantly their tables. Those who lack these resources, when hunger presses them, work for their neighbors, branding and caring for the herds, and are paid in animals. In the months of May and June they hunt deer and wild cattle, which abound in the woods where they have multiplied.

The Californians themselves do not work the fields; for this they obtain Indians and pay wages to the missionaries. It is a pity that this labor is turned over to a kind of slave while the men and hearty youths pass their time racing horses and gambling away the little they own.

The California men are generally hospitable but also vain and oversensitive. Fathers require complete submission from their children, a dependence that often continues after marriage. Rarely does one see a child of one sex or the other sit at table with the father, who most often eats alone, served by wife, sons, and daughters. Although the habit of smoking is so strong with them that you seldom see them without cigars in their mouths, a son would not dare smoke in the presence of his parents. A young Californian is not allowed to shave his beard for the first time without permission from his father, who seldom grants this before the age of twenty-two, the usual time of marriage.

The women are formed proportionately to the men; that is to say, they are large and strong. Some have quite pretty faces and might pass for beautiful if they did not neglect their complexion, their hands, and their feet. They are generally well behaved and modest. The California vice is not lechery but gambling first of all. In this fatal occupation of almost all their waking hours they ruin themselves and lose the taste for work. The most skillful player is the one who cheats the most. When they say of someone, *sabe barajar*, he knows how to shuffle the cards, this does not mean that he handles them with grace and elegance, but that he is able to arrange them in such a way that he will win.

If gambling ruins them, drinking degrades them still further. The two vices, among them as among us, usually go hand in hand. They give themselves over to the latter without restraint; at their festivities brandy is almost the only refreshment. And to put on a ball, which they call a fandango without any knowledge of that dance, all they need is a few gallons of brandy and some candles.

The Catholic religion is observed by the Californians with much outward show, and it can be seen all too clearly that for them, as for their Spanish ancestors, it amounts to no more than pious ceremonies mixed with superstitions. The importance given by the missionaries to the visible aspects of religion, thus appealing to the eyes of the Indians, is one of the causes of this error. A Californian thinks himself a good Catholic when he conforms to the exterior marks of devotion, although he pays no attention to what religion demands or prohibits. He has no notion at all that genuine faith is needed for the proper participation in the mass, in festivals, and in Sunday services. Fast days are distinguished from other days only in that a person should eat only fish or meat without mixing the two; on these days even the tables of the padres are set as usual with meat, fish, and vegetables, and each, according to his taste, partakes of one or the other of these dishes. Fasting, to the missionaries, means only that they do not eat their ragouts in the morning or evening; they patiently await dinner with a cup of chocolate and a tart.

The missionaries are almost the only ones to eat bread. The Californians make a substitute from wheat flour, small cakes they call tortillas, as I have said previously. Those made from corn meal are less good. Their table is generally quite simple; beef, or rather cow meat, which they prefer, is the basis of their cuisine. They don't care for game, although they could easily procure hare or deer, and they claim that venison is not healthful. It is, they say, a cold meat (*carne fria*); they never eat it. Cheese is much to their taste, and they make several kinds, but their cows give little milk.

They serve a good table at some of the missions, and if a gastronome would still find them lacking, the fault lies not in any lack of will by the missionaries but in the lack of development in this country of the culinary art. I have the sweet satisfaction however of thinking that the Luculluses of California will be congratulating themselves on the visit of the *Héros* to their shores, and perhaps someday they will erect an altar to the good and wise Dorrey, where his bust, crowned with thyme and laurel, will forever receive their homage in memory of the two Indian disciples whom he initiated into the secrets of his art.* [8]

There are two classes of Indians in Alta California, the Christian and the heathen, or gentiles as they are called in this country. The first group, as we have seen, are not numerous since there are only twenty thousand of them on this long stretch of coast. It is not possible to reckon the number of the others, whose land is bounded only by the territories of the United States and by the Northwest Coast of America. Without doubt that immense land contains a considerable number of nations or rather of different tribes, all as yet unknown. Here we will take notice only of those who live near the coast and have populated the missions.

The Indians have never formed themselves into a nation. Even their languages exhibit great variation over small distances; often the Indians of one mission do not understand those of the neighboring mission. They are scattered into separate villages or *rancherías*. Two or three rancherías make up a tribe. Sometimes a single one of these hamlets will have a chief who is quite independent of the others and speaks its separate language.

It is not surprising that war often breaks out among these small groups. The possession of a spring or a grove or a hillside becomes a source of dispute. For the skin of a rabbit or a beaver the bow is bent, and the lethal arrow does not fly through the air with impunity.

To avoid danger from the expeditions that have often been sent against them unjustly the Indians usually choose to place their villages on firm ground surrounded by those marshes known to the Spaniards as *tulares* on account of the great quantity of reeds [tules] growing in them. There the California riders cannot go on their horses. The boats

* Dorrey was the cook on board the *Héros,* and the padre at San Luis begged me to have him give culinary lessons to two of his Indians, who spent several months on the ship. Today he keeps a very good hotel in Le Hâvre.

8. The padre was probably Antonio Peyrí of San Luis Rey but may have been Luis Antonio Martínez of San Luis Obispo. Duhaut-Cilly never visited the latter mission but may have met Martínez, who was there from 1798 to 1830 and whose ambition it was that no mission should set a better table or treat visitors with greater hospitality.

they use for traversing the water or for fishing are surely the worst in the world, each made of two bundles of reeds eight feet long and tied together by cross-pieces of wood. This kind of raft, called a *balsa* in the country, is maneuvered by means of double-bladed paddles that they dip into the water first on one side and then on the other.

The natives of Alta California are not prepossessing in appearance. Some of the men are tall, but for the most part they are of a height below the average. Without being over-laden with flesh, their limbs are robust and their chests broad. While athletically formed, they have neither grace nor beauty. In color they are a dark red-brown; the face is lighter than the rest of the body, and the women are more yellowish than the men. Supported on a short neck, the head is large and crowned with a thick mane of straight and bushy hair of the blackest tint; tied high around the forehead, a band holds back this forest and allows an unrestricted view. Except for a light beard on the chin they are not hirsute; the skin is supple and smooth, and it appears that they are not ravaged by the smallpox. The forehead is low and receding; the eyes, not very open and quite black, harmonize with the savage character of their other features. Wide nostrils go with an unprominent nose. Two rows of large and strikingly white teeth fill the very wide mouth. Their lips are not thick; the upper one, larger than the other, is drawn back close to the nose; the cheek bones are prominent. And finally, the ensemble of their crudely fashioned features is a sign of stupidity, an overall characteristic of their appearance. But some exceptions must be granted; without being handsome, some young people of both sexes exhibit an appearance of spirit and good health that is most agreeable.

The women are short, thick-set, and ugly. Their hips are wide but not well formed, and their legs lean and lank. In both sexes the broad, square foot is armed with a thick and hoof-like sole from going barefoot over rocks and through the brush.

This race of Indians is one of the dirtiest in the world. Their huts, of conical form, are revolting hovels where they pass a filthy, brutish, and precarious life. Instead of making beds of straw or moss they all lie down around the fire in the dust and ashes. However, they make themselves cloaks of rabbit fur or bird skins, skillfully worked and decorated with bands of various colors. They also make fine baskets from reeds, ornamented with mother-of-pearl and partridge crests. Since the country does not provide gourds suitable for vessels, as in other lands, and since they do not know the common art of fashioning pots from baked clay, they use reed baskets so finely woven that they hold water. Since these containers cannot be put in the fire they cook their food by throwing hot stones into the water, causing it to boil at once.[9]

Their bows and arrows are so perfectly made that any attempt to improve them would be in vain. The flattened wood of the bow is covered on the convex side with deer or bull tendon fixed so tightly that the two materials become indivisible, and the two ends, slightly longer than the wood, are turned back in a loop for attaching the bowstring. When the bow is unstrung the tendon contracts and the convex side becomes concave. From this one can judge the strength and skill needed to bend it. To prevent the sound of the string from warning the game, they wrap a small part of it with a sleeve of beaver skin, which stops the vibration so well that the whistle of the arrow is the only sound heard by an animal that is missed, while the one hit has no time to perceive it. Probably it would be no improvement to replace the flint arrowhead with one of iron. As for the elegance of the shaft and the way in which it is feathered, these cannot be bettered. When they go to war or to the hunt they put some dozens of these into a pretty fox or beaver pelt, the animal having been skinned from the rump; the arrow heads protrude through the mouth while the other ends, adorned with feathers, stick out behind, giving this quiver an aspect at once wild and graceful.

To make poisonous the arrows used in war, these Indians, some say, cause one or more rattlesnakes to strike a piece of meat from a recently killed deer or ox, and they then thrust into it several times the point that is to be made deadly. Others say that they dry the meat by the fire, grind it up, mix it with blood, and use this concoction for the same purpose.

9. Some California Indians, especially those living near the Colorado River, made clay pots. Most of the coastal tribes encountered by Duhaut-Cilly did not.

There are several methods of testing the effectiveness of the venom. The first consists in touching with the arrow point a fresh piece of meat; if this becomes livid and greenish, the poison is sufficiently active. The second method is to make a small cut in the arm with a knife or other sharp instrument and touch with the arrow point the blood that runs from the wound. Then, they claim, as soon as the poison moves toward the wound, coagulating or decomposing the blood, they quickly wipe this off before it can harm them. But there is still another and even more certain test, one that costs the life of a woman whom they wound with the poisoned point of the arrow. The Indian who gave me this information spoke quite good Spanish, and when I showed my indignation at such a barbarous procedure, he said to me with a look of stupid indifference, "In such cases we choose an old woman who is no longer good for anything (*una vieja que no sirve*)." The unhappy woman, however, may sometimes be a relative or mother; among these native peoples family ties are broken as soon as the child is able to take care of itself. In this matter they differ sharply from their neighbors on the Northwest Coast, where even the oldest women retain the greatest privileges.[10]

To some old women the Indians attribute the art of sorcery; these then become objects of veneration and fear. They cast spells on pregnant women, giving them decoctions made from magical plants; those who have incurred their wrath soon become victims of the witchcraft without anyone knowing the true cause. No doubt they mix secret poisons into the food, while appearing only to be touching the hair of the hated ones with a mysterious wand, sending them into a kind of frenzy and causing them to go mad. On other occasions, it is said, they cause them to encounter a snake, which transfixes them with its eyes and brings on death. These old enchantresses refuse obstinately to discuss their occult science with strangers, no doubt for the good reason that their most effective secret is their way of working on the credulity of their primitive compatriots.

10. It is not clear whether the author believed these stories about the uses of rattlesnake venom. Investigators before and since then have had their legs pulled by native informants.

When an Indian feels indisposed he has recourse to a singular kind of cure. Each village has a health house or rather a health cavern; this is a sort of oven excavated in the ground and covered over with a roof of thatch. A fire is lit inside near the entrance, and all the sick people squat naked in the back of this almost airless and smoke-filled cave. One can imagine how quickly these poor patients break out in perspiration. Sweat rolls from all parts of their bodies, and when they are bathed in it and all their pores are wide open they run out and jump into the cold water and stay there for quite some time.

Nothing certain can be said about the religion of these aborigines. To questions on this subject they respond in a vague manner, and their answers almost never agree with each other. They believe that the sun is a man, master of the world, and the moon his wife, and they explain in quite a coarse way what it is that makes them think the moon a woman. They also say that the sun had a son and in a fit of anger chased him from the sky; the son, in the form of a marten, hid himself under the mountains. Storms are the wrath of the father, thunder is the voice of the son, and earthquakes are caused by his efforts to escape the prison where he is confined. It is only from the older mission Indians that one can extract details of this kind. Day by day the traditions are vanishing and being lost.*

The mission Indians who have embraced Christianity understand this religion less well than they might since it has been expounded to them by other Indians converted before them; the purity of the dogma can only be much altered as it passes through one ignorant mind to another and in a language that has no words to express our metaphysical ideas; thus they have retained many of their tribal superstitions. In each mission there is a sort of Indian preacher whose function is to repeat in the language of the region and phrase by phrase the instructions spoken by the padres in Spanish. After several years all the neophytes are able to understand and speak this language

* This account of the Indians of California and of the Californians themselves does not come entirely from my own investigations. I owe part of it to Mr. A. Bourdas, my brother-in-law, who made the voyage with me and whose inquiring mind has been of great help in this work.

more or less correctly. They succeed quite well in what is shown them. In the missions one encounters workmen who have acquired considerable experience in the crafts taught to them, as I have pointed out in my earlier description of some mission buildings. The Indians imitate the Californians in their horseback maneuvers and are equally good riders.

The same plan that governed the establishment of missions in Baja California under the Dominicans has been followed by the Franciscans in Alta California, and like the first named, the latter have not held to their compact. That is to say, they have not, after ten years, seen fit to distribute the land to the neophytes and so grant them their liberty. One must not, however, place the entire burden of this oppression on the fathers; they have made efforts that did not succeed. At several missions they selected some of the most intelligent Indians and placed them with their wives and children on lands more than sufficient for each family. They provided them with herds, cultivating tools, and food for the first year; their needs were fully met and their fortunes could have grown quickly, but the opposite happened. They let themselves slide into indolence and vice; they allowed the animals to perish or sold them for something to dissipate in gambling; weeds crowded out the vegetables in their gardens; their houses fell into ruin; and at the end of a few years they have had to return to the missions in order not to die of hunger and misery. There at least they lack nothing. They are obliged to work but are given food and shelter.

What must we conclude from this? That these peoples are not born to the agricultural way of life. As savages their life is in truth precarious but it suits their nature; as tillers of the soil they languish and die in want.

Chapter 17

GENERAL DESCRIPTION, II.

TRIP TO PERU

October 1827–May 1828

SLAVERY MAY WRAP ITSELF in the cloak of benevolence or of betterment of man's condition, but it is still slavery, a state incompatible with the inner intelligence that animates us. The desire for freedom may be stifled in a people but cannot be extinguished. While a chain may hold a man back from the abyss, he will nonetheless regard it as a fetter and will seek to break it, even at the risk of his life.

What do the padres require of the Indians of Alta California? A little work in return for plentiful nourishment, good clothing, and the benefits of civilization. In spite of these evident advantages, the instinct for freedom is there crying out against this tranquil but monotonous existence and urging them to prefer the poor and uncertain life of their forests and swamps.

From time to time these ideas stir in the heads of the Indians, and many of them run off to return to the wilderness. There are also those who, reduced to frightful misery by their local wars, come of their own accord to seek in the missions a subsistence that is never refused them. But the largest number of neophytes are retained only by their respect for the padres and by their fear of being recaptured. If they could all join together, they would certainly destroy the missions and take up again their former life. The Franciscans are the sole tie that binds them, and it is awareness of this that has so far held the Mexican government back from taking over these valuable properties, sending away the friars who founded them.

In 1820 the Indians of the missions of Santa Barbara, Santa Inés, and La Purísima revolted. The conspiracy was widespread and broke out at the same time in these three places. The intent of the insurgents was to burn the missions and flee to the tulares with what they could carry off; they had no wish to do harm to the missionaries. But when two of the latter joined with the soldiers resisting the Indians, they ran the risk of being killed. The padre at Santa Inés in particular, a man of great courage commanding four soldiers, held off for an entire day the siege of his house by two hundred assailants.[1]

This plot could not have been hatched with entire secrecy; the Indians had been seen to pile up a great stock of bows and arrows. Thus, notice had been given to the presidio of Santa Barbara, the nearest to these missions, and help arrived in time to prevent much of the disturbance.

At the approach of reinforcements the insurgents took flight and retired to the tulares. On that occasion three Californians and a larger number of Indians lost their lives. At Santa Barbara the insurrection took place in a quite orderly fashion with no attempt to burn the mission; it is true that it could have been quickly saved from the presidio, only two miles away. The insurgents chose themselves a chief, and he, at their head, began by ordering Fray Antonio Ripoll to retire into the church with all the sacred vessels. The band, after seizing everything that came to hand and loaded down with booty, set off in an orderly way on the route to the tulares. This revolt had for origin the cruel punishments inflicted by the soldiers on a number of Indians, whose resentment awakened in them the spirit of liberty.

---

1. The Chumash uprising of 1824 (not 1820) began at Santa Inés after the flogging of a neophyte, spread immediately to nearby Purísima and a day or two later to Santa Barbara. The padres were not harmed, but Indians and soldiers both suffered casualties. This complex event is described in a number of contemporary accounts and has been the subject of recent reappraisals. It seems likely that Duhaut-Cilly had the story directly from Father Ripoll of Santa Barbara.

Such an example could have been harmful to the other missions, and yet one could not punish so many delinquents. The padres chose to use persuasion and kindness to bring them back. So they went to seek them in their retreat and, throwing all the blame on the soldiers and making a great show of pardoning, they persuaded them to return. The wrongs of both sides were forgiven, and life resumed its usual course, but the event revealed the inner feelings of the Indians.

Commerce in Alta California, because of the small population, is not important; it can exist only in relation to consumption. The principal and almost the only means of exchange are tallow and hides. These two articles are in lesser supply in Baja California, but since that province produces pearls, silver, and gold, the ability to buy is almost equal. The missionaries of Alta California sell only in order to maintain their establishments; few of them hoard riches. As a result their wealth in herds is increasing constantly, the slaughter being less than the multiplying. In 1827 the number of cattle on all these properties amounted to two hundred two thousand; since private parties owned from twenty-eight to thirty thousand, the total for the province was two hundred thirty thousand. The harvesting at that time was no more than forty thousand hides and could have been almost doubled without diminishing the base.

Each animal, when slaughtered at the right time of year, should furnish two or three arrobas of tallow (an arroba equals twenty-five Spanish pounds); but since not all are killed in the best season and since a part of the product is consumed in the country, the number of arrobas exported is about equal to the number of steer and cow hides.

The other articles of trade, after these two principal products, are hardly worth mentioning. I have already noted that the pelts of the Saricovian otter are now quite scarce and of inferior quality. There is little or no marketing of grains since the missionaries sow only for their own needs. The Russian establishments of the Northwest Coast were the only places that bought provisions of grain in California, and after the settlement at Ross began obtaining good wheat harvests, this branch of trade has almost disappeared.

The American traders, who for a long time have been exploiting the commercial resources of the country, have concerned themselves only with the two most important products. If the French were to send ships here they could also deal for horse hides and manes. These animals, whose numbers can hardly be reckoned, have sometimes become so much of a problem that it has been necessary to kill thousands of them without deriving any gain. During a ship's stay on the coast one could also and at little expense make gelatin, bouillon tablets, and bone black, but would the importation of these things into France be allowed? If deer and bear skins are of some value in Europe, it would not be difficult to procure them in California.

A resident of the pueblo of Los Angeles brought me one day some specimens of fossil alum, assuring me that he had collected them from a nearby mountain almost entirely composed of it. The pieces he gave me were quite transparent and extremely caustic.

There is no trade in sheep's wool; in the missions it is used to make coarse cloth for the Indians. Each of these establishments has its spinning wheels and looms, places of employment especially for the young people of both sexes.

I think it will be of interest to show in a table the annual production of the missions of Alta California, followed by a summary of their export trade (p. 171).[2]

From the second table (p. 172) it can be calculated that the exports of Alta California come to about twelve hundred tons, that is to say, the cargo of four ships of three hundred tons each. Or in other terms a value of one million spread over four import cargoes, which means for each the sum of 250,000 francs. And since one must count on an import duty of at least 40 percent, it follows that in no case should the value of a cargo for this country exceed 180,000 francs.

It is clear also that if more than four cargoes are sent there in a year's time, business will be bad for all of them. One hundred eighty thousand francs are hardly enough capital to support an expedition that requires a considerable time. Also, I would not advise anyone to limit his trading to Alta California; the operation must be extended to the

2. The two tables contain errors, but since it is not always possible to tell whether these are in the detail or in the totals, we leave the figures as Duhaut-Cilly's book has them.

Missions	Fanegas Wheat	Fanegas Barley	Fanegas Maize	Fanegas Beans	Live Cattle	Live Sheep
San Diego	5,400	2,740	640	111	11,760	9,000
San Luis Rey	4,000	3,600	7,000	360	24,950	21,507
San Juan Capistrano	1,600	56	1,280	76	1,700	4,500
San Gabriel	4,070	210	1,200	00	22,807	7,100
San Fernando	4,000	00	1,400	220	6,850	3,500
San Buenaventura	1,600	1,000	1,800	100	6,850	5,600
Santa Barbara	1,740	400	206	60	2,050	2,500
Santa Ynés	1,200	600	800	24	9,940	2,400
Purisima Concepcion	2,200	00	240	00	17,140	6,000
San Luis Obispo	1,120	00	00	60	12,000	5,000
San Miguel	2,400	24	124	12	7,000	11,024
San Antonio	2,710	420	180	88	10,420	9,000
Soledad	2,040	486	00	78	7,200	57,007
San Carlos	428	1,600	50	288	3,420	5,400
San Juan Bautista	4,740	1,134	750	10	10,830	9,300
Santa Cruz	2,636	742	1,950	1,044	5,140	6,000
Santa Clara	4,000	500	1,000	216	12,000	13,500
San José	5,000	300	80	80	15,420	15,000
San Francisco	1,008	206	90	22	4,290	4,366
San Rafael	2,600	1,400	385	80	1,540	3,000
San Francisco Solano	1,000	00	400	12	1,880	4,000
Fanegas	56,532	15,418	19,180	2,941	195,187	214,704
½ kilogr.	7,056,400	1,927,250	2,414,000	367,625		

Alta California

Steer and Cow Hides	40,000 at 2 piasters	80,000	
Tallow, arrobas	45,000 at 2 "	90,000	
Otter Skins	200 at 20 "	4,000	
Wheat, fanegas	3,500 at 1½ "	4,250	
Silver Coins in Circulation		22,000	
			196,000

Baja California

Hides	25,000 at 1¾ piasters	43,750	
Pure Silver		43,000	
Gold Dust and Bars		50,000	
Fine Pearls		25,000	
Tortoise Shell		5,200	
Cheese and Soap		10,000	163,950
Total Exports in fr. 1,799,750		piasters	359,950

entire peninsula as well as to the Mexican ports on the Vermilion Sea,[3] Guaymas, Mazatlán, and San Blas.

The soil of Alta California is eminently fertile, but the long dry summers are a great disadvantage to cultivation. From the month of March until October no rain falls. The streams stop flowing, the ground dries up, pastures turn yellow, herds suffer and grow thin. During this entire season, at least eight months of the year, the wind blows steadily from the northwest. It is quite strong from ten in the morning until eight at night; it then dies down, and is often followed by a light land breeze. At the port of San Francisco the northwest wind often continues all night, blowing in gusts, and during the day it is sometimes so strong that ships have trouble communicating with the land even in the cove of Yerba Buena, where they are anchored quite close to the shore. The farther one travels to the south the less strong is this northwest wind except, however, at Point Conception, where it always blows with great force.

---

3. The present-day Gulf of California or Sea of Cortés.

When leaving one of the ports and sailing directly away from the shore, one perceives that the wind, from the northwest or west-northwest at first, gradually veers to the north, and at forty or fifty leagues from the land it settles down and blows steadily from the northeast. It follows that a ship, tacking to the north from one port to another, must avoid long tacks to the open sea, which would entail much beating into the wind and lead one far from the intended goal. A course close to land is always the best; one must be wary of any route that leads out to sea.

In the winter it is often quite rainy, especially with winds from south to east, which scarcely ever blow without bringing storms; these are especially dangerous since all the open roadsteads of the coast are turned in that direction and offer no defense against the wind's fury. It was this wind that made us abandon so precipitately the anchorage at Santa Cruz; it almost brought on our destruction at San Pedro; and it also, on an occasion I have not yet mentioned, caused us to pass an anxious night in the roadstead at Santa Barbara.

When it does not rain in the winter, the entire country is enveloped in a dense and almost permanent fog. The weather is cold and damp, but it does not freeze even in San Francisco. The Réamur thermometer hardly ever goes below 7°. The high mountains are sometimes white with snow, but it does not fall in the plain. The inhabitants suffer the more from cold as their houses are not well sealed and have no fireplaces; they are forced to wrap themselves in cloaks and woolen blankets.

By the time winter is half over the country takes on a new life: the rivers swell and go over their banks; springs burst out everywhere; streams reappear; the ground is moist; hills and pastures are covered with a thick and lush growth of grass; and by March the land exhibits freshness and plenty.

The seasons in Baja California are almost the opposite of what I have described. Forty leagues south of San Diego there is established a kind of equilibrium. The peninsula's fine season begins in November and lasts until June. During this period of about eight months the weather is magnificent; when it is calm, the heat is oppressive, but almost always there is an even and moderate wind from the north that cools and purifies the air while taking away its humidity.

During that time the poorest roadsteads provide security for navigation: the sky, of the utmost purity, brings neither clouds nor storms. This state of things extends along the entire west coast of Mexico, making it generally healthful, but the change of seasons comes earlier in the southern parts. For example, along the coast of Sonora toward the ports of Guaymas and Mazatlán it is still safe at the beginning of June, while in the region of Acapulco and to the south the change comes by the 1st of May.

During this ominous season the sky is covered with thick and stormy clouds, the wind varies and blows often from the south. Soon deluges of rain pour down on all this coast, battered by frightful hurricanes. Night and day the atmosphere is kindled by the fire and flash of lightning and the air reverberates with the almost unbroken sound of thunder. If by chance the sun comes out, its humid and stifling heat makes one regret the darkness. Deathly illnesses, putrid and burning fevers are spread along all this littoral of Mexico, which truly becomes uninhabitable. In several places the people betake themselves to the interior, where the higher and drier ground protects them at least from floods. The residents of San Blas spend this frightful season in Tepic.

Not only do the navigators run great danger who insist on remaining in this chaos of the elements but they can do little or no business; commerce ceases in almost all places. It is of the greatest importance, then, for those who intend to trade on this coast to calculate their time in such a way that they arrive no sooner than November in the southern ports and in December for those of San Blas, Mazatlán, Guaymas, and Baja California. To avoid the rigors of this winter season one must be at least two hundred leagues from the land; within that line one struggles against all sorts of difficulties, as we learned in sailing from Salango to San José del Cabo in October 1826.[4]

After this long digression on California, a digression that is part of my planned narration, I resume the voyage to Peru, on which I will

4. Salango is a small bay in northern Peru. In sailing north from there in 1826 the *Héros* went through almost continuous storms.

have few observations to make, that country having been perfectly described by Captain Hall in its political and commercial aspects, the only ones that I could have examined. This excellent observer, who is also a historian, has left nothing to be desired on this score. His navigational remarks on the seasons of the west coast of Mexico are no less judicious; I have had the opportunity to check their accuracy. If, in recording my own observations, I appear to be borrowing his, the coincidence derives from a conscientious description of the same conditions.[5]

A crossing from California to Lima cannot be done quickly. The indirect route that one must follow nearly doubles the distance, and the opposing winds that must be contended with for more than half the way are the other causes of the inherent length of the voyage.

Driven at first by a favorable wind from the northeast, some captains may be tempted to take a more direct route, passing between the Galápagos Islands and the coast of Colombia; this mistake would add to the difficulties instead of diminishing them. Before reaching the equinoctial line they would begin to encounter southeast winds and strong currents bearing to the north, which together would render the rest of the crossing tiresome and almost interminable.

The most suitable route is also the simplest: to cross the equator at 110° of west longitude, leaving the Galápagos group to the east. We took this course and found it good. As in the Atlantic we had some difficulty in passing the line. A small wind from the south and a current bearing to the north held us in those waters for almost a week, but after that we went along rapidly to the south, crossing the Pacific with a fine easterly breeze and good weather. At 27° latitude south and 101° longitude west the wind changed to the southeast, allowing us to tack about for Lima, where we arrived on 26 December 1827 after a passage of sixty-seven days with no unusual happenings.

We remained two months in the port of Callao, waiting to sell and collect for the cargo of tallow, which sold less well than expected. It

5. Basil Hall, *Extracts from a Journal, Written on the Coasts of Chile, Peru, and Mexico, in the Years 1820, 1821, 1822.* 2nd ed., 2 v., Edinburgh, 1824. The translator has examined this edition.

also suffered a considerable loss in weight from leakage caused by the equatorial heat that made it melt and run out the seams of the surons that held it and through holes made by insects during the voyage.

Lima, at the time I arrived, was far from presenting a happy or brilliant aspect. The revolution that had recently overthrown the constitution given to Peru by Bolívar . . . had at the same time thrown open the door to other ambitions. . . . The uncertain and unsettled state of the republic, spreading unease and fear everywhere, paralyzed a commerce that was already reduced to a state of constraint by the shortage of money and an accumulation of merchandise.[6]

The inertia of the government brought on another affliction; all the roads leading into Lima were infested with bandits, so that one might have said that the capital was under siege. No day passed without word of some assault of this kind. When business affairs obliged a man to take the road to Callao, he could give thanks to heaven if he were not plundered on the way, for this stretch of two leagues, nearly always filled with travelers, was not safe even in midday. It appeared that the weak patrols assigned to this road took care to avoid coming face to face with the evildoers. If by chance they arrested some suspect and took him to prison, he was released the next day and thus returned to his banditry with all the insolence of impunity. When someone had a large sum to transport to the harbor, he obtained, for a fee, a police escort, but this merited so little confidence that he found it wise to gather several well-armed friends, more to watch over the escort than to assist it.

On 28 February I took myself to Callao, and on the same day, at three o'clock in the afternoon, we got under sail to return to Monterey. On the way I had intended to drop anchor in the pretty little bay of Salango to obtain some building timbers for which we had several uses, but when we came near this place the weather was stormy, with squalls from the north, and I gave up the project. These conditions may have been temporary, but at the time it would have been imprudent, for a purpose of no great importance, to enter a bay where

---

6. From this passage we have omitted three paragraphs about Peruvian politics.

the anchorage, as I have noted, is so close to the shore that a ship can hardly avoid running aground with gusts from the open sea.

We passed once more between the archipelago of the Galápagos and the coast and from there, steering more to the west than on our first trip, we crossed the equator for the fourth time and continued our way in quite good weather and with a fine breeze from the northeast.

During this monotonous crossing our only distraction was provided by a huge number of birds. The most numerous ones and those coming closest to the ship were the boobies, ring-tails, and frigate birds. We often amused ourselves by shooting at them when they flew over the ship, aiming to make them fall on board. This was difficult to achieve; it was necessary to calculate the strength and direction of the wind and relate these two factors to the position of the bird at the moment of firing. If these factors could be combined for success, it was also necessary to kill the creature outright. If it retained the least breath of life it would use this to direct its fall so as to land in the water.

One morning in calm weather, when a number of frigate birds were wheeling above the ship in what appeared to be magic circles in the air, one of them alighted on the truck of the main masthead and there looked the perfect picture of the weathercock on a village steeple. While the others with their cries, or rather their croakings, seemed to upbraid him for the post he had assumed, a gunshot rang out and he fell dead at the feet of the officer of the watch. None of his envious companions judged it wise to accept the heritage of this dangerous throne, from which he had been cast down by a thunderbolt in punishment for his pride. This bird had a wingspan of six and a half feet.

On 6 April we found ourselves within view of a small island shown on the English map of Norie with the name of Clouds Island.[7] We came no closer than five leagues, and at that distance we could not, even with the telescope, examine it in detail. As it showed itself to us, that is from east-southeast to west-northwest, it appeared to be one league in length. Even had we come closer it would still have ap-

7. John William Norie (1772–1843), who published *Epitome of Practical Navigation* (1805) as well as charts and sailing directions for several parts of the world.

peared, I think, only a naked and sterile rock, a retreat for sea birds and sea lions. However that may be, in such cases one regrets not being able to spare a day to explore such a savage place, where nature, perhaps in horror, chooses to exhibit a kind of primal virginity that travelers seldom have occasion to experience, since the sea is furrowed in all directions by so many ships.

We were becalmed for two days in sight of this island; the weather was fine, the sky clear, the sea tranquil. As if to assuage our regret at not being able to explore the island, we decided to profit from the favorable conditions to verify, insofar as we were able, its longitude. With ten series of distances from the moon to the sun, we obtained a longitude of 116° 25′ 42′ west of the meridian of Paris. On the English chart it was placed at 117° 3′ west of the same meridian.[8]

The rest of the crossing provided nothing of interest. We made land at Point Conception and from there, with a strong northwesterly breeze, tacked our way to Monterey, where we dropped anchor on 3 May 1828 after a passage of sixty-four days.

8. The original book contains two tables not reproduced here: one listing the ten observations made from the ship and the other showing how these were used to calculate the longitude of the islet. The latitude is not provided.

Chapter 18

THE RUSSIANS AT ROSS. EXPULSION OF
THE SPANIARDS FROM CALIFORNIA

May–July 1828

ON ARRIVAL IN MONTEREY I was hoping to find Mr. R____ returned from the Northwest Coast. Not only was this hope dashed, but I learned on the contrary that instead of undertaking this voyage as agreed with me, he had changed directions and gone with the *Waverly* and the cargo to the coast of Mexico. I will not go into particulars about this unhappy affair, which can be of no interest to the reader. I shall say only, once and for all, that, having waited in vain for his return beyond the time set in a letter I found in Monterey, I was obliged by the conduct of this man to abandon him, while holding him responsible for the value of the goods he had taken with him. I took back on board the people that I had left in charge of the warehouse and the small quantity of merchandise still there. I then resolved, while waiting out the time set by Mr. R____, to visit the entire coast one more time in order to sell the rest of the cargo. To improve these prospects I decided also to visit the Russian establishment of Bodega, situated on the same coast at some distance northwest of San Francisco. On 30 May we left Monterey to go there, still quite poorly informed about the location of this settlement.

On 2 June toward evening we found ourselves a few leagues from land on that part of the coast where I supposed the Russian colony to be, and in fact we discerned with the telescope something that re-sembled a group of houses. At sunset we lay closer. Convinced now that we were not mistaken, I ran up the flag and shot off a cannon. Al-most at once a puff of white smoke told us that they were responding in the same way, and we could make out a Russian flag. But since it was too late for a landing before nightfall, we shortened sail and main-tained our position until the following day.

On the morning of the 3rd, as we were lying to at a distance of sev-eral miles, examining the coast without discerning any opening or re-cess that might indicate a harbor, we suddenly noticed three baidarkas coming toward us, each carrying three persons. Several minutes later these boats arrived alongside, and we were paid a visit by the Russian commandant himself, Paul Shelekhov, to whom I communicated my reasons for coming there. At the same time I requested permission to anchor in his harbor in order to display those things in the cargo that might suit him. Although he was not in need of much and was rather short of trading goods, he welcomed my proposal and, ordering one of his men to serve us as pilot, he said he would accompany me to the port of Bodega, the only anchorage in use by the colony. He sent two of the boats back to shore and asked me to have the other hoisted on board, after which we took our way parallel to the coast.[1]

From where we had been lying to the settlement had quite a differ-ent look from that of the presidios of California, models of rude de-sign and indifferent execution. Houses of elegant shape with roofs well constructed, fields well planted and surrounded by palisades gave this place an appearance that was quite European.

After fifteen miles we reached a small peninsula that sheltered the roadstead of Bodega. Three hundred cables to the east of this point there is a small, flat island where we could see some greenery. The sea was breaking violently on the rocky peninsula [Bodega Head] and against a cliff on its east-southeast side. Our Russian pilot had us pass in mid-channel between the island and the peninsula with a depth of

1. Pavel Ivanovich Shelekhov was the hospitable manager of the Russian colony from 1825 to 1829. Where fertile land was limited, he is credited with having cultivated every avail-able spot.

four to five fathoms, and we soon anchored inside in the middle of a sort of bay surrounded by land from south to east-by-north, that is to say on three-quarters of the horizon.

Toward evening Commandant Shelekhov returned to shore where horses had been brought for him, having made me promise to visit him the next day.

On the morning of the 4th, remarking the horses he had sent for us, I went on shore with Dr. Botta and our pilot. The landing place is in a small harbor at the mouth of a saltwater lagoon, sheltered from all winds. Ships drawing little water could find haven there. There they have built some fine wooden storehouses for use by the Russian ships.

Mounting our horses we began the journey, accompanied by several Russians and by our pilot; after having performed skillfully his nautical functions on the previous day, he steered us equally well over a different element, bearing now the modest title of guide. Having crossed the isthmus of the peninsula, we rode for a league along a fine sandy beach and then ascended a cliff of moderate height. After that we took our way over an esplanade carpeted with grass mixed with strawberry plants bearing fruit and ensplendored with a multitude of flowers of every color. The sea was breaking at the base of the cliff, its snow-white foam contrasting with the dark color of the rocks and the rich green of the fields, which our horses trod with no more sound than if they had been stepping on eiderdown. Two leagues along this plain brought us to the bank of a considerable river, called Sacabaya by the Indians and Slavianka by the Russians. It was too deep even in the summertime to be forded, and in winter it becomes fearsome, swiftly carrying off immense tree trunks uprooted by storms. The retreating water had left some huge ones on both banks.[2]

The crossing has been disastrous for many travelers; two years before this an American captain was drowned here. As for us, we passed over safely enough in a baidarka that Mr. Shelekhov had sent for the purpose. Since this boat, made of sealskin, held only two persons, it

2. The river was called Slavianka, or Slav Woman, by the Russian colonists according to Otto von Kotzebue, who visited in 1824, and it was known to others from the 1840s as the Río Ruso, or Russian River, its present name. Kotzebue spells the Indian name *Shabaikai*.

was necessary to make a trip for each one of us. Conducted skillfully by a Kodiak Islander, it had more than one point of resemblance to the bark of old Charon. Its lightness and instability could make one think that it was meant only for the transporting of shades, and the guttural grunting of the Kodiak when he pointed out the person who was to enter the baidarka with him must have sounded like the hoarse voice of the pitiless boatman of Hades, scolding souls on the banks of the Styx.

One had to exercise great care in sliding oneself into a round hole up to the middle of the body, when the slightest movement to right or left was enough to make the light craft tip in a disquieting way. Nevertheless, I had no wish to sit idly while we crossed, and in my capacity of seaman I seized a paddle and wielded it in a way to satisfy the old pilot of the Slavianka. It is in these cockle boats of skin that the natives of the Aleutian Islands, braving the high seas, hunt the Saricovian otter [sea otter] and do battle with the most monstrous whales, whose flesh and oil are their favorite food and drink.

In this dangerous hunt they rely more on skill than on strength. When they have decided to attack a whale they gather together several hundred baidarkas to pursue the monster. They manage to stay always close to it, and each time it has to come to the surface to breathe they immediately pierce it with a great flock of small harpoons, to each of which is attached an inflated bladder. The attack continues until the whale, bristling with harpoons, can no longer overcome the combined resistance of so many bladders. It must then fight on the surface without being able to dive, and they finish it off with longer and stouter lances. They also employ harpoons to hunt the sea otter, but need only one to take that animal.

Our horses were accustomed to the passage of the river and they swam across by themselves as soon as they were relieved of their saddles. Starting out once more we ascended by so steep a road that we found it hard to believe that the horses could avoid falling back on their riders.

The mountain whose summit we reached, not without difficulty and even some danger, was covered with enormous conifers, mixed

9. Aleutian sea otter canoe, or baidarka.

with sycamores, bay trees, and several species of oaks. At a height of two thousand feet we looked out over the sea, which was beating against the land below; the waves, silent at this distance, looked like small whitish patches scattered over a cloth of azure.

We descended the far side by a slope as steep as the first one, and at every opening we could see through the trees or over their tops and more and more distinctly the Russian establishment, lying below us and on the northwest side of the mountain. Fearing that our horses, after a journey of four leagues, would not be able to carry us over both dangerous slopes, Mr. Shelekhov had had the foresight to post fresh ones at the high point.

At eleven in the morning we arrived at the colony called Ross by the Russians. It is a large square enclosure surrounded by a thick wooden palisade twenty feet high, strongly constructed and topped with iron spikes of proportionate size and weight. At the northeast and south-west angles are two hexagonal towers pierced with ports and loop-holes. On the four sides, which correspond to the cardinal points, are four gates, each defended by a carronade of fixed breeching set in a port as on a ship. Within there were also two bronze field pieces with caissons. A handsome house for the commandant or governor, pleas-ant lodgings for the subalterns, large storehouses, and workshops oc-cupy the square. A newly constructed chapel serves as a bastion in the southeast corner. This citadel is built near the edge of the cliff on an esplanade about two hundred feet above the sea. On the left and right are ravines that protect it from attacks by the Indians from the north and south while the cliff itself and the sea shield it from the west. The ravines open onto two small coves which serve as shelter and landing place for the small boats of the colony.

All the buildings at Ross are of wood but well built and well main-tained. In the apartment of the governor are found all the conve-niences valued by Europeans but still unknown in California. Outside the compound are lined up or scattered the pretty little houses of sixty Russian colonists, the flat huts of eighty Kodiaks, and the conical huts of as many native Indians.

East of the settlement the land rises gradually to great heights cov-ered with thick forests that block the wind from the north to the southeast. All these slopes are partitioned into fields of wheat, beans, oats, potatoes, and the like, fenced off to protect the crops not from thieves but from farm animals and wild beasts.

In spite of its military appearance the colony is a commercial establishment owned, along with those of Sitka and Kodiak Island, by a company of merchants. It appears, however, that the emperor has granted it great privileges, and that many in the Russian court own an interest, large or small. The governors have military rank, and the ships of the company fly the national flag and are commanded by officers of the imperial navy.[3]

There appears to be great order and discipline at Ross, and although the governor is the only officer, one notes everywhere the signs of close supervision. After being busy all day in their various occupations, the colonists, who are both workers and soldiers, mount guard during the night. On holidays they pass in review and drill with cannon and musket.

Although this colony, in existence for fifteen years, appears to lack nothing, it cannot be of great account to the company that founded it. As the principal source of revenue they counted on the hunt for sea otters and seals. The first of these is nearly exhausted and no longer provides anything; as for the second, the governor keeps about a hundred Kodiaks on the Farallons throughout the year, as I have said elsewhere, but that hunt, once quite productive, declines with every passing day and in a few more years will amount to nothing. Looking on these products as now secondary, the governor has for several years concerned himself primarily with husbandry. Not only does he grow the wheat and vegetables that were once obtained from California, but he also provisions the larger colony of Sitka. With only six hundred cows he was producing more butter and cheese than all of Alta California with its countless herds.

---

3. Ross was established north of San Francisco in 1812 as a supply depot for the base at Sitka and a potential beachhead for future expansion. Unable alone to satisfy northern needs, the Russians promoted trade with California, which, although illicit, was carried on to the mutual benefit of both parties. The nearest port, except for small craft, was at Bodega Bay eighteen miles to the south.

In spite of all these advantages the colony of Ross inspires in the traveler's mind only somber and melancholy thoughts. The reason, I believe, is that this society is incomplete. The governor is a bachelor and has no woman in his house; all the Russian colonists live in the same state. In this establishment there are only the women of the Kodiaks and those of the Indians. No matter what relations may exist between them and the Russians, the visitor, to whom these women are objects of disgust, cannot help regarding this little community as deprived of that sex whose sole presence makes life bearable. The tasks that usually fall to women are here the portion of men, and this difference shocks the eye, weighs on the heart, and causes a pain that one feels in spite of oneself and before discovering the true reason for it.

We went with Mr. Shelekhov to view his timber production. In addition to the needs of his own settlement he cuts a great quantity of planks, beams, timbers, and the like, which he sells in California, in the Sandwich Islands, and elsewhere; he even builds entire houses and ships them disassembled. The trees felled are almost all conifers of several kinds and especially the one called *palo colorado* (redwood). The only virtues of this tree are that it is quite straight and splits easily; for the rest, it has little resin and is very brittle. It is the largest tree that I have ever seen. Mr. Shelekhov showed me the trunk of one that had been felled recently; it was twenty feet in diameter measured two feet from the ground and from one burl or buttress to the other; the main trunk was more than thirteen feet in width. I measured two hundred and thirty feet from the stump to the crown, lying where it had been parted from the bole. Imagine what a huge quantity of boards can be obtained from a tree of this size. The stacks of them from one such covered a considerable stretch of ground. Not all the palos colorados are this prodigious, but one can see many that three men would have difficulty stretching their arms around and that would make, as a single piece, the lower masts of our largest ships of war.

Mr. Shelekhov treated us with the most refined hospitality, and we passed a comfortable night with him. Unfortunately neither Dr. Botta nor I understood Russian, and the governor spoke neither French nor English nor Spanish. This inconvenience caused us to miss much of the charm that his company should have provided. It was in Spanish that we made ourselves understood best. I did only a little business with him; an American ship had preceded me here and had taken nearly all the pelts possessed by the establishment. I sold him only the value of a few hundred sealskins. Arising early the next day I positioned myself on a hillside to the east and sketched the citadel, as shown in the plate that accompanies this volume. After breakfast we mounted our horses to return to the port, from where we set sail the next morning.

During the three days that we remained in the bay at Bodega the wind blew fresh from the northwest, and although the ship was sheltered and the waters there were calm we broke our best bower cable. This was the second such accident to it; on our return from Peru to Monterey it had broken in a strong northwest breeze. At that place we found a smith who was skillful enough to repair it and who also changed seven links that were unsafe. This iron cable had been in excellent condition on our departure from Le Hâvre, and during two years of use we had on numerous occasions remarked its strength. But after having held in big winds and heavy seas it now failed us under quite ordinary circumstances. We must not believe, then, that chains are everlasting; they wear out like everything else.

The accident led me to discern two principal causes for the deterioration of cables like this one. The first arises from the rust that, beyond a certain point, cannot be avoided and is constantly acting upon iron. Finding it desirable to measure the thickness of this cable, I noted that in two years its diameter had decreased by a line and a half without the links having changed shape.[4] This examination led me to discover the other factor that shortens the life of chains. I noticed that those links that had been in the water were riddled with small holes like worm holes and that were often a line deep. The end that always remained on board and the one that customarily rested on the bottom had not suffered this change, which appeared to have affected only the middle part. After long reflection on this singular fact, I was persuaded that it came about either from the action of copper on iron, an action that is well attested and has made it necessary to use copper nails and rivets on vessels sheathed with this metal, or from the

4. The line, or ligne, a French measure, equals 2.26 mm, between 1/11 and 1/12 of an inch.

10. View of the Russian establishment at Bodega (Ross) on the coast of New Albion in 1828. By Auguste Duhaut-Cilly.

galvanic effect of contact between these two materials. When a vessel is anchored on chains one of them is almost sure to touch the sheathing or come quite close to it, and this is not the only way in which contact may take place. It is at these times that the iron of the chain is exposed to the corrosive power of copper oxide, which acts all the more rapidly when the contact takes place in the water.

I leave to those better versed in chemical science than I am to judge the value of these observations. But if their truth be recognized, a way of partially avoiding the trouble would be to leave quite slack the cable that is not holding and in such a way that, falling vertically to the bottom, it remains as far as possible from the hull of the ship. Another method, used up to now for a different reason, may accomplish the purpose more effectively; that is to have the two anchors clinched to the two ends of the same cable, stretched out along the bottom; a second and quite short cable meets the first at the spot judged most suitable and is attached to it by a swivel ring in such a way that the ship, while fully moored, appears to be on only one anchor. It can be seen, in this way, that the cables will never come close to the sheathing.

The day after our departure from Bodega we dropped anchor at Monterey. There we remained only long enough to collect some funds owed to our business, and we left again on 14 June for Santa Barbara. Since it was now summer and the offshore winds were not to be feared, we moored three cable lengths from the beach in six fathoms and in the kelp bed. My purpose in coming to this presidio was to take on the powder and guns that Mr. R____ deposited there and to continue disposing of the remaining cargo.

I learned on arriving that the superior of the mission, Antonio Ripoll, perhaps anticipating disasters to come and unhappy with his situation, quite different from what it had been at first, had escaped with Padre Altimira. They had made their plans together with great secrecy and embarked on the American brig *Harbinger,* which was returning to the United States.[5]

5. The *Harbinger,* a brig of 180 tons, Joseph Steele master, was on the coast from 1826 to 1828. Although the governor ordered its seizure, it did not enter another California port.

This event explained why, on my preceding stay, Fray Antonio, knowing that I was the bearer of a draft for seven thousand francs on the English government, had begged me earnestly to let him have it in return for piasters, an offer that I accepted. Doubtless he already had in mind a plan to leave California. In buying this letter of credit he declared that the money belonged to him, deriving from the yearly stipend of four hundred piasters allotted to each missionary by the Spanish government. I had too high an opinion of this friar to believe it otherwise, and when some persons told me that in leaving he had carried off huge sums, I put no credence in this derogatory claim. Padre Ripoll had been replaced by a young Mexican trained to less strict standards, politically speaking, than the Spanish Franciscans.[6]

On the 24th they celebrated with great pomp the festival of Saint John. All residents of the presidio and strangers were invited to dine at the mission. After the repast the entertainment began with the obligatory bullfights, and at the end of two hours of this cruel and barbarous sport the Indians devoted themselves to happier and less dangerous games.

In the middle of the square a greased pole had been set up and loaded at the top with articles of clothing and pieces of fabric. We were amused for quite a time by the vain efforts of the first who tried to climb it; finally, after the pole had been scraped and treated with ashes and dust, the prizes were attained by an Indian from Baja California, endowed with a quickness of which he gave proof several times that afternoon. He took part in and won several kinds of races, and it was in vain that the best runners of the mission leagued themselves against him. He was a young man of twenty-two, perfectly formed; although he did not appear robust, the several parts of his body left nothing to be desired for harmony of proportion or beauty of form. He ran with a thin piece of cloth about his loins, so that nothing hid from view the strength and grace of his movements.

6. Ripoll's successor was Padre Juan Moreno who, although a Spaniard, became a Franciscan in Mexico and came to California in 1827 when twenty-eight years of age. First at Mission San Carlos, he arrived in Santa Barbara on 26 January 1828, three days after Ripoll's departure.

Profiting from the occasion, the padre distributed gifts to his Indians, and they all ran to win these prizes; women and children, old men and young girls, all demonstrated their agility, each according to his age and ability. Those whom age had weakened displayed the strength still left to them, and those whose powers were not yet developed gave proof of what time would someday grant to them.

After the races came the Indian dances, which pleased us greatly. As I have said elsewhere these exercises are a kind of pantomime accompanied by monotonous and melancholy songs in perfect time. The grotesque costumes of the dancers, decked in feathers and painted in all sorts of colors, lend to their features so wild a look and so strange a character that one is tempted to think they are rousing themselves to battle rather than to pleasure.

On the next day, having nothing further to do in Santa Barbara, we raised the anchor and twenty-four hours later dropped it in the bay of San Pedro. On the 27th some men and horses appeared upon the cliff; I went on shore and made my way to the pueblo of Los Angeles and to Mission San Gabriel.

With Padre Sánchez I found the president of the Dominican missions of Baja California, a priest named Luna, who was visiting there along with Fray Félix Caballero, one of his colleagues;[7] two other Franciscans were there also. It appeared that this convocation of friars had been called expressly to hear read the famous decree of expulsion of the Spaniards, which had arrived from Mexico.[8]

This decree, drawn up in a great number of articles, required all Spaniards, with very few exceptions and regardless of rank or condition, to leave the territory of the republic within the short time of one month.[9] The reader may imagine the effect that this had to produce

7. Padre Domingo Luna was president and vicar forane of the Dominican missions, and Padre Félix Caballero was his secretary.

8. After the separation of Mexico from Spain in 1821 and its establishment as an independent republic, California became a territory of Mexico under the constitution of 1824. California citizens of all classes were required to take an oath of allegiance to the Mexican constitution. A federal decree banning Spaniards from Mexican lands was issued 20 December 1827 and arrived in California the following year.

9. The decree exempted Spaniards who were disabled, those older than sixty, and those

on the persons I have just spoken of; nevertheless, this was not the same for the Franciscans as for the Dominicans. The first uttered loud cries against the law and called the Mexican government base and tyrannical; in the first stage of their righteous discontent they proposed that I take them to Manila in the *Héros*. But the others, the Dominicans, raised and nourished under different principles, were seeking to find among the clauses of the decree some word that might save them from the general proscription. Padre Luna, born in Mexico, was exempt from the law, and while gently associating himself with the indignation of the Franciscans, it is possible that he was not unhappy with the misfortune that had befallen those whose conduct condemned his own. He sought to comfort Fray Félix, counseling him that he might, by a frank acceptance of republican principles, be spared by the government.[10]

I myself deplored the sad fate that awaited the Spaniards in Mexico, for it was easy enough to discern in the derogatory words of the decree the animosity that had inspired it as well as the personal interest of these patriots. The congress general, in adopting the law, had granted to the executive the power to extend to six months the time limit for departure, but the president of the republic, acting with unprecedented severity, had ordered it fixed at one month only. How was it possible in such a short time for these unfortunate people to settle their affairs and take ship? There could not even have been enough ships for so many passengers. Not only was their ruin certain, but it was much to be feared that, when they gathered in too great numbers in the ports and found no immediate means of transport, they might fall victim to local mobs stirred up by their mortal enemies, the Yorkinos.[11]

---

married to Mexican wives or with children who were not Spaniards. A second and more stringent decree, dated 20 March 1828, ordered immediate expulsion of all Spaniards except the physically disabled and sons of American-born parents. In California the chief application of both decrees was to those Spanish friars who did not take an oath to the Mexican constitution.

10. Most padres were Spanish and had sworn allegiance to Spain. Some did not mind taking an oath to Mexico as well; others refused and either escaped to Spain or were expelled. A few who refused were allowed to remain in order to ensure the continued cooperation of the Indian workers, who disliked the Mexicans.

11. For the Yorkinos see Chapter 11, note 11.

For a time I thought seriously of taking to Manila those missionaries who might want to leave as well as the few private individuals established in California and affected by the proscription. But although the decree was as explicit for the friars as for the others, it seemed unlikely that the commandant-general would let them leave before others had arrived to replace them, convinced as he must have been that if the missions were left to the mercies of the Indians they would soon be pillaged and destroyed.[12]

The Indians are certainly not capable of much reasoning, but they are not unaware that, according to the conditions under which they were made Christians, the missions belong to them; and they need little discernment to see that the government looks on these properties as belonging to the state. If from regard and respect for the padres, they remain submissive to them, this would no longer be the same if they had to work for the Mexicans, whom they hate. But on the off chance I wrote to the *padre prefecto* in Monterey to inform him of my disposition and of the conditions of passage if his wishes and his circumstances might lend themselves to the project.[13]

After doing some business with the padres and with the residents of the pueblo, I returned to the harbor. On the next day, 3 July, as we began to haul in the cable to raise the anchor, we saw coming into the anchorage an American ship that I recognized as the *Courier,* Captain Cunningham.[14] I let the cable run out again, thinking to sell him several hundred hides that I had taken in trade. As soon as his ship was moored I went on board and concluded the deal. The hides were quickly transferred, and we then set sail for San Diego, where we arrived on the following day.

12. A few years later it was the Mexican government and civilians who did the pillaging.

13. The *comisario prefecto* at Monterey was Vicente Francisco de Sarría. For a discussion of Sarría's troubles with the government, see Chapter 9.

14. William H. Cunningham, master of the *Courier* from 1826 to 1828, was like Duhaut-Cilly one of the active traders on the coast, spending much time on the shore and visiting all the ports. The California part of his log was published as *Log of the Courier 1826–1827–1828* (Los Angeles: Glen Dawson, 1958). It contains little about his experiences on shore.

Chapter 19

―――――――――・―――――――――

THE AFFAIR OF THE 'FRANKLIN'.
FIRST DAYS IN THE SANDWICH ISLANDS

July – September 1828

THE LONGER A MAN IS OUT of his own country, the more he feels the need of support. To a Parisian, then, every Parisian is a relative; to a Frenchman all Frenchmen are friends; to a European, any European is a compatriot, a fellow citizen. And a sailor extends even further this community of feeling. Any man whose name is inscribed on the muster roll of a ship is a child of the same great family, almost a brother. The sailor greets him, defends him, makes sacrifices for him, and, above all, will consider it shameful to be made use of in any way that might harm a man of his own craft. The reader will find in this chapter a manifestation of this solidarity that united the entire crew of the *Héros*.

Entering the port of San Diego, we anchored in the same place we always had, but at once and without being given any reason for a change, I was ordered to move farther in. I had noticed, however, that three American vessels were lined up as in an echelon along the whole length of the channel; farthest in was the three-masted *Franklin*, anchored five miles from us; in the middle was the schooner-brig *Clio*, and nearest us the brig *Andes*.

Only a few minutes after we had dropped anchor, an officer named Ramírez appeared on shore and called for us to send a boat; this I sent manned by four seamen, but they returned without him, reporting that he insisted on the presence of an officer. Suspecting a misunderstanding, I myself went on shore and asked him why he had not come in the boat. "I judged it not fitting," said he. "You should have sent an officer to receive me." This pretentious and unreasonable demand set me greatly against him. "The boat I sent you," I responded, "and which I have just come in, should be quite sufficient for the messenger of a government that does not have even a canoe at its disposal. Such vanity does not please me; if you have orders to take my declaration you may embark with me, but there will be no officer to accompany your return to land. You now have the privilege of choosing what you should do."

Seeing how I meant to deal with him, he made some awkward excuses for his conduct, claiming that he had been badly treated by some other captains. He finally decided to come on board, and after he had accomplished his mission I sent him back to shore with no other retinue than the boatmen. I was all the more uncompromising with this republican, knowing that he enjoyed a bad reputation, having recently been accused of murder. I was not displeased to find occasion to show my small respect for him.[1]

When I went to the presidio next day, the commandant-general, after some moments of conversation, asked whether I could sell him a boat.[2] The port had none, he said, and could not do without one. My dressing-down of Ramírez on the day before, I told myself, had been the chief stimulus for this request, which came conveniently enough since I had on board the materials for construction of a twenty-four-foot boat and was intending to have it made during our stay in San Diego. I therefore acceded to his wish, and we quickly agreed on a price for the boat in the condition it was in. If I mention a fact of so little importance at first glance, this is because it was the occasion, a few days later, of some genuine regret.

1. Alférez José María Ramírez, a cavalry officer, probably came to California with Governor Echeandía in 1825. In a personal quarrel in September 1827 he had indeed killed Vicente Gómez, a convict and assassin who had been exiled to California.

2. Governor Echeandía, although a lieutenant-colonel of engineers, was the commanding general of California. See Chapter 10, note 11.

In San Pedro I had been informed that the American ship *Franklin,* Captain Bradshaw, was suspected of smuggling in the Gulf of Cortés and now found herself under a kind of arrest in San Diego. That is to say, the commandant-general would not permit her to continue trading in California except under quite awkward conditions. Among other things, Captain Bradshaw found himself required to deposit in the government storehouses a quantity of merchandise valued at 13,000 piasters (65,000 francs) as surety for the duties that he would need to pay in the future.[3]

Nevertheless it appears that an agreement was about to be reached when a vagrant named William Simpson—of the same nationality, I regret to say, as the cruel mayordomo of Santa Barbara—whom Captain Bradshaw had kindly welcomed on board his ship, feeding and clothing him, went before the general and declared under oath that the *Franklin* had defrauded the government of duties at Loreto and San José del Cabo. In this accusation he made many statements, true or false, that greatly compromised the captain.

That is where matters stood when we arrived in San Diego, but I had not known about that last incident when the general purchased the boat in question. When I learned that they intended placing a garrison on board the *Franklin* and were taking precautions to prevent her leaving the harbor, I felt at once how unfortunate it was that I had made a deal that might do harm to Captain Bradshaw by providing the general with the means of transporting troops to the ship. On that very night I went on board the *Franklin* and described my situation to the captain, promising to do everything possible to delay delivery of the boat.

The affair went from bad to worse, and the discussions grew so heated that they tried to seize the captain and threatened to fire on him when he withdrew in his boat. Finally, when the general asserted that he must unload all his cargo, he resolved to leave the port come what may. During the night of 10 July the *Franklin* changed its an-

---

3. John Bradshaw, a well-known Boston trader, was on the coast in 1827 and 1828 as master of the *Franklin,* a ship of 300 tons. His is one of several documented cases of smuggling in the record.

chorage, moving to a place near us and ready to sail. This put the presidio into an uproar.

On the morning of the 11th a troop of horsemen appeared opposite the *Héros* and came to a halt before the tent where our carpenters were working. My men at once raised the signal agreed upon to call for me. Going to the shore, I found the general himself surrounded by his staff of officers. He informed me that he wished me to deliver the boat I had sold him and of which he had the most urgent need, but without telling me what he needed it for. Prepared for this request, I responded that I considered the boat of no present use to him because I did not think I could furnish it with oars.

"Try to find some," he said. "You will render me a notable service."

In order not to arouse his suspicions, I promised to look for some, but in my heart of hearts I was resolved not to find any until after the *Franklin* had departed.

At the moment when I was about to return to the ship an aide-de-camp drew me aside and tried to obtain from me one of the boats we had on board in order, he said, to deliver a letter to the *Franklin*. This attempt, whose true purpose was clear enough, was also of no avail.

"Say to the general," I told him, "that considering the situation of that ship, I cannot, without compromising myself with my own government and with that of the United States, grant his request. If the general wishes to use force, he may, on his own responsibility, take possession of my boats when they come to shore, but I will not lend them to him under these circumstances." To avoid putting temptation in his way I got back into the boat and returned to the ship.

Several hours later I wrote to him that my efforts had been in vain and that I had not been able to find oars for the boat without stripping my other boats. In consequence his boat could be of no use without oars, and I begged him to regard the sale as not having taken place. Thus I gained part of the day, hoping from moment to moment to see the *Franklin* set sail, but she did not do so.

Early next morning I received a letter from the general, who asked me to deliver the boat at once and in the state that it was in, reminding me of my pledged word. There remained no further way to hold back without compromising myself. I therefore had it taken to shore, but since it leaked,* needing to be caulked, I had it hauled up on the beach while the tide was in so that it rested high and dry at a considerable distance from the water.

Meanwhile in the fort they had found four galley oars thirty feet long that had been there since the arrival of the Spaniards. The carpenters of the presidio set about shortening them and giving them the proper shape, but while they were still wondering whether to trim the blades or shorten the handles, Captain Bradshaw, now fully prepared, slipped his cable, spread all sails, and made for the entrance to the harbor, leaving officers and soldiers dumbfounded and quite unable to comprehend how a ship, seemingly so firmly fixed on her anchors, could in a trice be made ready to depart.

I might describe here the ingenious maneuvers employed by Captain Bradshaw to hide his intentions from the attentive eyes of the Mexican officers; how his sails, which appeared as closely bound to the yards as on a parade day, were suddenly spread without any man seeming to put a hand to them; and by what means the ship, whose prow faced toward the inner harbor, could turn itself quickly, as a man might, to face in the opposite direction. But I leave to the clever Fenimore Cooper to render with touching verisimilitude the nautical scenes that only he knows how to paint—except perhaps for the author of *Le Négrier* [the slaveship].**

In departing, the *Franklin* had to pass within two hundred fathoms of the fort, a distance from which good cannoneers could have done her much harm. As soon as the garrison took note of her maneuver they began a fusillade that continued for the twenty minutes that it took the ship to reach the critical point and withdraw beyond cannon range. From thirty-six to forty balls were fired during this time and caused no other apparent damage than bringing down the flying jib, whose halyard was cut.*** Captain Bradshaw committed an error on

---

* The ship's caulker, entering into the game, had taken care to make this evident.
** Mr. E. Corbière, editor of the *Journal du Hâvre*.
*** We later saw the ship in the Sandwich Islands and learned that the Mexican artillerymen had been more accurate than we at first thought. She received two balls in the hull and two others in the rigging, which made it necessary to replace the main and mizzen yards.

this occasion; he replied with two cannon shots as he went by. Thus ended an affair that spread alarm in all of California.[4]

Toward the end of July I received the response of the padre prefecto, who thanked me for my offer. "I am resolved," he wrote, "not to abandon the flock that Heaven has entrusted to me unless they use force to separate us. To God I have made the sacrifice of myself, my freedom, and my life, all for the salvation of my soul. I will take no step that is not directed to this end. I have written to all my subordinates to make known this sentiment and to pledge them to follow the same line of conduct. It would be quite something else if, instead of driving me from this place, they should try to make me do something contrary to the testimony of my conscience: let come then what J. C. said to his disciples: 'When they shall persecute thee in one city, flee ye into another.'"

This letter took from me all hope of having the padres for passengers because I well knew that they would not go against the principles of their bishop or of the priest who was acting for him. I therefore changed plans and, in order to make good use of the ship, decided to transport to the Sandwich Islands as many horses as possible with the number of water casks I could procure. I had been informed that these animals could always be sold there at a good price, and it would cost little to feed them. I immediately set the crew to cutting hay in the neighborhood and engaged a trusted person to buy the horses while the casks were being filled and the carpenters were putting the last touches to the new boat.

On 23 August all was prepared for departure: hay and water were on board, the horses purchased and ready to embark, my accounts settled with the general and the customs. We were about to bid an eternal farewell to California when there occurred an incident that obliges me to return to the subject of Mr. R____ and that delayed our leaving for several days. It was distressing to me to leave behind the rather large sum he had in his control; although I could not be held responsible

4. The *Franklin* affair is described at some length in Bancroft, *California*, v. 3, pp. 132–34.

for the loss, it was not without regret and hesitation that I found myself impelled to leave California without having recovered it. But there was still no word from this strange person who had allowed much time to pass beyond the date he himself had set for his return. I might have thought him lost, but instead was ascribing the delay to the fickleness and levity of his character, which could have led him to change his plans once more.

There remained only a small amount of merchandise, residue of the cargo. The provisions that I had renewed in Lima were being consumed day by day; very little biscuit remained and we had been obliged to purchase flour in the missions at quite a high price in order to reach the Sandwich Islands, where I was sure we could procure biscuit from the whaling ships that put in there. I could therefore stay no longer to wait for Mr. R____; even less could I go in search of him at this time of the year. Thus, as we have seen, I had resolved to hesitate no longer, and then the *Waverly* appeared. Contrary to my every hope, Mr. R____ was not on board. From letters addressed to me and from the captain I learned just what had happened to him since his departure from Monterey, and my fears proved only too true. All the goods he had taken with him had been squandered, lost, as a result of his imprudence and incompetence. I felt confirmed in my decision to leave; there was nothing for it but to pursue my plan, the only suitable one under the circumstances and one that would serve the interests of the owners.[5]

The *Waverly* brought back the captain, supercargo, and crew of the English ship *Teignmouth* of Calcutta. The total loss of this vessel in the bay of San José del Cabo, where she tried to take on a cargo of horses in the month of July, confirms what I have said about the seasonal weather in Baja California. A hurricane from the southeast had surprised her at anchor, and it was a miracle that the crew was saved from the frightful catastrophe.

5. It appears that most or all of these goods were confiscated by the Mexican authorities. Rives died of cholera in Mexico in 1836. According to John Dunmore in *French Explorers in the Pacific: II, The Nineteenth Century* (Oxford, 1969, p. 267), the Mexican government in 1838 agreed to pay his heirs an indemnity of 90,000 francs. "No one seems to have worried about the fact that the goods in dispute had not belonged to [him] in the first place."

The supercargo and captain came on board and requested passage to the Sandwich Islands for them and their men. To me there was only one problem, the difficulty of obtaining an additional supply of water. When the supercargo procured several casks from other ships in the harbor, we agreed on a very moderate price for the passage. And on the 27th we took final leave of California, where we had spent nearly two years.

The crossing was uneventful; on the seventeenth day we came in sight of the island of Oahu and we then sailed along the southeast shore past Koko Head. All this coast appears quite arid at first, but on coming closer one soon perceives greenery and human habitations. This point projects prominently to the southeast and then, the coast turning sharply to the west, forms a shallow bay two leagues around and terminated by Diamond Head. This low mountain is all the more remarkable in that it stands isolated alongside the sea, arising out of a low terrain a league from the first high ground of the interior. Its shape, quite round and truncated horizontally, is that of a volcanic crater; it doubtless owes its origin to one of those fire-belching eruptions. At the summit there is a small lake of fresh water filled with excellent fish.

West of Koko Head the island takes on a more pleasant aspect; the mountains, cut by deep valleys, are covered with forests of densely growing trees. As soon as we had passed the Diamond we found ourselves opposite a magnificent grove of coconut palms whose broad leaves cast shade on the pretty village of Witite or rather Waytité, where ships used ordinarily to moor before the establishment of the port of Anaroura, one league farther west. At a distance of one mile and in a depth of eight or nine fathoms we coasted along the line of reefs that borders the shore and came to cast anchor at eleven fathoms in front of the harbor, where we could see a number of ships.*6

---

* I will not attempt to transcribe Sandwich Island words in a precise way but will seek to render pronunciation rather than spelling.

6. Two place names in this paragraph will hereafter be given as Waikiki and Honolulu. In the previous paragraph three names have been corrected from the author's spellings of Wahou, Pointe des Cocos, and Diamond-Hill. Hereafter such corrections will be made silently

Seldom can one enter the harbor of Honolulu in the middle of the day. The narrow channel leading in is a tortuous opening in the reef, two miles long. If there is not a favorable wind, which there rarely is, one must await the calm of early morning and let the ship be towed in by small boats. This difficulty has created in Honolulu a tradition dear to the fraternal alliance of all seamen among themselves. On the day a ship is to enter the port, boats from all the other ships arrive before sunrise ready to perform this service. A captain who refuses this touching ceremony would cover himself with shame in the eyes of all others. The harbor of Honolulu itself is a twisting channel where twenty-five ships can be moored in safety over a mud bottom in from three to six fathoms.

When the ship was settled in its mooring berth we shot off a salute of thirteen guns, which was returned immediately from the fort in the same number. I then called on the young king Kauikeaouli or Kamehameha III. He was at the house of the regent Boki, seated with no special marks of honor in an armchair similar to the one offered me. He was dressed quite simply in white with a yellow neck-piece of pandanus seeds. Even this was not, as I thought at first, a sign of distinction since many other people, both men and women, wore similar ones.[7]

This young prince, then seventeen years old, wore a melancholy air. His features were interesting, his face bearing several marks left by the smallpox, and his color was a dark chestnut brown. He spoke little and looked at me closely for a long time. I had on board portraits of the king, his brother, and of the queen, who had both died in London in 1824,[8] and I offered them to him through the interpreter. He accepted with little show of feeling at first; it was only several days later,

---

except where the author's form has particular interest. Hawaiian names will be spelled, where possible, as given in R. S. Kuykendall's *The Hawaiian Kingdom*, v. 1 (Honolulu, c. 1938).

7. Kauikeaouli was the younger brother of Liholiho, who had died in London. Boki, who had survived the London trip, was governor of Oahu, the island where Honolulu is situated. Accounts differ as to Kauikeaouli's legal position in relation to that of Kaahumanu, queen regent and leader of the opposing faction. Boki disappeared at sea in 1830.

8. See the author's introduction.

Vue du Port et de la vallée d'Anaroura dans l'île de Wahu.

Lith de Loretta quai d'Orleans.

J. Duhaut-cilly del.

H. Loretta Lith.

11. View of the harbor and valley of Honolulu. By Auguste Duhaut-Cilly.

when they had been delivered to him, that he was struck by the perfect resemblance and fine execution. For several days these two pictures excited great emotion among all his people; by shedding real tears they demonstrated the great attachment that they felt for their sovereigns. Almost all the women had broken off the two incisors of the upper jaw, a sign of mourning in these islands for the death of the monarch.

The house where I found the young king was, as I have said, that of the regent Boki. In exterior appearance it was quite the same as all other houses in the town of Honolulu. The interior, carpeted with mats like the others, differed only in its European furniture, standing in every corner and mixed with the native furniture. Nothing could have been more strange than to see a magnificent porcelain vase of French manufacture paired with a calabash, a work of nature; two splendid twin beds with curtains of embroidered stuff and quilts of eiderdown; two hanging mirrors with gilded frames meant to display beauties in their most elegant toilette but reflecting instead dark skin half covered with dirty tapa cloth.

However that may be, this dwelling would have been clean and decent if it had not been crowded with officials and servants stretched out on the mats and so close to each other that you could scarcely take a step without putting a foot on someone. There was barely free space for four or five people. Since the king was no more than a child, the regent Boki was the most considerable person in the realm; he was always surrounded by the principal chiefs of the archipelago, some of whom lived at his expense.

One might think, to observe them, that positions of authority derive directly from size; the highest in rank are also the fattest, and as they are generally tall, we appeared to be pygmies beside them. I often inquired about the extreme obesity of the chiefs, and this was always attributed to the lack of exercise and the abundance of food. These must have something to do with the matter of weight, but why are they taller than the others? There is reason to believe that their origin is different from that of the lesser people and that they are descended from the conquerors of these islands as the feudal seigneurs of medieval France descended from the Frankish chieftains who invaded the land of the Gauls, or like the Saxons and later the Normans who became by conquest the privileged nobles of England. The tradition mingled with fable, on which is based the history of the Sandwich Islands, seems to indicate that they were conquered in some remote time by strangers of a race different from that of the first inhabitants. That they do not now have the same facial structure is support for this conjecture. The profiles of most of the chiefs, instead of being straight or even pointed like most of the native people, are concave in form; if you put a straight rule to forehead and chin, it would hardly touch the nose. I do not wish, however, to state as fact a matter so little attested. As for Kauikeaouli, he had purely indigenous features, and he was afflicted by being thin so that the embonpoint of the others was a continual source of jealousy to him.

Among the chiefs and courtiers who surrounded the king and regent and who overfilled the house, some were dressed in the European style, that is, in pantaloons and white shirts, while others had wrapped themselves in a tapa, a piece of cloth made in this country from the bark of the paper mulberry. But most of them go naked, wearing around the waist only a *malo,* a band of cloth so narrow that it is nearly always insufficient for the use intended.

Some of the women wore dresses and had combs in their hair as our ladies do, but the most usual garment of the sex is a large and billowing white chemise—I speak only of its color. Princess Boki, having accompanied her husband to London when he went there with King Liholiho, had a greater taste for European style than the others and was thus better attired than they. All of them retained one feature of their national costume, a band of feathers, usually red, green, and yellow and worn sometimes around the neck and sometimes on the head like a crown. The latter manner becomes them marvelously.

Almost all travelers have been pleased to endow with surpassing beauty the women of the different archipelagos of the South Seas. I cannot speak of those in the Marquesas or Society Islands, but if one may judge by the Sandwich Islanders, on whom they have heaped the same praises, I am obliged to say that they are far from living up to this portrait. But I must agree that they possess a natural grace that, without matching the fine and regular features of a white and delicate skin, has nevertheless an almost irresistible attraction. Their movements are smooth and supple, their postures enchanting and easy, and their glances, more than anything, are indescribably alluring.

The freedom they enjoy means that they are strangers to anxiety or constraint, and this state of tranquillity is reflected in all their bodily manners. If they suffer storms of the heart these must be of a passing nature because there is no need for these to persist. Their ways appear to be based on inconstancy; they need never suffer the boredom of an ill-matched union. Amused by the veriest trifles, they wear only smiles on their lips, and their mouths never open to say no. It is not surprising then that the stranger, finding such an easy welcome among them, lets himself paint them with flattering praise if only to enlarge on and embellish his own conquests.[9]

When, several days after our arrival, the young king wished to visit the *Héros,* we prepared a small collation, and he came on board with the regent and a numerous suite. Kauikeaouli drank with pleasure our best liquors and ate our cakes with eagerness. We noticed that he did not touch the poi that he always has brought along wherever he goes;[*] he preferred our good bread. When he got into his boat to return we saluted him with thirteen guns, a courtesy that he found quite flattering. On the quay his bodyguard awaited: a score of fine young men fitted out simply but uniformly in blue pantaloons, short blue jackets, round hats, guns, bayonets, and ammunition pouches.

---

9. In his account, published four years before that of Duhaut-Cilly, Edmond Le Netrel, lieutenant on board the *Héros,* wrote: "The women, who are quite pretty and are perfectly formed, have changed nothing in their conduct toward foreigners. On the day of our arrival we observed a spectacle entirely new to us and quite unexpected. Hardly was our work done when there arrived on board from sixty to eighty women of Honolulu. At first the captain intended to prevent this kind of visit, but when he saw that this was impossible, since these beauties almost always swim out and come aboard without being noticed, and since moreover this was a custom of the island and of all ships anchored in the harbor, he allowed the crew to receive on board as many women as they wished but only after the work was done and on express condition that they not proceed past the main mast, an order that was punctiliously obeyed, although there were always more women than the crew desired. The between-decks was wide, spacious, and comfortable." (Le Netrel, *Voyage autour du monde . . . ,* p. 172.)

* A kind of paste made from the tuberous root of the taro plant.

The king's house is located in the same compound as that of the regent and is of the same style and size. It has a very high roof supported by low sidings that incline to the inside. This shape imparts to these dwellings of wood and straw more strength than if the sustaining walls were perpendicular. The king has another house built according to the rules of our architecture but he never lives in it, preferring this one of thatch. In fact, this sort of dwelling is better suited to their mode of life. They love to stretch out on mats, letting themselves drop wherever the fancy strikes them, and there they spend the greatest part of the day lying together helter-skelter on these rush carpets. This could not be done in lodgings furnished like ours, where they would need a sofa for each person. The young king sleeps in his thatched great house only in bad weather; when the night is fine he stays in a small hut that has to be entered on hands and knees and that is barely large enough for four people sitting or stretched out. Those of his young court follow his example; each constructs a small hut close to his, all of them together forming a sort of camp around the principal house, which hardly serves for more than to store the furniture.

The king and the regent are not the only principal authorities in the archipelago. A wife of the famous Kamehameha I, Queen Kaahumanu, exercises much power in fact if not legally. She has her private court and her own coterie of followers. She lives in the city during the winter but passes the summer in a pretty valley a league to the east of Honolulu.[10] Along with the English consul[11] I went one day to see her at her residence, which consisted of two main houses and a number of huts.

We found her seated on a mat and leaning back on cushions covered in silk. Although she was not much interested in us, she received us in a dignified way. A woman of forty-two, she appeared to have once had much embonpoint, but bad health, caused by her well-known excesses, had brought on premature old age, which left her little hope of a long life. Thus the adherents of the young king were

10. Nuuanu Valley. The name means cool height.
11. Richard Charlton, who will appear at greater length in the next chapter.

X

being patient while awaiting the death of Kaahumanu, which they expected soon and believed would deliver him from a feminine yoke.[12] She had on a dress of gray silk and wore a kerchief on her head in the manner of our creoles. Few important chiefs were there except for Kaou-noua, colonel commanding the troops, who had reached this high rank by marrying one of the princesses, but some women of the highest distinction were around her, all remarkable for their great height and their obesity.

Among them I noticed a young woman of twenty to whom they gave the title of princess. Even at that age she had become so enormous that she could not walk without being helped. She much resembled that huge seal, the sea elephant, which because of its great weight remains for weeks at a time in the same place, its soft body molding itself to the irregularities of the rock.*

These women and these chiefs have more than one point of resemblance to the amphibian with which I compare them. Just as the seal, so heavy and apathetic on the rocks or on the beach, is endowed when back in the water with an astonishing suppleness and vivacity, so these men and women, quite lethargic on their mats, are the most skillful and intrepid swimmers.

We have often seen them lying belly down on a board six feet long and fifteen inches wide and waiting, more than a mile out from the village of Waikiki, for the most powerful wave and then, with feet to the wave and head pointed toward shore, swimming with hands and feet to keep the board always in front of the wave, allow themselves to be propelled in a few minutes and with the speed of an arrow to the beach, where the wave dies out. But if they perform this journey with

12. Kaahumanu was queen regent from the departure of Liholiho in late 1823 until her own death in 1832. Kauikeaouli reigned until his death in 1854. Of Kaahumanu, Paul-Emile Botta, physician on board the *Héros,* wrote: "The most influential person in the Islands, the one who really rules them, is the old queen Kaahumanu, one of the wives of Kamehameha. After having been a veritable Messalina, this woman in her old age is trying to expiate her past sins in the fanaticism and bigotry inspired in her by the missionaries." (Botta, *Observations sur les habitans des Iles Sandwich,* p. 144.)

* On my return, reading the interesting voyage of J. Arago, I found that he makes use of the same comparison. [About Arago, see the Editors' Introduction, p. xvi and note 5.]

incredible speed and agility, they must exert even more skill when they wish to go back and repeat the game, for then they must overcome the speed and power of all the succeeding waves, and in doing this they prove whether or not they are good swimmers. To accomplish the return they must plunge through each wave as it unfurls, swim strongly as soon as it has passed, then do the same with the next wave and the next until they have reached the last one. Then they can let themselves be carried once more to the beach. They employ canoes for the same game, but these must be handled with even more dexterity because the smallest paddle stroke done wrong is enough to turn them over. When that happens the only consequence is that they are delivered over to the ridicule of their fellows whose laughter, so easily aroused, is then at its height.

This amusement, pursued with equal skill by men and women, might be considered analogous to our game of Russian mountain [roller-coaster] if they did not have another that is much more similar. Above the town of Honolulu there rises to a height of about two hundred meters an old volcanic crater covered with loose earth and grass; this is a truncated cone, hollow in the center and for that reason called by the English, in honor of a gentle custom, the Punch Bowl. The last conqueror of the Sandwich Islands, Kamehameha I, caused to be dragged up there by hand several cannon of large caliber that can still be seen perched on the lava points along the side of the mountain almost like chamois on the ledges of Mont Blanc. This wily and suspicious tyrant, using the pretext of defending the harbor entrance, thus constructed a fort from which he could, in case of a revolt, blow away the people of the town.

In the rainy season when the land was damp and lush the sporting enthusiasts used to make use of the grooved channels that run down the steep side of the mountain from the summit to the plain below. Lying face down on wooden sleds they let themselves slide down head first with a speed that may be judged by the angle of the slope, which is not less than fifty-five degrees. Having reached the flat ground, they continued sliding for a long way, almost to the town before losing speed from the rapid descent.

I cannot claim to have witnessed this entertainment since it is forbidden today for a reason that I will give later, but it was described to me by persons who had no reason to deceive and who could be trusted. Moreover, it is no more astonishing than what used to be practiced on the Matterhorn, I think, before the strong mind of a man of genius determined the proper routes there and saw that they were adhered to. The Chileans still make use of the same means to descend the cordillera of the Andes in the snow of winter with this difference: in the Alps they use a sled while in the Andes they slide on a cowhide.

Chapter 20

MISSIONARIES AND ISLANDERS

September—November 1828

DURING THE FIRST DAYS of my stay in Honolulu I went to see the three French missionaries who had been brought out by the ship *Comète* a short time before. They were poorly housed but appeared to bear their situation with cheerfulness and courage. They recounted to me all the troubles they had experienced in getting admitted to the country, adding that it was only by a sort of ruse that they had avoided having to reembark. The captain, conforming to their wishes, had set sail at the moment when he would have been required to take them back.[1]

Before my departure from France, when the minister of the marine spoke to me of this mission, I had foreseen that these men would not be received in the Sandwich Islands without strong opposition and that their presence might spoil the trading operation of the captain who transported them. Since several years, I knew, the Protestant missionaries had gained and were still enjoying great favor with the old Kaahumanu, but I did not know how great their influence had be-

1. About the *Comète* and Captain Plassiard, see Chapter 15, note 1, and the Editors' Introduction.

come. They so dominated the mind of this woman that she saw only through their eyes and acted only on their prompting. It was natural then that they would look with jealousy on missionaries of the Catholic faith. It was only for this reason that I declined the request of the minister that I bring them to these islands. My prudence was well justified later by the situation of the captain who brought them to Oahu and who, to avoid taking them back on board, had to get under sail at once without engaging in any trade.

Despite the power of the Protestant missionaries, who sought to prevent a landing by the Frenchmen and then to have them put back on board, the religious indifference of Boki and some maneuvers by the English consul brought about a partial failure of these designs; the precipitate departure of the *Comète* did the rest. Since then they have remained without much notice being paid, avoiding with care anything that might call attention to themselves. When I visited them in their quiet retreat they were devoting themselves without rest to the study of the native language in order that later on they might employ resources quite superior to those of their rivals, poor artisans who could scarcely read the Bible but who enjoyed the privilege of interpreting it to the islanders.

One cannot deny, however, that these American missionaries have contributed much to the civilization of the archipelago as we understand that word, and if the pure Christian doctrine is not the basis of their instruction, they have at least enabled these people to enjoy some of the benefits of Christianity in teaching them the ethics of the Gospels. They have been able to adapt the English alphabet or a part of it to the Sandwich Island idiom and they have succeeded in teaching these people to read and write their own language. There is a printing shop where they print in the Sandwich language the works judged proper for the people to read.

This is all that can be said in favor of these propagators of Methodism;[2] the evils they have brought about are far greater than any good they may have done. It is incontestable that, since they gained a cer-

2. The first missionaries were Congregationalists and Presbyterians; all are called Methodists by Duhaut-Cilly.

tain influence in these islands, agriculture has decreased by a third. What plague could be more harmful and destructive?

Instead of commencing with the instruction of the new generation, they have wished to bring into their schools the entire population: women and children, old men and adults, all have been required to take lessons and to spend whole days at them while leaving their fields untilled and their plantations overgrown with weeds. This waste and misuse of time has been so great that the irrigation ditches are filled in almost everywhere and the small ponds where taro once grew are now dried up. The unfortunate people, appalled to see how much work is needed to restore the fields to production, have abandoned them. One encounters large stretches of land where the remains of dikes, already reduced almost to ground level, show in an incontestable way that here there once were cultivated fields.

The missionaries obtain these sacrifices by means of the taboo, or *kapu,* which is a law, either permanent or temporary, that the islanders only rarely dare to transgress. Through the influence of Kaahumanu they receive kapus from the king for everything they want: to build their churches, their houses, their cloisters, their walls, and the like. At such times all the people are required to perform the prescribed tasks. Another kapu fills the schools. In addition to these kapus for the benefit of the missionaries others are used by the king, the queen, and the chiefs to get work done for themselves. A great part of the year is devoured in this way. From this comes a shortage of food and the difficulty of nourishing a family, and from that a decreased desire to have children and the noticeable decrease in the population of the archipelago. Before the Europeans came with their industrial products the chiefs in particular and the people in general had fewer needs; the former exacted less labor, and agriculture flourished. There was only the cutting of sandalwood on behalf of the nobility, a third or fourth of the population.

The Methodist preachers are also merchants of a kind who know how to make profit from their influence. They own a number of small ships intended, they say, for communication among the islands in the sole interest of what they call religion, but these packet-boats also carry merchandise and return with loads of sandalwood. The missionaries are even stronger in the other islands than in Oahu. One of them was pleased to call himself King of Ottawa.[3] A number of ships that had once put in there for provisions, especially for potatoes, which had always been abundant, could no longer find a single sack. The "king," having noticed that his trade declined when ships came to his island, had forbidden the growing of this tuber so that it would no longer attract the foreigners who provided harmful competition to his business.

We observed the cruel treatment inflicted by these missionaries in the name of religion on the islanders who rebelled against their strictures—cruelties, I say, quite comparable to those charged against the inquisitors of Spain and Portugal. I was shown a young woman of eighteen whose neck, limbs, and body were furrowed with scars imprinted by their irons. Her crime, they told me, was fleeing from a husband assigned to her by the Methodists. What an outrage against a poor Sandwich Island woman who had no other idea of marriage than the one learned from her father and mother—that is, to be faithful until it no longer suited her.

But it appears that the Sandwich Islands are in only the first stage of decline. The Society Islands, subject to Methodism for a longer time, have reached under the same system such a state of decay and abandon that their population is perhaps less than a third of what it was when Cook visited there. When the great navigator arrived foodstuffs were abundant and the fields in such a prosperous state of cultivation that he could scarcely procure firewood. Today the gardens have been replaced by forests and the woods have advanced to the edge of the sea. The inhabitants, reduced in numbers by two-thirds and knowing happiness only as an old tradition, flee and emigrate from all parts, seeking a soil that will nourish them in lands not yet reached by the American missionaries.[4]

Calculating the probabilities, one is led to conclude that the moral means of our French missionaries should be at least equal to the ma-

3. The island was Kauai, sometimes spelled Tauai. Samuel Whitney was the early missionary there. We have made no attempt to verify this story.
4. The Protestant missionaries in Tahiti were English.

terial means and self-interest of their competitors. As soon as they are sufficiently versed in the Sandwich language to make use of their persuasive powers there must occur a struggle between the apostles of the two religions. This time will surely come upon the death of Queen Kaahumanu, protectress of the reformers. If, before that calamity takes place, the Catholics manage to profit from the differences between the two courts and obtain the support of the young king, they will easily triumph over their rivals. If not, it may well happen that both parties will be expelled, since their principles are equally opposed to the manners and the passions of the court.[5]

One of Kauikeaouli's principal grievances against the American missionaries was that they were opposed to his marriage with his sister [Nahienaena], whom he loved very much. Such unions, forbidden by us, are a common custom in the archipelago of the Sandwich Islands, but Kaahumanu, fearing the power and influence of a young and beautiful queen, was using religion as a pretext for preventing the marriage, and in order to make Kauikeaouli forget his desires she had separated the two young people, sending the princess to the island of Maui and confining her there.[6]

There has taken place in the Sandwich Islands what nearly always occurs in Europe during the minority of future rulers. Those who wish to retain authority try to prolong the childhood of the heir to the throne. They surround him with seductions and easy pleasures in order that amid this dissipation he may forget his destiny and neglect the duties demanded by his birth. Using all possible means, they hold back the moment when his emancipation will take away their power. Fortunate are the people when these shameful maneuvers do not corrupt the heart of the monarch.

Before ending this account of the Methodist missionaries I should

5. Fathers Bachelot and Short, the last two French missionaries, were put on the *Waverly* in 1831 and sent to California. They returned in 1837 and were again expelled. The French government did not like this, and in 1839 the frigate *Artémise,* Captain Laplace, under threat of bombardment, forced the island government to put up a guarantee of $20,000 and sign a decree granting freedom of entry to the Catholic religion and to French citizens.

6. The marriage was prevented but the couple were not kept entirely apart. In 1836 Nahienaena bore her brother a child that did not live and she herself died a few months later.

add that it was they who prohibited the sledding on the Punch Bowl, innocent as that was. One might applaud this measure if the game had caused some serious accident and they were acting for reasons of human concern. But no: it is merely that the principles they profess, in public and hypocritically, are extremely rigid. According to them no pleasurable activity can be proper; all the time that is not employed in work, sleep, and eating should be devoted to prayer or to religious meditation. In their strictness they have even wished to set a kapu against bathing, as important to the health of a Sandwich Islander as his food and the air he breathes. To deny a man all recreational exercise is to weaken his body and impoverish his spirit, thus the better to dominate him.

In Honolulu I traded what remained of the cargo in exchange for sandalwood. Stowing this wood on board is a long and careful task if one is to make full use of the space. After ballasting the ship to a sixth of its tonnage, one begins stowing at both ends, stacking together the pieces of equal length, even under the deck, and then forcing into each stack as many other pieces as possible, driving them in with a mallet.

While this work was proceeding on board the *Héros,* I accepted the invitation of the English consul to make a short trip to the north of the island in a small schooner that belonged to him and was going to obtain sandalwood in a place called Waialua. We left at three in the afternoon, and in order to double Koko Head and the eastern part of the island, we tacked until noon the next day when, finding ourselves sufficiently to windward, we let the ship fall off northwest toward our destination.

For some while the chain of mountains that appears to traverse the island from east to west and falls away on the side of Honolulu to form a number of fine valleys appeared from the north as a steep wall hemming in a plain of two or three leagues in width and stretching from this barrier to the edge of the sea. But soon the mountains, turning abruptly to the north, advanced to the water, leaving only a very small space between themselves and the shore, where a great number of huts stood everywhere.

We were less than a mile at sea, ranging along the coast in somber and rainy weather. The setting sun, about to go down on the opposite side of the mountain, left in the shade all that we could see. It is hardly possible to imagine anything more imposing than the spectacle before us at that moment.

These massive shapes, suspended over our heads, were composed of fearsome precipices, one towering over the other, of impenetrable forests rising in great steps above other forests, dark chasms of frightful depth, steep and slippery slopes, bare wet rocks mingling their dark color with the somber green of the old trees. High and gleaming cascades, after descending for hundreds of yards, threw themselves onto the tree tops, where they burst into foam only to reunite and fall again until some fissure in the rocks provided a channel for a gentler descent to the sea. If I add that the progress of the ship was continually changing and varying the scene for us, the reader may form an idea of this spectacle. But one must see it with one's own eyes, see the heavy clouds, now motionless over the forests that they drench with their showers, now eddying swiftly, rising and falling at the will of the wind that was whirling around behind the mountains. One must see this turbulent chaos of clouds, moving, dissipating, and reappearing in different form as the ship advances if one is to sense how magical and mysterious was this scene to us.

In the far distance the mountains opened up as if some great hand had torn them apart; narrow valleys, well peopled, wound among the openings. A large number of fishing canoes could be seen close to us, and we called to one of these light craft for a pilot to show us the port of Waialua (place of two streams). The pilot pointed it out, several miles ahead, and we lost no time in entering through a wide opening in the reef, where we found no less than four fathoms of water.

It was almost dark when we went ashore and were received by the village chief, who invited us to sup with him and sleep in his house. We had some provisions brought from on board along with some bottles of wine, and these we added to the excellent fish that he served.

Although the house was very large it barely sufficed to hold the numerous guests who were gathered there, for we were no fewer than forty men and women under this hospitable roof. I and my companion, the English consul, stretched ourselves out on mats as did the others, but the night was far advanced before we could sleep. In addition to the insects, flying, jumping, and crawling, that tormented us, the chief, after reciting a Christian prayer in the language of the country, kept up a long conversation with several others. Although I did not understand a word, this eternal colloquy held me awake for a long time.

Even the sleep was not peaceful; with my imagination overwhelmed by the grandiose and sublime spectacle of the mountains, I dreamed that I was pursued by a torrent and took refuge under an overhanging rock that then broke loose and collapsed on me. Awakening with a start, I found on my chest the two heels of a fat Sandwich Islander, my neighbor on the bed, who slept profoundly in that position and who had been the cause of my nightmare. Day was breaking. Taking my gun I went for a walk, intending to shoot some birds, but could not reach the base of the mountains; the entire landscape was cut into a labyrinth of taro fields separated by slippery dikes covered with high, wet grass and difficult to walk on without tumbling into the muddy ponds. After killing only a few plover and a duck, I returned to the port. Our little schooner was loaded early, and in the evening we set sail for Honolulu.

During our stay in the Sandwich Islands I often went with Dr. Botta to the hills and valleys of the region, hoping to obtain specimens of some handsome birds. The number of species is not great and the forests so impenetrable that it was only in persevering that we managed to collect a few. We were seeking especially a fine fruit-eater of singular form and very bright colors. This bird, about the size of a sparrow, has tail and wing tips of black while the rest of it is of the most beautiful red, sometimes mixed with a little yellow on the underside of the neck near the mandibles. The most remarkable part of this bird is its beak, a pale red and ten lines long, very sharp and curved along its entire length. The natives call this bird the *i-i-vi*.[7] We also shot another bird of the same genus, smaller and more elongated;

7. The *i-i-vi* or *iiwi* is one of the Hawaiian honeycreepers. Most species feed on nectar and insects, including fruit flies. Ten lines is less than an inch.

its beak has the same structure but is proportionately shorter. Its plumage of mingled black, blue, and red appears violet overall.

We encountered a third of the kind but as large as a blackbird and with plumage entirely black except for some yellow feathers along its sides. The Sandwich Islanders put great store in these yellow feathers, which, along with red ones from the i-i-vi, are used in the making of fine cloaks. These are the only remarkable species to be found in the woods, but there are tomtits whose plumage is more or less a mixture of gray, yellow, and green. On the plain are found only owls and plover, and the latter are birds of passage.

On fresh water we saw only a small species of duck and some rails. On the seashore we found a small gray heron, some curlews, sand-pipers, oyster catchers, and a godwit with flattened beak and long stilt-like legs. This was the only place on the entire voyage where we saw no seagulls.

If birds are scarce in the animal kingdom of the Sandwich Islands, native quadrupeds are even fewer. Besides pigs, rats, and mice, I know of none that do not originate in other lands, thus horses, cows, goats, sheep, asses, and dogs. It is said that there are no venomous or other snakes.

The Sandwich Islands—seven principal ones of which the most fertile is Oahu—merit today the attention of any nation that maintains a navy or a merchant marine. They seem destined by Providence to become a general entrepôt between Asia and America, as well as a place for sailors to rest and recuperate after long and perilous voyages, and also a haven for ships that need refitting before resuming their journey.

The population at the time of discovery is said to have been two hundred thousand souls, but is now, I believe, no more than one hundred fifty thousand including foreigners. The town of Honolulu in southern Oahu contains six thousand inhabitants, they told me, and is the largest concentration in the archipelago. Except for a number of houses of more than one story and constructed of wood and stone by foreigners, the town is made up of thatched huts of varying sizes with high roofs, steeply pitched. The framework is made of small tree trunks, fitted perfectly together without the use of nails. The huts are

X

enclosed in palisades of stakes of unequal length; each forms a square or parallelogram.[8]

The gentle character of the islanders causes them to be loved by all who know them well, and their intelligence fits them for all kinds of work, especially the maritime. It is no exaggeration to say that there are in these islands at least eight hundred excellent sailors. On the English and American whaling ships they are taken on as replacements for those who have died or deserted. The ships that deal in furs on the Northwest Coast come here to fill out their crews, and it is a remarkable thing that these men, born in the torrid zone, endure the temperatures of that glacial coast more readily perhaps than do the sailors from Boston. On the king's ships, seven brigs in number, the only white men on board are the captain and the officers; all the others are Sandwich Islanders.

The native sailors come before the commandant of the fort to make engagements with foreign ships and to have their wages set. The captain must declare under oath that he will return them to their country, and on that return he pays them before the same commandant, who withholds a part of their pay for the government.

But if these islands are to remain a permanent resource for all maritime nations, it is necessary first of all that their independence be assured by a treaty or convention among all the interested states and that this same treaty establish the permanent neutrality of all the island ports in time of war. We no longer live in an age when a power may seize, without scruple or respect for property, any land that it may discover. Today such an act will arouse the indignation of the entire Christian and civilized world.

Nevertheless, and in spite of the wide sway of this sane and liberal philosophy, there are three redoubtable powers that have attempted, one after the other, if not to seize the islands then to establish over them an improper hegemony. One of them, Russia, went even further

8. According to a Dutch visitor in the same year of 1828, the palisades were intended to keep out the herds of pigs that roamed the town. (Jacobus Boelen, *A Merchant's Perspective . . .* Honolulu, c. 1988.)

a few years ago; without the firmness of Kamehameha the world might have had to deplore a great violation of international law. It is possible that the ideas I here profess, and which are those of the entire world, may be the only rampart that stands between the Sandwich Islands and a second invasion on the part of that nation.

The Americans have had recourse to more subtle methods. As we have already seen they have sent there, and maintain there, a group of missionaries who under the pretext of religion, it is claimed, pursue a more worldly and political goal; and if a better understanding had prevailed between these individuals and the consuls of their country, they might be quite far along with their designs. Fortunately for the islanders, these ridiculous apostles of the Methodist sect do not wish to share their influence with anyone; and instead of joining forces the two parties block each other and do to each other as much harm as they can. This rivalry has existed ever since there have been American missionaries and consuls in the Sandwich Islands. The animosity has been pushed so far that, during my stay there, the diplomatic official, although far from wishing to raise his children as Catholics, had one of them baptized by the French missionaries in order to mortify those of his own country.[9]

Meanwhile England has declared herself protector of the Sandwich Islands, and one need not remember that Napoleon took the title of Protector of the Confederation of the Rhine to understand the political meaning of the words *protector, protectorate, protection.* From time to time you may hear British subjects slip into the conversation a few phrases about the claimed grant made by Kamehameha to the king of England as represented by Captain Vancouver. It is possible that this sagacious navigator was convinced in good faith that the Sandwich Island king had conceded to him, as he said, the island of Hawaii, but these two men were able to communicate only through quite unskilled interpreters; and it is doubtful that Kamehameha, who had sacrificed everything to attain sovereignty over the entire archipelago,

9. American influence continued to increase, and the islands were annexed in 1898.

would have given up the largest parcel of it to a man whom, in his limited vision, he must have looked on as an adventurer.[10]

However that may be, England has so far shown herself quite liberal in her dealings with the Sandwich Islands, and in justice to the English consul, Mr. Richard Charlton, I testify that no one knows better than he how to join the duty owed to his own country with a human consideration worthy of all praise. Any foreigner, of whatever nation, will be welcomed by him and afforded protection.[11]

It is much to be desired then that all maritime nations renounce in good faith any kind of domination for ulterior purposes. If that happens, one may watch with no envy and even with approbation an effort by the English, so skilled in amelioration, to augment the prosperity of these islands. A splendid people, a delightful climate, a spacious land, and a soil fertile to the highest degree—these elements may bring on a state of human happiness provided that there be adopted a better set of laws, an outcome that seems to me not impossible. I speak not of the criminal or administrative codes, but of the basic legal system itself.

The basic change would be simply to convert the present feudal government into a true monarchy. The change should not be too abrupt and should serve for a long period of time. Only the king would lose anything. The chiefs would become a nobility, privileged in certain respects, the principal one being a larger role in the distribution of land. This property, until now belonging entirely to the king, would be divided among all the inhabitants with the provision of a land tax. Hereditary succession would be established, with each owner allowed to dispose of his property although not to sell it to for-

10. Vancouver wrote that the king and his party "assembled on board the Discovery, for the purpose of formally ceding and surrendering the island of Owhyhee to me for His Britannic Majesty, his heirs and successors . . ." He then records the sense of Kamehameha's speech in making the cession. The date was 25 February 1794. (W. Kaye Lamb, ed., *The Voyage of George Vancouver, 1791–1795*, London, 1984, v.3, 1180–81.)

11. Charlton was British consul of the Sandwich, Society, and Friendly islands, 1824–43. Duhaut-Cilly made at least two excursions with him and seems to have known him well. But there was bad blood between Charlton and the American missionaries, who accused him of numerous sins.

eigners. The abolition of the corvée would follow as a natural consequence of this revolution.

In this way the inhabitants would no longer regard themselves as precarious cultivators of another's land; each would find new courage in fertilizing his own soil both for himself and for his descendants. Agriculture would experience a new impetus. Each person being free to sell his products, the markets would be better supplied than they are today, and foreigners, attracted by this abundance, would provide ready purchasers.

These ideas, inspired in me by a desire for the well-being of an excellent people, will doubtless need to be elaborated by a better legislator than I; but while acknowledging my own lack of capacity, I persist in believing that such a revolution, felt by the large majority only in its happy effects and at the same time assuring irrevocably the rights of the great people, would truly give more than it might take away. And I think that if England pushed for it, she could bring it about.

When the Sandwich Islands were visited, not discovered, by Cook,[12] he found plains and valleys cultivated as they are today, perhaps much better; and had not the people, led astray by idolatry, offered human sacrifices to their imaginary gods, one could not in justice have classed them among the uncivilized. An agricultural people should not be considered such. For if they behaved barbarously toward some navigators, there was reason to feel distrust of strangers who came acting as masters and whose conduct merited all too often the resentment of the islanders. And Cook himself, did he do nothing to provoke vengeance?

Their principal crop, then as now, is the taro, a broad-leaf plant whose bulbous root grows in the water and produces a farinaceous tuber, substantial and with an agreeable flavor. It is served in two ways: simply boiled like yams or made into a mucilaginous paste and eaten with the fingers, to which it adheres. The taro grows well only in a kind of pond where the water flows continuously in channels. These

12. Cook's "discovery" or first European visit to the island of Hawaii was made in 1768. He was killed there in the following year.

fields, divided by narrow dikes, rise in a sort of amphitheater, one above the other, and the water that has irrigated one flows down to the next below. Nearly all these ponds serve also as fish reservoirs where they put small mullet, which quickly grow large and are quite delicious. This is the best fish that can be had here but is almost always reserved for the chiefs.

Toward the end of October I made use of the same schooner that had taken me to Waialua in order to visit a village called Pearl River and situated to the west of Honolulu. Again I sailed with Mr. Charlton, and we left the port with a strong breeze from the northeast. We had with us the former high priest of the island, who in the time of Kamehameha had the entire confidence of that prince and enjoyed a favor that has almost disappeared since the arrival of the missionaries. Nevertheless, he is still highly regarded by his compatriots, who address him with no other title than that of King, conferred on him by Kamehameha. We were told that he was a man of high probity and great abilities, but we could scarcely judge this since he was so drunk during the time he was with us that, had he had a hundred times as much wit and reason, neither the one nor the other could have held out against the many assaults he made upon them during the day. This priest can no longer live on the proceeds of his abandoned altar; he had come to the port to ask some presents of Boki, and the latter, more from politics than from generosity, and to "close the mouth of Calchas," had given him eight hundred piasters. He had converted this sum into cloth and strong liquor, but when he reached home, I thought, there would be little left of these things, since he had distributed the one to his numerous retinue and drunk the other during the voyage. Thus passed one of the periodic visits of the high priest, always embarrassing to the chiefs, whom he could reproach with having abandoned the religion of their fathers and who had always to fear an uprising in favor of the idolatrous cult.[13]

13. Calchas was the talkative high priest or soothsayer of the *Iliad,* who predicted many things, including the need to sacrifice Iphigenia to obtain fair winds for Troy, and that Chryseis must be given back to her father by Agamemnon. Later he was bested by another seer, Mopsus, and died of mortification. The high priest of 1828 may have been Hewahewa, the

After an hour and a half of sailing we found ourselves opposite Pearl River and we proceeded there through a wide opening in the reef, where there was only eight or nine feet of water. This lack of depth prevents the use of a place that without this fault would be one of the finest harbors on the globe. Scarcely had we passed this shallow spot when we found ourselves in a mile-wide channel with everywhere from ten to twenty fathoms of water. Our schooner was to take on a load of salt in front of a small village near the entrance, but the high priest wished to be taken nearer to his dwelling, and we did not stop but continued into the harbor, which widened out and split into several branches, all of them as broad and safe as the one we followed. One turned to the northeast, another to west-northwest, and ours to the northwest. The land through which these channels run is low and flat, and the banks are cut vertically like wharves or levees.[14]

We advanced thus for nearly three leagues into the interior and after disembarking the pontiff, his retinue, and his baggage, we returned to drop anchor at the village close to the entrance. We went ashore with a native interpreter named Tupia, who had accompanied me on all my excursions. Going to the house of the chief, we found him seated beside his wife in a very clean hut, where the two of them took up almost half the space. To judge from their height and embonpoint they were clearly nobles. These good people received us like childhood friends and did everything possible to provide us a good supper; indeed, they soon served us an excellent repast, including especially that delicious mullet that one might almost call a domestic fish. It was cooked to such perfection that when we removed the banana leaves in which it had been braised, it had suffered only a slight change in form and color.

We spent the night in this little house, men and women stretched out pell-mell on mats, as in the Golden Age. The next morning we went to observe the salt works that are the wealth of this village and

---

last of that breed in the islands, who had advised Liholiho to abandon the ancient gods. The identification is not sure.

14. Thus Pearl Harbor as it appeared 113 years before the Japanese attack.

there admired the cleanliness and skill with which the salt is produced. The sea water, arriving in pretty canals and spreading out to crystallize in a number of square ponds, is as limpid and transparent as a diamond, and the salt formed therein rivals snow for its whiteness; refining would only soil it.

After breakfast, which was as tasty as the supper of the night before, we left the schooner to take on its cargo and, having had ourselves transported to the other side of the harbor, we made our return to Honolulu on foot, hunting birds as we had planned to do. We shot only a few plover, sole winged inhabitants of the white coral plains, partly covered with grass, that we had to traverse. We dined in the village of Maunalua (Double Mountain),[15] which occupies a pretty valley one league to the northwest of Honolulu and is shaded by a great grove of coconut palms. We reached town at an early hour.

It is in the months of October and November that the English and American whaling ships, having spent the summer off the coast of Japan, come to the Sandwich Islands to refresh their crews and put their vessels in shape to go back to sea, either to return home if their whaling is finished or to continue the work if they do not yet have a full cargo. And in fact there arrived many such ships belonging to these two nations.

One cannot help noticing a great difference between the one and the other. The Americans do not use ships of more than four hundred tons; they all arrive here in a state of uncleanness and disrepair that indicates a lack of discipline and care. The English ships, much larger and more difficult to maintain since they are almost all renovated warships, appear on the contrary pleasingly neat and orderly. We saw American whalers that remained a week in the harbor without loosing their wet sails to dry and others that let them flap in the wind for several days without furling them. On the English ships the oil casks are stowed away as they are filled and not touched until arrival in England. The Americans have to heave theirs onto the deck at least once in order to reseal them; without this precaution they would lose half

15. Spelled Mawona-Aroua by the author.

their contents. The English have perfected their casks, while the ship owners of Boston and Nantucket follow an old practice that they do not wish to change.

But if the English show more order and capacity to manage their ships, once the whalers have reached the Sandwich Islands the two groups compete with each other in dissipation. English and Americans, officers and sailors, all display the same manners. As soon as they set foot on land, the streets are full of drunken men; nothing is to be heard but quarrels and bickering. What a spectacle for the islanders; you see them run shouting toward the places where the Yankees and John Bulls dispute their differences. The captains arrive, sometimes more drunk than the men, and would send them back on board; the latter resist; the captains strike, and sometimes the sailors strike back; all shout at the same time; the *God damns* and *damnations* are like thunder; kicks and blows of the fist come down like hail; *black eyes* shine like lightning.[16] It is late at night before the storm abates, only to blow up again the next day. Few of these ships complete their voyages without some kind of mutiny or revolt, but there is good reason to believe that if the captains and officers were more sober, the sailors would be more obedient and peaceable. Every day the English consul finds it necessary to have some of them flogged.

In general and with very few exceptions the foreigners who have settled in the Sandwich Islands are the dregs of all countries, and they have brought their vices with them. There are always a number of them around the young king, corrupting and giving bad counsel. Among them are several who have escaped from Botany Bay,[17] having been branded for crimes in England. The consul is aware of this situation but has no way to prevent it. For the honor of his country, however, he would not suffer the executioner [flogger] to be a compatriot of his.

The season that brings English and American whalers to this archipelago attracts also those ships that trade for furs on the Northwest

16. The italics here indicate English words in the French text.
17. The penal colony near Sydney.

Coast of America, few of which wish to pass the winter on those frozen shores. During the month of October there arrived four of them, all of which had failed to prosper in this business. One of them, the *Louisa*,[18] out of Boston, staying through a winter and two summers, had been able to procure only eight hundred beaver pelts and one hundred twenty otter skins, and the latter had cost eight times what they were worth ten years before. It appears that this commerce, formerly so rich, is now quite done for, and the natives have turned sour in their relations with the whites. Continually at war among themselves, they have become more savage and intractable than ever; they now hunt the otter only for their own needs. During the years 1827 and 1828 ten vessels have traded for fewer than half the otter skins that a single ship could once have done in three months, and the ones they did obtain have cost them four or five times as much. All the ships that came to the Sandwich Islands during my stay in Honolulu were obliged to sell at public auction what remained of their trading goods. I myself used the same method to rid myself of three hundred muskets. These were offered for public sale at one piaster five reales each (about 8.6 francs), and the captain of the *Louisa*, a month later, obtained for his guns only seven reales (4.35 francs). The poor quality of these guns, made in Liège, the huge number brought here, and the ruination of trade on the Northwest Coast, these were what brought about the depreciation in value.*

The ill will of the Indians on the Northwest Coast had created such a grave problem that the Russians, no longer able to hold off their attacks without enlarging the garrison at their base in Sitka, now wished to abandon it. Captain Muke, who was returning from that colony, told me that at the time of his departure they intended to re-

---

18. Adele Ogden, in *The California Sea Otter Trade, 1784–1848,* p. 176, lists a bark of that name, 164 tons, Captain George Wood, which touched in California in 1831 on its way from Honolulu to New York. But the timing and cargo (400 otter skins) make the identification doubtful.

* The Liège muskets that I had on board the *Héros* were so poor in spite of their shiny appearance that when we tested them with a charge of powder only, more than half of them burst.

move to the island of Kodiak and to burn what they could not take with them.[19]

The inhabitants of that coast have always been described as ferocious by the navigators who have visited them; nevertheless, by observing some precautions they have found it possible to carry on trade with them. At first some tribes were most open and friendly, and the chiefs were usually true to their word. How has it happened then that they have become so unfriendly today? Must we point to the conduct of the captains who have gone there in recent years?

It embarrasses me to answer in the affirmative. Instead of recognizing and encouraging honest dealing among the natives, so important in trading operations, these navigators were the first to provide an example of bad faith. They have sought to deceive by all manner of tricks, sometimes in relation to the quantity, sometimes to the quality of the merchandise traded; they have even resorted to violence to seize the furs wanted; indeed, they have done everything to exasperate the natives. And once the fatal word "revenge" has been inscribed on the prows of their canoes, like the bestarred flag of the Union on the ships, the reign of confidence is forever ended.[20]

The whaling ships and those trading on the Northwest Coast were not the only ones to come to the Sandwich Islands during our stay. Vessels of divers nations stopped there on the way from various parts of the west coast of America to China, to Manila, and to other ports in the Indies. Several days before our arrival His Majesty's corvette *La Bayonnaise,* commanded by M. Legouarant de Tromelin, had departed from there for the island of Vanikoro, where had been discovered recently some traces of the shipwreck of M. de La Pérouse.[21] By its fine appearance and the good conduct of its crew this corvette had left in the minds of the Sandwich Islanders an excellent impression of the French navy; they never ceased praising the commander and his

19. Sitka remained the chief port of Russian America until its transfer to the United States in 1866.

20. Presumably a reference to the American flag.

21. The two ships of La Pérouse, the first foreign vessels to visit Spanish California in 1786, were lost on the reefs of Vanikoro in 1788. No trace of them was found until 1826.

officers. These reports, flattering to a Frenchman, were particularly pleasing to me as a friend of several of those gentlemen.

At the beginning of November the ship was loaded and we were ready to sail for Canton. But I did not wish to leave Honolulu without informing myself on the pretended authority claimed by Mr. R____. To clear myself of responsibility I asked the English and American consuls to be present at the explanation that I asked of the regent Boki, with whom I requested an interview on the subject. A Spaniard named Marin,[22] settled in the country for a number of years, also attended as government interpreter. There is no need to record here everything that I learned at this meeting; it will suffice to state that Mr. R____, while acting in the name of the government, had played the role of swindler and schemer. I obtained written proof of his bad faith, signed by the regent, the consuls of England and the United States, and by the interpreter.

On the morning of the 15th the ship was made ready to sail. The king wished to accompany us as far as the outer roadstead. When we loosened sails, the ships in the harbor as well as those of the government saluted us with all their guns, and we replied with seven carronades. When we had cleared the pass Kauikeaouli said his adieus, and we ran out to the open sea.

22. Francisco de Paula Marin, a Spaniard who arrived in Oahu in the 1790s, became a wealthy landowner, and acted as interpreter for the Hawaiian kings.

Chapters 21–23

CHINA AND THE WAY HOME[1]

November 1828–July 1829

[The crossing of the Pacific, writes Duhaut-Cilly, was monotonous, the weather variable, often overcast and stormy. The *Héros* stayed close to the 19th parallel north, deemed the quickest and least dangerous route to Canton. They passed near Asunción Island in the northern Marianas and south of Taiwan, then called Formosa, to the coast of southern China.]

ON 21 DECEMBER WE PASSED near the rock called Pedra Branca (White Rock) by the Portuguese. . . . We were then off the coast of the province of Fukien. A multitude of sampans surrounded us; they all had two plaited sails, the main one placed two-thirds of the way toward the bow and the smaller one on the poop.

On the next morning we were close to the Lema Islands. From one of the sampans around us there came a small skiff, and a Chinese man came on board the ship. If we had judged the entire nation by this first individual, we would have said, as did the English traveler arriving in Calais, that the Chinese are small, ugly, liars, and thieves. This man, who called himself a pilot, demonstrated all these qualities. He proposed to guide the ship to Macao for the sum of two hundred piasters, assuring me that this was the customary charge. Happily, I had better information and I offered him thirty. He cried out as if I had blasphemed the name of the emperor. At this moment a furious squall struck us; the ship was lying to, and the wind beat at the sails with

---

1. The last three chapters of the original book are here condensed into one. Brief omissions are signaled by three dots within a paragraph, longer ones by asterisks between paragraphs. Editorial summaries are between square brackets.

great force; torrents of rain fell on the deck where the Chinese had laid out two hundred pieces of copper while showing me a piaster as if to render his claims more solid. But when he saw me firm in my resolution he gathered them up with a gesture of anger, climbed into his skiff and, pointing an arm toward the blackest part of the sky, he went away crying "ty-foon! ty-foon!" He was threatening me with a real hurricane as if the Heavens would punish me for not letting myself be duped by an inhabitant of the great empire.

But this little storm passed as quickly as it had come, and we were entering the channel between the Lema Islands and the coast when a real pilot appeared. But it was still necessary to dicker; after considerable discussion he agreed to conduct us for forty piasters to Macao, where we arrived the next day. I went on shore to arrange for a new pilot and to obtain the "chap" or permission to proceed up the river. The standard fee for pilotage from Macao to Canton, or rather to Whampoa, is sixty piasters.[2]

On the morning of the 25th we reached the Boca Tigris [Tiger's Mouth or Tiger Gate], where the river begins. There the pilot, relinquishing his post to a sub-pilot, went ahead of us in his boat and boarded a war junk stationed at that place, where he obtained a preliminary permit which he exchanged later at another office in a small town that we passed on our right. We followed him, slowing down so as not to pass him. China is the land of formalities; even this second permit was not sufficient; the pilot had to have it countersigned by the commandant of a fort built on a small island on our left and opposite another fort on the mainland.

It is this narrow spot that is properly termed the Boca Tigris, a passage easy to defend with crossfire from the batteries; but as they now stand they would be of no use against European ships armed in a manner quite superior to the Chinese system, which has in all likelihood

2. The Portuguese colony of Macao was on the estuary of the Pearl (or Canton) River. Canton, in Kwangtung Province and at that time the chief import and export city of China, is on the river, 65 miles north of Macao. Whampoa, or Huang-pu, is the outer port of Canton. The British crown colony of Hong Kong, 40 miles east of Macao, had not yet been established in 1828.

not been changed since the Tartar conquest or even since the very old invention of gunpowder. . . .

There the pilot came back on board to resume the duties that he had abandoned for two hours to take care of the formalities. Two Chinese soldiers came with him, and one of them demanded six piasters for the commandant of the fort. Suspecting that this was an extortion, I refused. But I was not sure of my rights and did not wish to prolong the discussion, which might have gone on for a considerable while, with the pilot refusing to move on until it was concluded. I gave the man half of what he had asked, and he left us.

The other soldier, a more important individual, appeared to be a guard who would accompany us to Whampoa. We amused ourselves by making him repeat several times in his bad English the orders he had received. To each of us who asked how long he would stay on board he replied with as many explanatory gestures as words: "Ship— Let go—Whampoa—me—go—Canton," trying to make us understand that when the ship arrived at Whampoa he would go on to Canton to render an account of his mission. That night, the tide having ceased running and the wind dying down, we anchored below a place known as the second bar near several ships of the East India Company which, because of their great draught, had to take on cargo there.

On the 26th we tacked about in a contrary wind and with the help of the tide. On arrival at the second bar, the pilot asked for six local boats to mark out the rocks and ten others to tow the ship. I found the request exorbitant; thinking that he himself had an interest in the matter, I discussed it with him a long time but without obtaining any reduction. It must be admitted that the ten boats were of great help in speeding up the ship's many maneuvers among the dangerous shoals that make up this passage, but I think that four boats would have sufficed to mark the channel. The pilot received a piaster for each boat, and I have reason to believe that he gave only a part of this to the boatmen.

The day was quite tiring for us who had to maneuver constantly in the rain. This part of the river is very wide, but it appeared that the right side was not navigable because the pilot kept us always on the left. The bank where we found ourselves is low and is occupied by rice fields; the right bank, on the other hand, runs near some high hills on which can be seen in the distance a number of those seven- and nine-story towers that are encountered, it seems, in all provinces of the empire and about which all travelers have written. On the way from Whampoa to Canton one passes close by two of them. They are of nine stories, and if we allow twenty feet to the story we must conclude that their total height is about 180 feet. To judge by the deterioration of the materials that form them they must be quite old, which shows that they were constructed with as much skill as elegance. Whatever the purpose for which they were destined, it seems that their usefulness has come to an end; for a long time they have been abandoned monuments.

About five in the evening we arrived at the first bar where we were again obliged to make use of sixteen boats, more necessary this time since the wind was down and night was coming on. This bar, like the preceding one, is a narrow passage between two rocky reefs under the water. At seven in the evening we reached Whampoa where we anchored in six fathoms in the midst of twenty-five or thirty large ships of several nations but mostly English and American.

✿   ✿   ✿

The esplanade or quay that runs in front of the *factories*[3] along with a few narrow streets occupied by small merchants, these are virtually the only places where a European is able to go, but these are a very small part of Canton; the rest of this great city is almost unknown to us.[4] It is no easier for us to judge the population of the city than it is for a European ambassador to calculate that of all China; he will have gone to Peking on a route designated in advance by the emperor and passing by only those things that deceive and fascinate his eyes. All that one can say about the number of people in Canton is that it is enormous. Some put it at a million, others at two million; the second

3. The European trading houses along the river. The merchants were called *factors.*
4. Edmond Le Netrel, lieutenant on the *Héros,* says that he and others were insulted by the Chinese whenever they went ashore and so preferred to remain on board in spite of the ennui. "They are with reason proud of their country," he wrote, "and they despise completely everything that is foreign to them." (Le Netrel, *Voyage autour du monde,* 176–77.)

estimate would not surprise me more than the first, so difficult is it to judge the matter and so great is the swarm of people wherever one goes.

It is easier to estimate that part of the population living on the river. One can, without exaggeration, put at twenty thousand the number of boats, large and small, moving and stationary, that crowd its several branches within and around the city; and if you suppose only five people on each, you reach a total of one hundred thousand people living on the water. It appears that this riverine population makes up a kind of separate caste and that those who are part of it do not enjoy the privilege of choosing whether to live on shore or on board. Several Chinese told me that people of this class, when found in the city at night, are subject to a fine that is not reduced by well-placed strokes of the bamboo. The necessity of living on the water has no doubt taught them how to pack into their floating dwellings all the conveniences found in a house, so that even the smallest boat is a marvel of orderly arrangement.

As for the numerous pleasure boats where wealthy Chinese gather for excursions, to smoke opium, or indulge in pleasures of another kind, nothing can equal their richness of decoration and the luxury on board. To form some small idea of this, one need only imagine an elegant Parisian saloon bar put down on a long vessel and ornamented in a fashion that, while Chinese, cedes nothing to our own.

Among the stationary boats that comprise another city on the river (divided into streets, squares, and avenues) where circulate constantly a great number of smaller boats that provide the inhabitants with all things needed and desired, one may notice especially those in which the women reside who in China as in Paris ply a trade whose capital fills out, well or less well, their silken robes, women sought out by vice and awaited by the hospital: courtesans, since one must call them by their name. These boats are larger and even more highly decorated than the others. A handsome wooden staircase leads to a gallery at bow or stern, richly pavilioned and arranged with flowers and shrubs. It is on this kind of balcony that these ladies display their charms and where, painted and rouged, they solicit the attention of passersby. Their hair, with entwined jasmine flowers, is always put up with care, and some have the lower lip gilded. But these Sirens are not dangerous to foreigners. To avoid their snares one need not employ the wiles of Odysseus; it would be at great damage to his fortune and his shoulders should a European attempt to board this Paphos.[5]

○   ○   ○

The quays where are the factories of Canton are almost everywhere occupied by small booths and stalls where you find cook-shops, bakers, hairdressers, and, circling around them all, a great crowd of idlers. There is always a huge number of barbers, whose equipment consists of a chair surmounted by a parasol or a kind of chandelier, a water bucket and basin, a razor, comb, and small instruments for clearing the ears. Everyone knows that the Chinese shave their heads except for a toupee that hangs in a great queue over their shoulders or which they roll up on top of the head. To maintain this style they have to shave their hair as often as we do our beards.

Here there is not the variety of colors seen on our public squares. The dress of the ordinary people consists of wide pantaloons of blue or brown cotton and a long and ample jacket of the same material with a sky-blue collar closed at the neck. Some, instead of pantaloons, wear breeches tied at the knee over white stockings. On their feet they wear babouche slippers with toes that are square and raised.

○   ○   ○

On 21 February we had completed our loading at Canton but still had some goods to take on at the island of Lintin, situated off the mouth of the river. In the evening we left Whampoa and on the 23rd anchored in the roadstead of that island and close to an American ship from which we were to receive the rest of the cargo.[6]

The anchorage at Lintin, about six leagues to the northeast of Macao, is frequented by ships that do not wish to go at once up to Canton. On the island that shelters the roadstead there are stationed

5. Odysseus passed the singing Sirens by sealing the ears of his men with wax and lashing himself to the mast. Paphos was a city in Cyprus, sacred to Aphrodite.

6. Duhaut-Cilly says no more about unloading and loading in China, but Le Netrel wrote that they got a good price for their furs and sold the sandalwood at nine piasters per *picul,* which he considered low. The new cargo, he said, consisted of sugar, tea, cinnamon, camphor, silk, etc. (Le Netrel, op. cit., 178.)

no permanent Chinese officials, and although the small town on the western side is inhabited by Chinese, the foreigners who anchor here consider themselves outside the limits of the government's authority. Many trading houses in Canton keep ships anchored here the entire year; these serve as warehouses where one can pick up at a moderate charge all sorts of merchandise. Ships that have to go up the river pass by Lintin and employ their available cargo space to carry goods up. The usual freight charge from Lintin to Canton is half a piaster per *picul,* or about forty francs a ton.

This practice is followed especially in the opium trade. Since the importation of this valuable stuff is prohibited by Chinese law, it has to be smuggled in. It is first deposited in these warehouse ships, and to them the Chinese boats come to procure it in small packets for sale in Canton. Death is perhaps the mildest punishment meted out to a Chinese who is convicted of bringing in opium, but this has not prevented the sale from reaching thirteen million piasters in the year 1828 and probably more in 1829. The habit of smoking this gum has become so general throughout the empire that everyone, from the merest boatman to the mandarin minister, has an interest in seeing that no one is arrested for the offense.

        ❂   ❂   ❂

[On 25 February the *Héros* moved from Lintin to Macao and on the 26th, after two months in China, raised anchor for the last time there and departed for home. In their hurry to regain France after an overlong voyage, captain and crew sailed down the South China Sea and, without stopping, passed through the Sunda Strait between Sumatra and Java and so into the Indian Ocean. After a short pause in mid-April at the island of Bourbon (La Réunion), preferred by Duhaut-Cilly to Mauritius, by then in British hands and holding memories both proud and painful for him, and after weathering the most dangerous storm of the voyage, they doubled the Cape of Good Hope and turned north toward France.][7]

---

7. At La Réunion, says Le Netrel, they were visited by Captain Camille de Roquefeuil, who had made the same voyage ten years before. (Le Netrel, op. cit., 180.)

We wished to take on a supply of water at the island of St. Helena, where that is done easily. And in fact, after two hours at anchor there we were ready to put to sea again. Another French ship had arrived at the same time we did, and the passengers asked to be granted a day to visit the tomb of Napoleon. Almost no captain returning from the Indies today refuses this permission to his passengers, and the visit has become a veritable pilgrimage. We were invited to join the company that was about to mount horses for the trip, but after more than three years of absence from home every hour was precious to us, and in spite of the entreaties of the party we did not accept. But a vague sadness seized on our hearts at sight of the barren rock that will remain for centuries a monument to a great misfortune, a shameful injustice, and a mean vengeance.[8]

Near the Azores we experienced several days of calm and made use of them to paint and polish our ship, which arrived in Le Hâvre on 19 July 1829 as fresh and clean as she had left there. This was a subject of astonishment to many people who imagine that a ship returning from a voyage around the globe will be a broken wreck.

8. Napoleon had died only a few years earlier, in May 1821. His remains were removed to Paris in 1840.

SELECTED BIBLIOGRAPHY

This list includes only the most pertinent references together with a few out-of-the-way items that may not be familiar to the reader. The translators have seen all these titles except for two that were examined for us by others.

I. THE VOYAGE OF THE *HÉROS*

Duhaut-Cilly, Auguste Bernard. *Voyage autour du monde, principalement à la Californie et aux Iles Sandwich, pendant les années 1826, 1827, 1828, et 1829.* 2 vols. Paris and Saint-Servan, 1834–35.

———. *Viaggio intorno al globo principalmente alla California ed alle Isole Sandwich negli anni 1826, 1827, 1828, e 1829 . . . con l'aggiunta delle osservazioni sugli abitanti di quei paesi di Paolo Emilio Botta.* Traduzione del francese nell' italiano di Carlo Botta. 2 vols. Torino, 1841. The translator was the father of the physician-naturalist on the *Héros.* See below.

———. "Duhaut-Cilly's Account of California in the Years 1827–28." Translated from the French by Charles Franklin Carter. *California Historical Society Quarterly* 8 (1929): 130–55, 214–50, 306–56. A literal translation of the Alta California chapters only.

———. "Shadows of Destiny: A French Navigator's View of the Hawaiian Kingdom and its Government in 1828." Translated by Alfons L. Korn. *The Hawaiian Journal of History* 17 (1983): 1–39. A translation of chapters 19 (partial) and 20 of Duhaut-Cilly's *Voyage.* The introductory remarks are concerned primarily with political conditions in France during the captain's career after 1815.

Botta, Paul-Emile. "Observations sur les habitans des Iles Sandwich. Observations sur les habitans de la Californie. Observations diverses faites en mer." *Nouvelles annales des voyages,* Paris, 22 ser. 2 (1831), 129–76. An Italian version of these three pieces by the naturalist on board the *Héros* was later printed in the Italian translation of Duhaut-Cilly's book, as listed above. An English version of the first of the three, along with an account of Botta's life, may be found in Edgar C. Knowlton, Jr., "Paul-Emile Botta, Visitor to Hawaii in 1828." *The Hawaiian Journal of History,* 18 (1984), 13–38. More on Botta's life may be found in a long article by his friend, Charles Levavasseur: "Paul-Emile Botta," in *Le Correspondant,* N.S. 82 (1880), 745–62.

The second of the three was translated into English by John Francis Bricca and published as *Observations on the Inhabitants of California, 1827–1828* (*Early California Travels Series,* 5). Los Angeles, 1952.

The Bancroft Library, Berkeley, possesses a manuscript journal of 196 leaves written by Botta in French. This is similar to the three Observations, which were probably taken from it, and includes additional descriptions of animals, shells, and plants. The manuscript was examined for us by Robert Ryal Miller of Berkeley.

Le Netrel, Edmond. "Voyage autour du monde pendant les années 1826, 1827, 1828, 1829, par M. Duhautcilly commandant le navire *Le Héros.* Extraits du journal de M. Edmond Le Netrel, lieutenant à bord de ce vaisseau." *Nouvelles annales des voyages,* Paris, 15 ser. 2 (1830), 129–82. This partial account, first-person excerpts mixed with third-person summaries, was published four years before the captain's full account.

———. *Voyage of the* Héros *around the World with Duhaut-Cilly in the Years 1826, 1827, 1828 & 1829.* Translated by Blanche Collet Wagner. (*Early California Travels Series,* 3). Los Angeles, 1951. In this English version of the item above, four engravings are reproduced from the Italian version of Duhaut-Cilly's *Viaggio intorno al globo.*

2. THE CAPTAIN OF THE *HÉROS*

Cunat, Charles. *Saint-Malo illustré par ses marins . . .* Rennes, 1857. Pages 434–38. The name is given here as Auguste Bernard-Duhautcilly.

Levot, P. "Biographie des frères Bernard Duhaut-Cilly." *Revue des provinces de l'ouest,* I, pt.I (1853–54), 305–9.

Répertoire générale de la bio-bibliographie bretonne, v. 489, p. 9. Rennes, 1889. Several paragraphs on the family Bernard du Haut-Cilly, commencing in the 17th century.

Information on the captain's immediate family was provided in a manuscript genealogy, courtesy of M. and Mme. Alain du Haut-Cilly, Paris, who also own the portrait reproduced as our frontispiece. An eight-page untitled and handwritten biography of the captain, giving the names and destinations of the commercial ships he commanded, was supplied by the Service Historique de la Marine in Brest.

3. THE OTHER VOYAGE: THE *COMÉTE* AND JEAN B. RIVES

Morineau, Philippe-Auguste. "Précis historique de l'expédition des Iles Sandwich et des causes de sa mauvaise réussite." *Nouvelles annales des voyages* 61 (1834), 313–34. This appears to be the only contemporary account of the voyage of the *Comète*. Morineau was in charge of a small agricultural colony. He also published in the same volume of the same journal a "Notice sur la Nouvelle Californie," where he stopped briefly on his way home.

Blue, George Verne. "The Project for a French Settlement in the Hawaiian Islands, 1824–1842." *Pacific Historical Review*, 2 (1933), 85–99.

Jore, Léonce. "Le voyage du trois-mats bordelais 'La Comète' de Bordeaux à Honolulu (1826–1828)." *Revue Maritime et des colonies* 101 N.S. (1954), 1183–96.

Whelan, Harold A. *The Picpus Story*. Pomona, 1980. Priests from the Congregation of the Sacred Hearts of Jesus and Mary were known as the Picpus Fathers from the site of their headquarters on the Rue de Picpus in Paris. Three of them went to Honolulu on the *Comète* in 1827, where they were visited by Duhaut-Cilly. When expelled from the islands in 1831 they spent several years in Alta California.

4. GENERAL REFERENCES

Dunmore, John. *French Explorers in the Pacific. II: The Nineteenth Century*. Oxford, 1969.

Geiger, Maynard. *Franciscan Missionaries in Hispanic California, 1769–1848: A Biographical Dictionary*. San Marino, 1969.

Jore, Léonce. *L'Océan Pacifique au temps de la Restauration et de la Monarchie de Juillet (1815–1848). I: Politique française*. Paris, 1959.

Kuykendall, Ralph S. *The Hawaiian Kingdom. I, 1778–1854: Foundation and Transformation*. Honolulu, 1980.

Nasatir, Abraham P. *French Activities in California: An Archival Calendar-Guide*. Stanford, c. 1945. Several of Rives' letters to government officials are quoted here.

Ogden, Adele. "Trading Vessels on the California Coast, 1786–1848." Typed manuscript in the Bancroft Library, Berkeley. Examined for us by Doyce B. Nunis, Jr. of Los Angeles.

BIBLIOGRAPHICAL ADDENDUM

Since publication of the limited edition, we have seen two French studies that pertain to the voyage of the Héros.

Perilhou, Jacques. "Dans le sillage des navires marchands français le long des côtes occidentales de l'Amérique au début du dix-neuvième siècle." *Jeune marine*, 109–11 (1993–94). A three-part article on merchant marine voyages to the west coast of the Americas. There are extended quotations from the accounts of Roquefeuil, Duhaut-Cilly, and others.

Robichon, Jean-Pierre. "Un Tour du monde commercial à la voile: le voyage d'Auguste Bernard Duhaut-Cilly à bord du *Héros, 1826 à 1829.*" *Recueil de l'Association des Amis du Vieux Hâvre* 48 (1989), 33–80. A remarkable study of the voyage as a voyage and as a commercial enterprise. The author, a present-day sea captain and scholar, has dug up a wealth of detail about the ship, the crew, equipment and food, problems of navigation, and the like. Merchant voyages, he says, were many but little known because full accounts of them, such as those of Roquefeuil and Duhaut-Cilly, were seldom published. Thus, many commercial ships went around the world before Bougainville's voyage (1766–69), commonly thought to be the first French circumnavigation.

We have also seen two original documents now held by institutions in Normandy. A watercolor of the ship Héros *is in the Musée du Vieux Granville in Granville. It was done by Louis Montardier (1792–1856) of Le Hâvre, who painted portraits of ships. We have a color photograph courtesy of the curator, Mme. Michèle Chartrain.*

Another set of extracts from the journal of Edmond Le Netrel, somewhat different from that published in the Nouvelles annales des Voyages *and listed in section 1 above, is owned by the Bibliotèque Municipale in Le Hâvre. This manuscript was copied in the 1830s or 1840s by J.-B. Eyriès, whose book collection was sold in 1846. We have a transcript made by J.-P. Robichon.*

We failed to list the second edition of the Italian translation of Duhaut-Cilly's Voyage. The Viaggio . . . *was issued a second time in Naples in 1842, with the same title and virtually the same contents. It was, however, a new typesetting and came out in one volume without the four engravings. This edition was examined for us by Lynda Corey Claassen of the University of California Library, San Diego, and by Doyce B. Nunis, Jr.*

ABOUT THE TRANSLATOR AND EDITOR

AUGUST FRUGÉ is emeritus Director of the University of California Press, Berkeley and Los Angeles, and has written and published widely. His most recent book is *A Skeptic Among Scholars: August Frugé on University Publishing*, University of California Press, 1993. He lives in Twentynine Palms.

NEAL HARLOW was Chief Librarian at the University of British Columbia and then Dean of the Library School at Rutgers University. Among his many works are *The Maps of San Francisco Bay from the Spanish Discovery in 1769 to the American Occupation*, Book Club of California, 1950; *Maps and Surveys of the Pueblo Lands of Los Angeles*, Dawson's Book Shop, 1976; and *California Conquered: War and Peace on the Pacific, 1846–1850*, University of California Press, 1982. He lives in Los Angeles.

INDEX

Designer: Mark Ong
Compositor: G & S Typesetters
Text: Adobe Garamond
Display: Perpetua, Adobe Garamond
Printer and Binder: Thomson-Shore